25 to 36 Months
Rhyming Books, Marble Painting, and Many Other Activities for Toddlers

Creative Resources Infant and Toddler Series

Dedication

THIS BOOK IS DEDICATED TO:

My grandchildren, Jeffrey and Eva Herr.

J. H.

My son, Randy, and my nieces and nephews.

T. S.

25 to 36 Months
Rhyming Books, Marble Painting, and Many Other Activities for Toddlers

Creative Resources Infant and Toddler Series

by

Judy Herr Terri Swim

PHYSICAL

COGNITIVE

EMOTIONAL

LANGUAGE & COMMUNICATION

SOCIAL

DELMAR
CENGAGE Learning™

Australia • Brazil • Japan • Korea • Mexico • Singapore • Spain • United Kingdom • United States

**Rhyming Books, Marble Painting
and Many Other Activities for Toddlers:
25 to 36 Months**
Judy Herr, Terri Swim

Business Unit Executive Director:
Susan L. Simpfenderfer

Acquisitions Editor: Erin O'Connor

Editorial Assistant: Ivy Ip

Executive Production Manager:
Wendy A. Troeger

Production Editor: Joy Kocsis

Technology Project Manager: Joseph Saba

Executive Marketing Manager: Donna J. Lewis

Channel Manager: Nigar Hale

Cover Design: Joseph Villanova

Composition: Stratford Publishing Services, Inc.

For product information and technology assistance, contact us at
Cengage Learning Customer & Sales Support, 1-800-354-9706
For permission to use material from this text or product, submit all requests online at **www.cengage.com/permissions**
Further permissions questions can be emailed to
permissionrequest@cengage.com

Library of Congress Control Number: 2002031235

ISBN 10: 1-4018-1841-2
ISBN 13: 978-1-4018-1841-8

Delmar
10 Davis Drive
Belmont, CA 94002-3098
USA

Cengage Learning is a leading provider of customized learning solutions with office locations around the globe, including Singapore, the United Kingdom, Australia, Mexico, Brazil and Japan. Locate your local office at: **www.cengage.com/global**

Cengage Learning products are represented in Canada by Nelson Education, Ltd.

To learn more about Delmar, visit **www.cengage.com/delmar**

Purchase any of our products at your local college store or at our preferred online store **www.ichapters.com**

Printed in the United States of America
4 5 6 7 8 9 10 11 12 11 10 09

Contents

Preface

Responding in a warm, loving, and responsive manner to a crying infant or playing patty-cake with a young toddler both exemplify ways that caregivers and families promote healthy brain development. In fact, recent research on brain development emphasizes the importance of the environment and relationships during the child's first three years of life (Shore, 1997). With this in mind, *Rhyming Books, Marble Painting, and Many Other Activities for Toddlers: 25 to 36 Months* was written for you, the caregivers and families. The ultimate goal of this book is to assist in promoting healthy development of our youngest children. Thus, it should be part of all parents' and caregivers' libraries.

The book focuses on the growth of the whole child by including norms for physical, language and communication, cognitive, social, and emotional development. To support, enhance, and promote the child's development in all of these areas, this unique book includes specially designed activities for toddlers. Note that the book has several sections. The first section includes information for understanding, assessing, and promoting development, as well as suggestions for interacting with young children. The next sections include innovative activities to promote development for toddlers. The last section includes references for the material cited in the text. The appendices are a rich resource including, but not limited to, lists of recipes, songs, finger plays, chants, and books. They also contain a list of toys and equipment, as well as criteria for making selections.

To assist you, the experiences are grouped by age ranges and developmental areas. Each of these activities is designed to illustrate the connection between a broad area of development and specific goals for children. For example, physical development may be the primary area and eye-hand coordination may be one specific goal. The materials, preparation, and nurturing strategies for the activities are designed for easy and effective implementation. Moreover, variations and additional information have been incorporated to enrich the experience for both you and the child. Highlighting Development boxes provide valuable information for fostering an understanding of young children's development. Collectively, the information and experiences provided in this book will enhance your ability to meet the developmental needs of toddlers, fostering optimal development of the whole child. Furthermore, these early experiences will create a strong foundation for children's subsequent thinking, interacting with others, and learning.

ONLINE RESOURCES™

The Online Resources™ to accompany *Rhyming Books, Marble Painting, and Many Other Activities for Toddlers: 25 to 36 Months* is your link to early childhood education on the Internet. The Online Resources™ contains many features to help focus your understanding of the learning and teaching process.

- Sample Activities and Preface
- Developmental Milestones
- Books for Toddlers
- Books for Two-Year-Olds
- Criteria for Selecting Materials and Equipment for Children
- Materials and Equipment for Promoting Optimal Development
- Movement Activities for Children from Thirteen to Thirty-Six Months
- Favorite Finger Plays, Nursery Rhymes, and Chants
- Songs
- Rhythm Instruments
- Recipes
- Resources Related to Toddlers
- Developmental Checklist
- Sample Running Record
- Panel Documentation
- Lesson Plan
- Daily Communications
- A Summarized list of Web links is provided for your reference.
- On-line Early Education Survey – This survey gives you the opportunity to let us know what features you want to see improved on the Online Resources™.

The authors and Delmar Learning make every effort to ensure that all Internet resources are accurate at the time of printing. However, due to the fluid, time-sensitive nature of the Internet, we cannot guarantee that all URLs and Web site addresses will remain current for the duration of this edition.

 You can find the Online Resources™ at www.EarlyChildEd.delmar.com

ACKNOWLEDGMENTS

We would like to thank many people. First, our husbands, Dr. James Herr and James Daniel Swim, who supported us during this process.

To our families, who have continuously provided encouragement and facilitated our personal and professional development.

Furthermore, this book would not have been possible without the inspiration of the numerous young children who have touched and influenced our lives in so many meaningful ways. The children we have met in university laboratories and child care settings and their teachers and parents have all demonstrated the importance of the early years of life.

We want to acknowledge the contributions of the numerous colleges, universities, colleagues, and students that have fostered our professional growth and development:

College of William and Mary, Norfolk, Virginia; University of Akron, Ohio; Harvard University, Cambridge, Massachusetts; Purdue University, West Lafayette, Indiana; University of Minnesota, Minneapolis, Minnesota; University of Missouri, Columbia, Missouri; University of Texas, Austin, Texas; and University of Wisconsin-Stout, Menomonie, Wisconsin.

Specifically we would like to thank Carla Ahman, Carol Armga, Michelle Batchelder, Chalandra Bryant, Mary Jane Burson-Polston, Bill Carver, Linda Conner, Kay Cutler, Sandi Dillon, Loraine Dunn, Nancy File, Nancy Hazen-Swann, Debra Hughes, Susan Jacquet, Elizabeth Johnson, Joan Jurich, Susan Kontos, Gary Ladd, Julia Lorenz, Pat Morris, Linda Norton-Smith, Barbara O'Donnel, Diana Peyton, Douglas R. Powell, Kathy Pruesse, Julie Rand, Karin Samii, Jen Shields, Cathy Surra, Adriana Umana, Chris Upchurch, Lisa West, and Rhonda Whitman for their encouragement and support.

Also, special thanks to Carol Hagness, University of Wisconsin-Stout Educational Materials Collection Librarian, and Ann Salt, Children's Librarian at the Menomonie Public Library, who developed the list of books for toddlers that is located in Appendix A; Erin O'Connor, our editor from Delmar Learning who provided continuous encouragement, support, and creative ideas; and Deb Hass and Vicki Weber, who typed the manuscript.

The authors and publisher would like to thank the following reviewers for their constructive suggestions and recommendations:

Davia Allen
Western Carolina University
Cullowhee, NC

Alice Beyrent
Hesser College
Manchester, NH

Billie Coffman
Pennsylvania College of Technology
Williamsport, PA

Irene Cook
Taft College Children's Center
Taft, CA

Linda Estes
St. Charles County Community College
St. Peters, MO

Jody Martin
Children's World Learning Centers
Golden, CO

Introduction

S miling, crying, bicycling with their legs, and laughing at caregivers are all signals infants use to gain and maintain attention. Watching them is exciting. They are amazing. Each infant has an individual style; no two are alike. Differences in temperament are apparent from birth. Some infants are quiet, while others are active. Each is unique. However, all infants grow and develop in predictable patterns, even though the exact rate varies from infant to infant.

Development can be defined as change over time. According to Bentzen (2001), development refers to any "change in the structure, thought, or behavior of an individual that comes from biological and environmental influences" (p. 15). Human development occurs in two distinct patterns. First, development proceeds from the top of the body to the bottom. For example, control of the head develops before control of the torso or the legs. The second pattern is for development to proceed from the center of the body outward. To illustrate, the arm muscles develop before those of the hands or fingers.

UNDERSTANDING THEORIES OF DEVELOPMENT

Searching the literature, you will find numerous beliefs about or theories of child growth and development. Some beliefs are in direct opposition to each other. There are theories that state children are biologically programmed at birth. These theories purport that children develop according to their own individual timetable, regardless of environmental influences. In contrast, there are nurture-based theories that emphasize the importance of environmental factors. These theories assume that children enter the world as blank slates. According to these theories, the children's environment is instrumental in molding their abilities. A third set of theories incorporates aspects from both of these two extremes, nature and nurture. These interactional theories are based on the premise that biology and environment work in concert to account for children's development.

While reading this book, you will note that it celebrates interactional theories. Current research on brain development supports the belief that human development hinges on the dynamic interplay between nature and nurture (Shore, 1997). At birth, the development of the child's brain is unfinished. Through early experiences, the brain matures and connections are made for wiring its various parts. Repeated experiences result in the wiring becoming permanent, thereby creating the foundation for the brain's organization and functioning throughout life.

Your role is critical because early experiences significantly affect how each child's brain is wired. The child's relationships with parents, caregivers, and significant others will all influence how the brain becomes wired. Therefore, loving encounters and positive social, emotional, language and communication, cognitive, and physical experiences all influence the development of a healthy brain.

However, this influence is far from unidirectional. Children, for example, are born with different temperaments. Research has shown that children's dispositions influence their involvement with both people and materials in their environment. To illustrate, Quincy is a quiet, slow-to-warm-up child. He initially holds back and observes. Moreover, he becomes very distressed in new situations. To prevent Quincy from feeling distressed, his caregivers and parents sometimes respond by minimizing the introduction of new experiences or situations. Consequently, his physical, language and communication, emotional, social, and cognitive development are shaped by his characteristics and his caregivers' and parents' responses to these characteristics.

USING DEVELOPMENTAL NORMS

Research on human development provides evidence that infants and toddlers grow and develop in predictable sequences or patterns. Such predictable, or universal, patterns of development occur in all domains—physical, cognitive, language and communication, social, and emotional. The specific components of these universal patterns are called developmental norms. Norms provide evidence of when a large group of children, on average, accomplishes a given task. Because norms are averages, they must be interpreted with caution. There are differences from child to child in the timing for reaching developmental milestones within one specific domain and across different domains. For example, a child may reach all developmental milestones as expected in the cognitive domain but develop on a later timetable in the language domain. Hence, each child has a unique pattern of timing of growth and development that must be taken into account.

Notwithstanding their limitations, developmental norms are useful to caregivers and parents for three main reasons. First, they allow for judgments and evaluations of the relative normalcy of a child's developmental progression. If a child is lagging behind in one developmental task, generally there should be little concern. But if a child is behind on numerous tasks, human development specialists should be consulted for further evaluations.

Second, developmental norms are useful in making broad generalizations about the timing of particular skills and behaviors. Understanding the child's current level of development in relation to the norms allows predictions about upcoming tasks. For example, a child who can easily find a toy that is partially hidden is ready to begin searching for a toy that is completely out of view.

This knowledge of future development ties into the third reason why developmental norms are helpful. Developmental norms allow caregivers and parents to create and implement experiences that support and enhance the child's current level of development. Following the example just given, an adult playing a hide-and-seek game could begin by partially hiding a toy with a towel and then add the challenge of completely covering the toy.

The following table includes a list of developmental norms for infants and toddlers, highlighting significant tasks. Norms are grouped by areas of development, and within each area the specific tasks have been arranged sequentially. When using this table, please remember that it represents universal patterns of development. You will need to be cognizant of each child's unique patterns.

Developmental Milestones*

PHYSICAL DEVELOPMENT

Birth to Three Months	Four to Six Months	Seven to Nine Months	Ten to Twelve Months	Thirteen to Eighteen Months	Nineteen to Twenty-Four Months	Twenty-Five to Thirty-Six Months
Acts reflexively—sucking, stepping, rooting	Holds cube in hand	Sits independently	Supports entire body weight on legs	Builds tower of two cubes	Walks up stairs independently, one step at a time	Maneuvers around obstacles in a pathway
Swipes at objects in front of body, uncoordinated	Reaches for objects with one hand	Stepping reflex returns, so that child bounces when held on a surface in a standing position	Walks when hands are held	Turns the pages of a cardboard book two or three at a time	Jumps in place	Runs in a more adult-like fashion; knees are slightly bent, arms move in the opposite direction
Holds head erect and steady when lying on stomach	Rolls from back to side	Leans over and reaches when in a sitting position	Cruises along furniture or steady objects	Scribbles vigorously	Kicks a ball	Walks down stairs independently
Lifts head and shoulders	Reaches for objects in front of body, coordinated	Gets on hands and knees but may fall forward	Stands independently	Walks proficiently	Runs in a modified fashion	Marches to music
Rolls from side to back	Sits with support	Crawls	Walks independently	Walks while carrying or pulling a toy	Shows a decided preference for one hand	Uses feet to propel wheeled riding toys
Follow moving objects with eyes	Transfers objects from hand to hand	Pulls to standing position	Crawls up stairs or steps	Walks up stairs with assistance	Completes a three-piece puzzle with knobs	Rides a tricycle
	Grabs objects with either hand	Claps hands together	Voluntarily releases objects held in hands		Builds a tower of six cubes	Usually uses whole arm movements to paint or color
	Sits in tripod position using arms for support	Stands with adult's assistance	Has good balance when sitting; can shift positions without falling			Throws ball forward, where intended
		Learns pincer grasp, using thumb with forefinger to pick up objects	Takes off shoes and socks			Builds tower using eight or more blocks
		Uses finger and thumb together to pick up objects				Imitates drawing circles and vertical and horizontal lines
		Brings objects together with banging noises				Turns pages in book one by one
						Fingers work together to scoop up small objects
						Strings large beads on a shoelace

*The developmental milestones listed are based on universal patterns of when various traits emerge. Because each child is unique certain traits may develop at an earlier or later age.

LANGUAGE AND COMMUNICATION DEVELOPMENT

Birth to Three Months	Four to Six Months	Seven to Nine Months	Ten to Twelve Months	Thirteen to Eighteen Months	Nineteen to Twenty-Four Months	Twenty-Five to Thirty-Six Months
Communicates with cries, grunts, and facial expressions	Babbles spontaneously	Varies babble in loudness, pitch, and rhythm	Uses preverbal gestures to influence the behavior of others	Has expressive vocabulary of 10 to 20 words	Continues using telegraphic speech	Continues using telegraphic speech combining three or four words
Prefers human voices	Acquires sounds of native language in babble	Adds *d*, *t*, *n*, and *w* to repertoire of babbling sounds	Demonstrates word comprehension skills	Engages in "jargon talk"	Able to combine three words	Speaks in complete sentences following word order of native language
Coos	Canonical, systematic consonant-vowel pairings; babbling occurs	Produces gestures to communicate, often by pointing	Waves good-bye	Engages in telegraphic speech by combining two words together	Talks, 25 percent of words being understandable	Displays effective conversational skills
Laughs	Participates in interactive games initiated by adults	May say *mama* or *dada* but does not connect words with parents	Speaks recognizable first word	Experiences a burst of language development	Refers to self by name	Refers to self as *me* or *I* rather than by name
Smiles and coos to initiate and sustain interactions with caregiver	Takes turns while interacting		Initiates familiar games with adults	Comprehends approximately 50 words	Joins three or four words into a sentence	Talks about objects and events not immediately present
					Comprehends approximately 300 words	Uses grammatical markers and some plurals
					Expressive language includes a vocabulary of approximately 250 words	Vocabulary increases rapidly, up to 300 words
						Enjoys being read to if allowed to participate by pointing, talking, and turning pages

*The developmental milestones listed are based on universal patterns of when various traits emerge. Because each child is unique certain traits may develop at an earlier or later age.

Developmental Milestones* (continued)

COGNITIVE DEVELOPMENT

Birth to Three Months	Four to Six Months	Seven to Nine Months	Ten to Twelve Months	Thirteen to Eighteen Months	Nineteen to Twenty-Four Months	Twenty-Five to Thirty-Six Months
Cries for assistance	Recognizes people by their voice	Enjoys looking at books with familiar objects	Solves sensorimotor problems by deliberately using schemas, such as shaking a container to empty its contents	Explores properties of objects by acting on them in novel ways	Points to and identifies objects on request, such as when reading a book, touring, etc.	Uses objects for purposes other than intended
Acts reflexively	Enjoys repeating acts, such as shaking a rattle, that produce results in the external world	Distinguishes familiar from unfamiliar faces	Points to body parts upon request	Solves problems through trial and error	Sorts by shapes and colors	Uses private speech while working
Prefers to look at patterned objects, bull's-eye, horizontal stripes, and the human face	Searches with eyes for source of sounds	Engages in goal-directed behavior	Drops toys intentionally and repeatedly looks in the direction of the fallen object	Experiments with cause-and-effect relationships such as turning on televisions, banging on drums, etc.	Recognizes self in photographs and mirror	Classifies objects based on one dimension, such as toy cars versus blocks
Imitates adults' facial expressions	Enjoys watching hands and feet	Anticipates events	Waves good-bye	Plays body identification games	Demonstrates deferred imitation	Follows two-step directions
Searches with eyes for sources of sounds	Searches for a partially hidden object	Finds objects that are totally hidden	Shows evidence of stronger memory capabilities	Imitates novel behaviors of others	Engages in functional play	Concentrates or attends to self-selected activities for longer periods of time
Begins to recognize familiar people at a distance	Uses toys in a purposeful manner	Imitates behaviors that are slightly different than those usually performed	Follows simple, one-step directions	Identifies family members in photographs	Finds objects that have been moved while out of sight	Points to and labels objects spontaneously, such as when reading a book
Discovers and repeats bodily actions such as sucking, swiping, and grasping	Imitates simple actions	Begins to show interest in filling and dumping containers	Categorizes objects by appearance		Solves problems with internal representation	Coordinates pretend play with other children
Discovers hands and feet as extension of self	Explores toys using existing schemas such as sucking, banging, grasping, shaking, etc.		Looks for objects hidden in a second location		Categorizes self and others by gender, race, hair color, etc.	Gains a nominal sense of numbers through counting and labeling objects in a set
						Begins developing concepts about opposites such as big and small, tall and short, in and out
						Begins developing concepts about time such as today, tomorrow, and yesterday

*The developmental milestones listed are based on universal patterns of when various traits emerge. Because each child is unique certain traits may develop at an earlier or later age.

Developmental Milestones* (continued)

SOCIAL DEVELOPMENT

Birth to Three Months	Four to Six Months	Seven to Nine Months	Ten to Twelve Months	Thirteen to Eighteen Months	Nineteen to Twenty-Four Months	Twenty-Five to Thirty-Six Months
Turns head toward a speaking voice	Seeks out adults for play by crying, cooing, or smiling	Becomes upset when separated from a favorite adult	Shows a decided preference for one or two caregivers	Demands personal attention	Shows enthusiasm for company of others	Observes others to see how they do things
Recognizes primary caregiver	Responds with entire body to familiar face by looking at the person, smiling, kicking legs, and waving arms	Acts deliberately to maintain the presence of a favorite adult by clinging or crying	Plays parallel to other children	Imitates behaviors of others	Views the world only from own, egocentric perspective	Engages primarily in solitary or parallel play
Bonds to primary caregiver	Participates actively in interactions with others by vocalizing in response to adult speech	Uses adults as a base for exploration, typically	Enjoys playing with siblings	Becomes increasingly aware of the self as a separate being	Plays contently alone or near adults	Sometimes offers toys to other children
Finds comfort in the human face	Smiles at familiar faces and stares solemnly at strangers	Looks to others who are exhibiting signs of distress	Begins asserting self	Shares affection with people other than primary caregiver	Engages in functional play	Begins to play cooperatively with other children
Displays a social smile	Distinguishes between familar and unfamiliar adults and surroundings	Enjoys observing and interacting briefly with other children	Begins developing a sense of humor	Shows ownership of possessions	Defends possessions	Engages in sociodramatic play
Is quieted by a voice		Likes to play and responds to games such as patty-cake and peekaboo	Develops a sense of self-identity through the identification of body parts	Begins developing a view of self as autonomous when completing tasks independently	Recognizes self in photographs or mirrors	Wants to do things independently
Begins to differentiate self from caregiver		Engages in solitary play	Begins distinguishing boys from girls		Refers to self with pronouns such as *I* or *me*	Asserts independence by using "no" a lot
		Develops preferences for particular people and objects			Categorizes people by using salient characteristics such as race or hair color	Develops a rudimentary awareness that others have wants or feelings that may be different than their own
		Shows distress when in the presence of a stranger			Shows less fear of strangers	Makes demands of or "bosses" parents, guardians, and caregivers
						Uses physical aggression less and uses words to solve problems
						Engages in gender steriotypical behavior

*The developmental milestones listed are based on universal patterns of when various traits emerge. Because each child is unique certain traits may develop at an earlier or later age.

Developmental Milestones* (continued)

EMOTIONAL DEVELOPMENT

Birth to Three Months	Four to Six Months	Seven to Nine Months	Ten to Twelve Months	Thirteen to Eighteen Months	Nineteen to Twenty-Four Months	Twenty-Five to Thirty-Six Months
Feels and expresses three basic emotions: interest, distress, and disgust	Expresses delight	Responds to social events by using the face, gaze, voice, and posture to form coherent emotional patterns	Continues to exhibit delight, happiness, discomfort, anger, and sadness	Exhibits autonomy by frequently saying "no"	Expresses affection to others spontaneously	Experiences increase in number of fears
Cries to signal a need	Responds to the emotions of caregivers	Expresses fear and anger more often	Expresses anger when goals are blocked	Labels several emotions	Acts to comfort others in distress	Begins to understand the consequences of basic emotions
Quiets in response to being held, typically	Begins to distinguish familiar from unfamiliar people	Begins to regulate emotions through moving into or out of experiences	Expresses anger at the source of frustration	Connects feelings with social behaviors	Shows the emotions of pride and embarrassment	Learns skills for coping with strong emotions
Feels and expresses enjoyment	Shows a preference for being held by a familiar person	Begins to detect the meaning of others' emotional expressions	Begins to show compliance to caregivers' requests	Begins to understand complicated patterns of behavior	Uses emotion words spontaneously in conversations or play	Seeks to communicate more feelings with specific words
Shares a social smile	Begins to assist with holding a bottle	Looks to others for cues on how to react	Often objects to having playtime stopped	Demonstrates the ability to communicate needs	Begins to show sympathy to another child or adult	Shows signs of empathy and caring
Reads and distinguishes adults' facial expressions	Expresses happiness selectively by laughing and smiling more with familiar people	Shows fear of strangers	Begins eating with a spoon	May say "no" to something they want	Becomes easily hurt by criticism	Loses control of emotions and throws temper tantrums
Begins to self-regulate emotional expressions			Assists in dressing and undressing	May lose emotional control and have temper tantrums	Experiences a temper tantrum when goals are blocked, on occasion	Able to recover from temper tantrums
Laughs aloud			Acts in loving, caring ways toward dolls or stuffed animals, typically	Shows self-conscious emotions such as shame, guilt, and shyness	Associates facial expressions with simple emotional labels	Enjoys helping with chores such as cleaning up toys or carrying grocery bags
Quiets self by using techniques such as sucking a thumb or pacifier			Feeds self a complete meal when served finger foods	Becomes frustrated easily		Begins to show signs of being ready for toileting
			Claps when successfully completes a task			Desires that routines be carried out exactly as has been done in the past

*The developmental milestones listed are based on universal patterns of when various traits emerge. Because each child is unique certain traits may develop at an earlier or later age.

ASSESSING DEVELOPMENT

"All children have the potential, albeit in different ways, to learn and to develop their own ideas, theories, and strategies. All children also have the right to be supported in these endeavors by adults. Teachers and parents, therefore, should observe and listen to them" (Gandini & Goldhaber, 2001, p. 125).

Assessment is the process of observing, listening, recording, and documenting behavior in order to make decisions about a child's developmental and, thus, educational needs. This process is applicable for an individual child, a small group, or an entire group of children. Your observation skills are the main tools needed for assessing development. By observing and listening, you will discover much about children's needs, interests, and abilities.

This is a simple process. Your eyes and ears are like a video camera capturing children's behaviors, language, attitudes, and preferences. Most of the time you should be examining the children's abilities on worthy and meaningful tasks that you have created. Thus, your assessments will be directly tied to the curriculum that you have planned and implemented. For example, you do this when interacting with an infant or when assisting a toddler who is busy "working" at an experience. In other words, this is a spontaneous process that is continuously occurring. Authentic assessment requires your focused attention and some additional time for documenting your observation. To assist you in this process, a checklist has been included in Appendix K. If you are caring for more than one child, reproduce a copy for each.

Appendix L provides a sample running record. This method of assessment allows you to continuously observe and record, in narrative form, behaviors over a specific period of time. A running record provides a complete view of a particular time period or behavior.

You can also collect artifacts that represent the children's abilities. For example, collect samples of artwork, writing (scribbling), or sculptures. To record the children's performance during an activity that does not result in a product, use a camera to document behavior and abilities.

There are several reasons why caregivers and parents need to assess the development of young children. First, assessment tracks growth and development, noting progress and change over time, thereby providing evidence of learning and maturation. Each observation conducted by a parent or caregiver provides a "snapshot" of the child's development. Combining several snapshots over time provides a comprehensive composite of the changes in the child's growth and development. These changes can be in one of three directions. Typically, children's growth and development follow a predictable sequence. That is, infants coo before they babble. Likewise, they produce a social smile before they are able to wave good-bye. Children can also continue working on the same skills. For example, they may

spend several weeks or even months working on picking up objects with their thumbs and fingers. Finally, children can regress in their development. Although this happens infrequently, it can occur in times of great stress. For example, a toddler who had demonstrated proficiency at using a spoon at mealtime may revert back to using fingers to eat nonfinger foods.

Second, assessment provides insight to children's styles, interests, and dispositions. This information is invaluable in determining the correct level of responsiveness by parents and caregivers. It is much easier to meet a child's needs when you understand, for example, that the infant has difficulty transitioning from one activity to another. Knowing this assists you in preparing the infant for the next component of your daily routine, such as eating lunch.

Third, assessment data provides you with information regarding the normalcy of children's growth and development. This information directly impacts the experiences you create for the children. You should plan a balance of activities that support, enhance, and foster all areas of development. Some activities should be repetitious and represent developmental tasks that a child has accomplished yet still shows interest in and enjoys. Other activities should be a continuation of developmental tasks that the child is currently mastering. Still other activities should stimulate the child's development by requiring a higher skill level, thereby providing a challenge. At these times, children may need more adult support and assistance for scaffolding their learning as well as building their confidence as competent learners.

Fourth, developmental data must be gathered for effectively communicating the child's development with others. For example, if you are caring for children other than your own, you could discuss their progress with their parents or guardians. Likewise, if you are a parent, you will want to share this information with your child's caregiver, your significant other, or your child's pediatrician. Then, too, you may want to compile a portfolio or scrapbook containing a developmental checklist, photographs, videotapes, artwork, and other documents representing the child's growth and development.

Finally, assessment must be conducted to ensure that data is gathered for all areas of development. People have different biases and values. As a result, they may overlook or slight one area of development because of selective attention. If all areas are not assessed, experiences, toys, and equipment provided for children may not meet their developmental needs.

To undertake effective assessment, you will want to compile the data you collect into a meaningful form. The format you choose will depend on how you intend to use the data (Helm, Beneke, & Steinheimer, 1998). For example, if you wish to communicate with others about learning that occurred during a specific activity, you could display the artifacts collected, the photographs taken, and the dialogue transcribed while the children were working. If working in an early childhood program, this information could be displayed on a two-dimensional panel (see Appendix M) or a three-dimensional "Look at What I Did Table." Moreover, to communicate about one child's current level of development, you might want to create a portfolio containing significant artifacts, such as a developmental checklist, anecdotal records, running records, photographs, videotapes, and artwork that represents the child's growth and development.

RESPECTING TODDLERS

Respect. Regard. Honor. Value. These words are seldom used to describe very young children. Yet, these are traits or characteristics that are desired and valued in older children and adults. How better to teach such traits than to model them to infants and toddlers from the very beginning? Respect must be demonstrated in your behaviors. More importantly, respect for infants and toddlers must be something that emanates from inside of you. You have to believe that infants and toddlers are worthy of your time and attention as individuals, because a respectful relationship is vital to all aspects of child development. For example, when infants are respected, they learn to trust that adults can be counted on to meet their needs. This foundation of trust allows them to actively explore their environment during toddlerhood. Hence, trust leads to learning about the world and the toddler's place in it.

It may seem hard to demonstrate respect to infants and toddlers because we are unaccustomed to thinking about very young children in this manner. However, it is not difficult. Respect means believing in the children's abilities to explore, solve problems, or cause events to happen in their world. It also means setting and enforcing clear boundaries for behavior. This is not always easy to do as toddlers are gaining a sense of autonomy and want to do things by themselves. We think that this is the most important time to demonstrate respect. Watch them for cues on how to help. Monitor your own behaviors to avoid doing too much or too little. Toddlers need help that is "appropriate" to support their development and learning.

Furthermore, employing positive guidance techniques promotes a sense of autonomy and self-efficacy. To illustrate, when a toddler is exploring her body in space by climbing and jumping, ensure that she has a safe place for these behaviors. If the spot she has selected is not appropriate, guide her toward a safer location by saying, "If you want to jump, jump from this step onto the mat. It is safe to jump over here." This redirection technique recognizes the child's underlying desire for activity and finds a more acceptable, safer substitution (Marion, 1999). Moreover, setting clear limits allows toddlers to make decisions within a framework of boundaries. Demonstrating respect does not mean that the infants and toddlers have control over the adult. In fact, it is just the opposite. Adults who are respectful of young children have established clear rules and enforce them. These adults also explain the rules to children. Making rules explicit and clear has been found to assist toddlers with adhering to rules and developing a sense of morality (Charlesworth, 2000).

A great deal has been written for parents/guardians and teachers about toddlerhood. Unfortunately, much of the focus is on the "terrible twos." It is easy to see how this could happen. On one hand, toddlers can be challenging to be around because they want to do so many things on their own that they actively resist help, even when help is clearly warranted. They are also continuing to learn about emotions and ways to control them. Unfortunately, they do lose control, but we all have at some point in our lives. On the other hand, a two-year-old can be an absolute delight, full of humor and self-confidence, and a remarkable source of pleasure for adults. Within a framework of respect, both "hands" of toddlerhood are valued and cherished for what they are at any given moment and for what they can be in the future. Respectful caregivers of toddlers realize that important life lessons and foundations for future life lessons are being learned now.

Take the time to look through the eyes of toddlers. From their perspective, there is so much to see and the world is absolutely fascinating. No wonder they are so enthusiastic, energetic, and inquisitive. With this mindset, you will come to share their never-ending curiosity.

COMMUNICATING WITH TODDLERS

Parents and caregivers play a vital role in helping children master communication and language skills. Listen to the infant-directed speech people use while interacting with and speaking to infants. Originally, this speech was referred to as "motherese"; now it is called "parentese." This type of speech involves speaking slowly and exaggerating changes both in intonation and pitch.

When people use parentese while speaking to an infant, the higher pitch and slower pace capture the child's attention. Then, too, the careful enunciation and simplified style and meanings make the speech easier for the child to understand. By emphasizing one word in a sentence, the adult helps to provide a focal point for the child. When speaking parentese, adults consciously reinforce the infant's role in the conversation by encouraging turn taking and responding to the child's utterances. The following example illustrates the components of parentese:

Caregiver: *"Look at the kitteeee."*
Infant responds by cooing: *"Ahhhhh."*
Caregiver: *"The kitty is black."*

Infant responds by cooing: *"Ahhhh."*
Caregiver: *"The cat is eating now."*
Infant responds by cooing: *"Ohhhh."*
Caregiver: *"Yes, you knew the cat was hungry."*

Common features of parentese are highlighted in the following table:

Common Features of "Parentese"

Producing Sounds
- Exaggerates intonation and uses higher pitch
- Moves frequently between high and low pitches, occasionally whispers
- Enunciates more clearly
- Emphasizes one or two words in a sentence
- Parrots a child's pronunciation, correct or incorrect

Simplifying Meanings
- Substitutes simple words for more complicated ones: moo moo for cow
- Uses diminutives: doggy for dog
- Labels objects according to simplest category: bird for parrot
- Repeats words invented by child: baba for bottle

Modifying Grammar
- Simplifies sentences grammatically to use short sentences: daddy go
- Uses nouns in lieu of pronouns: mommy helping Jeffrey
- Uses plural pronouns, if spoken: We drink our bottle

Interacting with a Child
- Focuses on naming objects, sounds, or events in the immediate environment
- Asks and answers own questions
- Uses questions more than statements or commands
- Pauses to allow for turn taking
- Repeats own utterances
- Responds to the child's utterances through repeating, expanding, and recasting

(Baron, 1992; Snow, 1998; Zigler & Stevenson, 1993)

Once young children begin understanding language, they begin using it. Language comprehension occurs before production. In the beginning, new words emerge slowly, then suddenly there is a burst. Nouns are acquired more rapidly than verbs. Children's first words focus on their body parts, toys, clothing, and words for social interaction such as *bye-bye* and *hello*. After developing and expressing a repertoire of single words, between 18 months and 2 years of age, children begin to combine words to make two-word phrases for communicating.

Environments are powerful for facilitating toddlers' language development. One of the primary roles of the adult is to provide a literacy rich environment to encourage exploration and keep toddlers interested in listening and communicating. Toddlers need unlimited opportunities for conversing, reading stories, engaging in finger plays, singing, and pretend play where they construct their own version of reality. Therefore, provide them with toys and household items to stimulate their language development. Then, too, it is important to talk often to help them learn that talking is communication.

Because language is learned in authentic interactions, talk to toddlers in meaningful contexts as well as in social situations. Whenever possible, get down to their level and give them your full attention to reinforce the importance of the spoken word. Nonverbal cues, voice tones, and facial expressions convey important information. While communicating, provide the children with labels for objects, feelings, and ideas. To engage them, use prompting techniques by either asking a question or creating a situation that requires a response.

Kratcoski and Katz (1998) offer some guiding principles that can be used to support the children's language growth including:

- Use simple sentences.
- Speak slowly and clearly.
- Vary your tone/expression to emphasize key words.
- Use concrete vocabulary.
- Build from the child's utterance/phrase.
- Follow the child's topic of interest.
- Try to "comment" more than question. (p. 31)

Likewise, you need to:

- Provide the child with labels for objects, feelings, ideas, colors, and shapes.
- Give the child an opportunity to learn vocabulary in meaningful ways, and provide new objects and experiences to expand the child's language.
- Expose the child to a variety of books, catchy rhymes, and music.
- Connect the child's actions, ideas, and emotions with words.
- Engage in verbal interactions focusing on the child's interest. Prompt the child either by asking questions or creating a situation that requires a response.
- Engage the child in problem solving.
- Provide toys and household items that stimulate the child to talk.

APPLYING THIS BOOK

This book can be a wonderful companion when working with toddlers. To use it effectively, you will need to begin by reviewing the developmental norms and assessments. After this, you can use the checklist in Appendix K to begin gathering and documenting data. Once you have collected this developmental data, evaluate it to determine each child's needs, interests, and abilities. At this point, you are ready to begin searching for activities in this book that provide a balance of experiences to support, enhance, and foster all developmental areas.

When undertaking this process, you will need to narrow your selection of activities to prevent overstimulating the child(ren) in your care. This minimizes your preparation time and the amount of materials and equipment required; hence, you will have more energy to expend while interacting with the child(ren) in your care.

While working with toddlers, questions often arise. To support you, a list of resources related to infants and toddlers has been included in Appendix J. You may discover these resources can be very useful in supporting your role as a caregiver.

We hope you enjoy reading and implementing the activities in this book as much as we did developing them. We leave you with this thought:

> For a baby, those early weeks and months of growth, understanding, and reasoning can never be brought back to do over again. This is not the rehearsal. This is the main show. (Irving Harris)

Promoting Optimal Development in Toddlers

TWENTY-FIVE to THIRTY MONTHS

THIRTY-ONE to THIRTY-SIX MONTHS

PHYSICAL

LANGUAGE & COMMUNICATION

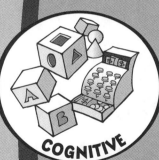

COGNITIVE

SOCIAL

EMOTIONAL

Physical Development

TWENTY-FIVE to THIRTY MONTHS

PHYSICAL

Square Ball

Child's Developmental Goals

✓ To practice throwing a ball

✓ To improve eye-hand coordination

MATERIALS:

❏ Masking tape

❏ Balls, approximately 12 inches in diameter.

PREPARATION:

♡ Sweep and clean an area of sidewalk.

♡ Make a rectangle (4' × 6') on the sidewalk with the tape. Use another piece of tape to divide the rectangle in half.

♡ Place one ball in each square.

♡ Use tape to mark spots approximately 1 and 2 feet away from square.

NURTURING STRATEGIES:

1. When a child shows interest, introduce the experience. To illustrate, say:

   "Stand on this piece of tape and throw the ball into the square."

   While speaking, reinforce your words with actions by pointing to the tape and square.

2. Observe the child's performance. If the child consistently misses the ball, he may need to move even closer to the square. If, on the other hand, the child is consistently accurate, encourage the child to move to the second piece of tape farther away.

3. In any case, providing positive reinforcement may result in the child remaining at the experience for a longer period of time.

☀ Highlighting Development

During the toddler stage play continues to be the primary vehicle for learning. Toddlers are learning many ways to move their bodies. At this stage of development, they enjoy throwing and kicking balls. By now, they should be able to throw a ball at a target from approximately 2 feet with some accuracy (Charlesworth, 2000).

VARIATION:

♡ As the toddler's skill level increases, make the box smaller to provide a challenge.

ADDITIONAL INFORMATION:

♡ Toddlers frequently have their own agenda, so introducing activities to them can be challenging. Avoid pushing them too hard, and do not be surprised if they resist following directions. Frequently described as "the terrible twos," in the eyes of adults, toddlers' behavior can be contrary, demanding, and unreasonable. Allen and Marotz (1999) describe this behavior as an early step toward establishing independence.

25 to 30 months

Fill 'er Up

Child's Developmental Goals

✓ To improve eye-hand coordination

✓ To increase muscle strength

✓ To continue developing special awareness

MATERIALS:

❏ 2 medium boxes without lids

❏ Packing tape

❏ Thick rope, cut into two pieces

❏ Scissors

PREPARATION:

♡ Remove any flaps from box and cover edges with tape to prevent scratches.

♡ Punch two holes on same end of the box. Insert one end of the rope through each hole and tie on the inside of the box. Wrap knot with tape to secure.

♡ Repeat with second box.

♡ Place boxes in an eye-catching location.

NURTURING STRATEGIES:

1. Observe the toddlers' use of the boxes. They will probably immediately begin to put items from their immediate environment into the box . . . even their bodies!

2. If a toddler happens to fill the box so full that he cannot move it, encourage the toddler to problem solve.

3. To illustrate, identify the problem by saying: *"You found many blocks to put in your box. It seems too heavy for you to move now."*

4. Encourage the child to generate solutions by asking: *"What can you do so that your box can be moved?"*

5. If necessary, model generating solutions by asking: *"What if you asked Payton to help move the box?"* *"What if you took some of the (blocks) out of the box?"*

6. Help the child select one solution to try.

7. Assist the child as needed in following through with the selected solution. For example, say: *"I'll take the blocks out of the box. You can put them back on the shelf. There, now you can try and move the box."*

8. Provide positive reinforcement for solving the problem.

☀ Highlighting Development

Young children will concentrate for long periods of time when interested in an experience. An example for children of this stage of development is "filling and spilling" which offers many learning opportunities. By participating in this activity, children develop fine motor skills, visual perceptual skills, and gain an understanding of concepts such as full, empty, light, heavy, more, and less.

VARIATION:

♡ Increase or decrease size of box to alter size and number of objects that fit inside.

ADDITIONAL INFORMATION:

♡ Toddlers enjoy repetition. They may wish to repeat this experience many times. Moreover, they may modify the activity by changing the manipulatives they put into the box.

25 to 30 months

Twenty-Five to Thirty Months

Screwing On a Lid

PHYSICAL

Child's Developmental Goals

✓ To practice eye-hand coordination skills

✓ To improve fine muscle skills in fingers and wrists

MATERIALS:

❑ Varying sizes of plastic containers with screw-on lids

❑ Basket

PREPARATION:

♡ Clean the containers, checking for sharp edges.

♡ If any sharp edges are discovered, cover them with masking tape.

♡ Put all lids and containers in the basket.

♡ Place the basket in a convenient location for the child.

NURTURING STRATEGIES:

1. When a toddler selects the materials, observe her behavior.

2. If necessary, provide a suggestion for using the materials. Say, for example, while pointing:
   "Kyra, can you find a lid that fits this container?"

3. If the toddler is having difficulty finding a lid that fits, verbally assist by saying:
   "The container in your hand is skinny. Look for the smallest lid."
   "Try the blue lid, Kyra. It might fit."

4. Encourage the toddler, if you notice the level of frustration rising. Comments to make include:
   "This is hard work. You can do it."
   "That is the right lid. Turn it a little more."

5. Continue the experience as long as the toddler shows interest.

Highlighting Development

Toddlers' motor skills continue to develop during this period. Recall that by 24 months, they were successful at removing snap-on lids from containers. By 30 months, they are often proficient with screw-on lids. This means that they are also able to open doors by turning the knob (Berk, 1999). Hence, adults must be constantly alert if the toddler is tall enough to reach the door knob. Door knob safety covers can be installed to protect toddlers.

VARIATION:

♡ If necessary, decrease the challenge by providing snap-on lids.

ADDITIONAL INFORMATION:

♡ Toddlers often modify an activity to fit their interests. So, do not be surprised if this activity turns into a fill and close, then open and empty exercise.

 Be sure to have available hazard-free objects that the child cannot choke on.

25 to 30 months

PHYSICAL

Kangaroo Jump

Child's Developmental Goals

✔ To practice jumping up and down
✔ To improve full-body coordination

MATERIALS:
❑ Compact disc player
❑ Compact disc, *The Ultimate Kids Collections: Favorite Sing-a-Longs Vol. 3* (2000). (Wonder Workshop, Inc., 2000)

PREPARATION:
♡ Select and clear an area that is large enough for full-body movements.
♡ Set the player in a safe and convenient place.
♡ Cue the compact disc to the song "The Numbers Jump."

NURTURING STRATEGIES:
1. Gather the toddlers and introduce the activity; model, if necessary. Begin by saying:
   "We are going to jump to music. Stand up. Put your arms out at your side. For this activity, we need plenty of space. If you touch someone, move your body. Good. Now everyone has enough space. Listen to the words, they will tell you how many times to jump."
2. Practice jumping up and down. Say a number and count while jumping.
3. Provide positive reinforcement throughout the activity. Comments to make include:
   "What a great song!"
   "This is fun!"
   "You are doing a great job of keeping your body safe."
4. Repeat the song as long as the toddlers seem interested.

 Highlighting Development

Older toddlers are quite skillful, especially when compared to their motor skills during the first two years of life. Gross motor skills often dominate their activities. Toddlers revel in repeating actions over and over again. Sometimes it seems as if they are practicing to master a skill. At the beginning, they have simple and separate leg-arm actions. Gradually, these actions develop into an integrated system of movement.

VARIATION:
♡ If the weather and facilities permit, perform this experience outdoors, preferably on a grassy area.

ADDITIONAL INFORMATION:
♡ Hopping is a fundamental motor skill that serves as a foundation for later skills. By age six or seven, children can integrate two or more separate skills into an action. For example, they can run, leap, and throw a ball at a hoop.

25 to 30 months

Drawing with Pencils

PHYSICAL

Child's Developmental Goals

✓ To refine grasping of tools with fingers and thumb

✓ To develop visual discrimination skills

MATERIALS:

❑ 8½ × 11–inch pieces of construction paper cut into 4¼ × 5½–inch rectangles

❑ Small and large diameter pencils

❑ Felt-tip, nontoxic, washable black pens

❑ Containers for holding marking tools

PREPARATION:

♡ Make sure all writing tools are in working condition.

♡ Arrange the tools in a container, and then place all materials so that they are easily accessible to the toddlers.

NURTURING STRATEGIES:

1. When a toddler selects the activity, observe the child's behavior.

2. Position yourself near the child, allowing the toddler to work independently.

3. If the child initiates interaction, respond promptly. Likewise, respond to sounds of distress with verbal support. Use your voice as a tool to communicate warmth and support. Comments to make include:
   "Reizo, push hard. There! The caps are tough to put back on sometimes."
   "Your pencil lead broke. Let's go sharpen it."

4. Describe what you see in the child's artwork. Say, for example:
   "You made a long curved line, Reizo. It stretches from one side to the other."

5. Encourage the child to talk about the artwork. Some questions to ask include:
   "Would you like to tell me about your picture?"
   "What were you thinking about while working on your picture?"
   Write the child's response on back of the artwork or on another piece of paper.

6. To develop responsibility, encourage the toddler to return all pens and pencils to the container before selecting a new experience.

☀ Highlighting Development

Young children are able to grasp a crayon with their entire fist by 13 to 18 months. By 30 months, they are able to hold a large-diameter pencil in their hand. They are also using instruments to make straight and curved lines and circles. These marks may be either random or controlled scribbles (Charlesworth, 2000) at this time.

VARIATIONS:

♡ Slowly increase the size of paper while providing the same tools.

♡ Use other writing tools such as watercolor markers and/or chalk pieces.

ADDITIONAL INFORMATION:

♡ Children learn through repetition. They must have, and enjoy, opportunities for repeating experiences. Therefore, leave out the small paper for at least one week.

♡ Notice how the toddler's use of blank space changes after repeating this experience numerous times.

♡ Save examples of the child's work for his portfolio.

♡ Because two-year-olds do not hold the paper with one hand, it is likely to move. If the paper moves, it most likely will not bother them.

♡ Study the toddler's movements while marking. They are large, muscular, and random. At this stage, the child enjoys the feel of the marking tool in his hand. With milestones in physical and cognitive development, his work will gradually become more controlled (Herr, 2001).

25 to 30 months

Shape Run

Child's Developmental Goals

✓ To practice running skills

✓ To improve full-body coordination

MATERIALS:

❑ Colored construction paper

❑ Masking tape

PREPARATION:

♡ Draw one familiar shape (e.g., square, apple) on each piece of paper. Make these shapes large enough to be viewed from about 10 to 15 feet away.

♡ Tape the shapes at the children's eye level on different areas of the outside play area. For example, tape one shape to a tree and another on the fence.

NURTURING STRATEGIES:

1. If you notice a child wandering or otherwise appearing to need something to do, encourage her to run over and touch the square.

2. Provide positive verbal and nonverbal reinforcement when the first direction is followed. Say, for example, while smiling:
   "Isadora, you ran very fast to touch the square."

3. Suggest that the child run and touch another shape.

4. If the child easily accomplishes one direction at a time, increase the difficulty by giving two at once.

5. If possible, invite another child to join in the activity.

6. Continue the experience as long as the children seem interested.

7. Make a notation of the child's running and/or listening abilities on a running record (see Appendix L).

☼ Highlighting Development

Fogel (2001) uses the 4 *E*'s to describe toddlers, calling them energetic, expressive, experimental, and exploratory. Toddlers are in a constant state of motion. Their coordination and, therefore, their running ability is changing. They are now more adult-like, meaning that their arms swing in opposition to their legs. Furthermore, their knees are slightly bent and their feet actually lift off of the ground. As any adult who cares for toddlers knows, they are also increasing in speed.

VARIATIONS:

♡ Change the color of construction paper and shapes to promote the development of additional concepts.

♡ Perform this experience indoors on a rainy day.

ADDITIONAL INFORMATION:

♡ This experience also fosters listening and auditory memory skills.

♡ Remember that the rate of skill attainment varies from child to child. Each child has her own unique rate of development.

25 to 30 months

Chair Maze

Child's Developmental Goals

✓ To move around an obstacle

✓ To improve full-body coordination

MATERIALS:

❑ Child or adult size chairs

PREPARATION:

♡ Select and clear a carpeted area.

♡ Place chairs in a maze-like fashion in that area.

NURTURING STRATEGIES:

1. When a child selects the area, observe his behavior. Allow him to experiment and problem-solve the purpose of the chairs. If he seems confused, introduce the activity by saying:

   "The chairs are arranged in a maze. Walk around them and try not to bump anything."

2. Supervise the area carefully. It may be necessary to redirect the child's behavior. To illustrate, if he is attempting to jump off of the chair, take him to a safe place to jump.

3. Provide positive reinforcement when the toddler walks around the chairs without bumping. Say, for example:

   "Yahto, you walked very close to the chair but did not touch it."

4. Encourage the toddler to take a different route in the maze by rearranging the chairs.

☀ Highlighting Development

Avoiding obstacles in a pathway is a tricky maneuver that requires both cognitive processing and physical coordination. Toddlers must see the object, decide how to solve the "problem," and then actually perform a selected behavior. Because of the difficulty inherently involved in maneuvering around obstacles, it is best to minimize such challenges unless a soft floor or ground covering is available.

VARIATIONS:

♡ Encourage the toddlers to move in different ways around the chairs. You might suggest crawling or hopping.

♡ Do this experience outside. Use bales of hay if available and no one is allergic.

ADDITIONAL INFORMATION:

♡ Toddlers enjoy climbing on and off of adult-size chairs. As a result, they may decide to climb on the chairs instead of walking around them.

25 to 30 months

Taping the Day Away

Child's Developmental Goals

✓ To improve fine motor skills

✓ To enhance eye-hand coordination

MATERIALS:

❑ Scotch tape with dispenser for each child

❑ Pieces of construction paper

❑ "Beautiful junk" to tape to picture, such as cotton balls, bottle caps, yarn

❑ Containers

PREPARATION:

♡ Place a piece of paper and a tape dispenser at each workstation.

♡ Aesthetically arrange "beautiful junk" in containers and place in easy reach.

NURTURING STRATEGIES:

1. When a child selects the area, engage her in conversation about the materials.

2. Observe the child's use of the tape and the dispenser. How is she using the materials? Is any assistance needed? Use answers to these questions to guide your behavior.

3. Provide verbal and physical assistance as necessary. For example, say:
   "Bryn, it might help to have me hold down the tape dispenser."

4. Engage the toddler in conversation about the tape. Questions to ask include:
   "Why is one side of the tape sticky?"
   "Have you ever used tape before? What did you do with it?"

5. Provide encouragement to help the toddler persist when frustrated. Verbal support is often effective in such situations. Comment, for example:
   "That tape keeps sticking to your fingers. How annoying!"

6. When the toddler is finished, write her name on the artwork. Also, write any comments she might make about it, such as "for Mommy."

☀ Highlighting Development

Toddlers enjoy moving their bodies and working on gross motor skills. They also work on fine motor skills. Gradually they will use their hands with more precision as the coordination of the thumb and fingers improve. This lays a foundation for later skills such as cutting with scissors and writing. Young children need ample opportunities to strengthen and develop their fine motor movements.

VARIATIONS:

♡ Use self-adhesive stickers instead of tape to make a picture.

♡ Provide a wide variety of tape such as clear packing, duct, double-sided, and colored masking tape.

ADDITIONAL INFORMATION:

♡ The magical powers of tape seem to be lost on adults, but luckily not toddlers. Observe them and share their enjoyment!

♡ Maintain a container of beautiful junk for the children to use creatively. Include items such as different types of paper, toilet and paper towel rolls, small boxes, and pine cones (see Appendix D). It's amazing how toddlers will think of 100 ways to use a cereal box!

25 to 30 months

Jumping Hose

Child's Developmental Goals

✓ To jump over an object

✓ To practice full-body movements

✓ To practice using one's body in space

MATERIALS:

❑ Garden hose with the metal ends removed

❑ Camera

❑ Notepad and pencil

PREPARATION:

♡ Select and clear an area outdoors, if possible.

♡ Lay the garden hose on the ground in a curved design.

♡ Place the camera so that it is easily accessible.

NURTURING STRATEGIES:

1. Introduce the experience to the toddlers before going outside. For example, say:
   "I've noticed that many of you have been jumping off the bottom step of the staircase. I have put a hose in the yard for you to jump over. Let's go outside so you can go try it!"

2. Take pictures of the toddlers as they are jumping. Note picture number and reason for taking snapshot in notepad for later documentation purposes.

3. Comment on the children's performance and enthusiasm. Statements include:
   "You pushed off with both feet."
   "Jacob Wayne, you seem proud of your landing. You didn't use your hands that time."

4. If necessary, model jumping over the garden hose and describe your behavior while doing so.

5. After the pictures are developed, make a panel (Gandini and Goldhaber, 2001; Helm, Beneke, & Steinheimer, 1998) to document the children's learning and/or abilities displayed during the experience. Such documentation allows children to revisit the experience as well as to help their parents/guardians better understand their children's development.

☼ Highlighting Development

Jumping skills are practiced and then improve greatly during toddlerhood. In the early stages, toddlers propel their bodies off the ground using only their leg muscles. In time, they will begin to swing their arms, as well (Berk, 1999). In fact, toddlers seem to take every opportunity to jump on and down from things. Because toddlers lack good judgment based on experience, it is imperative that they are constantly supervised.

VARIATIONS:

♡ Perform this experience indoors by having the children jump over tape adhered to the floor.

♡ Encourage the children to try other movements, such as hopping or crawling, to get across the hose.

ADDITIONAL INFORMATION:

♡ By two years of age, the typical child can walk in a straight line and jump off of the floor. Within the next six to eight months, other gross motor skills will emerge. The child will be able to walk on his tiptoes; hop on one foot for two or more hops; walk up and down stairs with alternating feet; and jump from a bottom and second step (Turner & Hammer, 1994).

♡ The pictures taken should be displayed at eye level for the children. In a home setting, the pictures could be displayed, for example, low on a refrigerator door; in a child care program, they could be mounted on a bulletin board or wall. Such displays help promote language and communication skills, memory skills, and self-esteem.

25 to 30 months

Arranging Flowers

Child's Developmental Goals

✓ To improve eye-hand coordination
✓ To practice fine motor skills

MATERIALS:

❏ Floral foam or Styrofoam™ piece for each child
❏ Plastic flowers or natural items such as leaves, twigs, etc.

PREPARATION:

♡ Clean a child-size table.
♡ Arrange objects at the center of the table.
♡ Set a piece of floral foam on the table in front of each child.

NURTURING STRATEGIES:

1. When a toddler selects the area, discuss the materials. Say, for example,
   "Josy, these twigs are from our nature walk yesterday. Do you remember which items you found?"
2. Providing hints or clues may help the child remember better. Comments to make include:
   "You were walking with Jaffa by the water's edge."
   "Do you remember what we saw under the evergreen tree?"
3. While naturally continuing the conversation with the child, begin to stick objects into the foam. Describe your behavior by saying, for example:
   "Wow! The pinecone stays in the foam when I press hard. I'm making a sculpture."
4. If the child has not already joined in the work, invite her to do so.
5. Continue to work as long as she seems interested.

 Highlighting Development

Although it may seem like toddlers spend the majority of their time perfecting gross motor skills, they are also working to refine fine motor skills. Fine motor development is defined as the ability to coordinate small muscles. During this stage of development, toddlers progressively improve the coordination of their wrists, thumbs, and fingers. In addition, they are able to use their hands with more precision.

VARIATIONS:

♡ Encourage social interactions by using one larger piece of foam to create a group flower arrangement.
♡ Encourage the development of kindness by having the child give the flower arrangement to a family member or friend.

ADDITIONAL INFORMATION:

♡ Preserve work by taking photographs and posting them on a bulletin board. Encourage the children to revisit their work experience, thus improving visual and auditory memory as well as language skills.
♡ Capitalize on teachable moments. In a home setting, explain the value of the experience to older siblings or other adults. In a child care program, place the flower arrangements on a "Look at What We Did" table. To teach center visitors the value of the activity, create a sign that reads "Flower Arranging," and under the title, list the developmental goals for this activity.

 If working with a child who still explores objects orally, substitute play dough for floral foam.

25 to 30 months

Language and Communication Development

TWENTY-FIVE to THIRTY MONTHS

Rhyming Books

Child's Developmental Goals

✓ To increase phonological awareness
✓ To hear rhyming words

MATERIALS:

❑ Cardboard book, *Hand, Hand, Finger, Thumb,* by Dr. Seuss

PREPARATION:

♡ Display the book on a child-size table or shelf to attract the toddler's attention.

NURTURING STRATEGIES:

1. When a toddler selects the book, observe his behavior. Notice book handling skills such as proper orientation of text (e.g., right side up, working front to back) and/or turning pages one at a time. Record observations in the form of an anecdotal record.
2. Ask the child for permission to join in reading the story. For example, ask:
   "May I sit down and read the story with you, Gian-Carlo?"
3. Respect the child's answer. For example, if the toddler says, "no," you may wish to reply, *"Maybe we can read together later."*
4. If, on the other hand, the child welcomes your involvement, make yourself comfortable and begin reading the book.
5. Use your voice as a tool to communicate delight in reading the story and its content.
6. Initiate a conversation about the rhyming words in the book. Comments to make include:
   "I noticed several words that sounded alike in the book. These rhyming words are fun to read. Which rhyming words did you like best?"
7. If the toddler is interested, read the book again.

Highlighting Development

The English language comprises 44 speech sounds, or phonemes. Young children must gain phonological knowledge, which includes the abilities to distinguish speech from other kinds of sounds, one phoneme from another, questions from statements, and so on (McGee & Richgils, 2000). Speaking and listening skills are acquired easily through many and varied experiences with adults. In contrast, phonological awareness is necessary for reading and writing. "This is a special kind of phonological knowledge that requires the ability to think and talk about . . . differences in speech sounds" (McGee & Richgils, 2000, p. 22). Children who have phonological awareness are able to decide if two words rhyme, for example.

VARIATIONS:

♡ Choose other rhyming books.
♡ Make up own rhymes or songs to describe the toddler's behavior.
♡ If possible, encourage another adult to read to the toddler while you record his behavior using a running record or a video camera.

ADDITIONAL INFORMATION:

♡ Toddlers enjoy a sound-rich environment. They like hearing songs, rhythms, and chants. Given enough experience with predictable rhymes, they may be able to supply a rhyming word when you pause to encourage such behavior. This will help them with acquiring spoken language.
♡ This experience also supports a print-rich environment, which is needed if toddlers are to develop early literacy skills.

25 to 30 months

Learning More about . . .

Child's Developmental Goals

✓ To gain information from a book

✓ To converse about a topic of interest

MATERIALS:

❑ Nonfiction book

PREPARATION:

♡ Select a nonfiction book with real photographs on a topic of interest to a child or small group of children.

NURTURING STRATEGIES:

1. When a toddler appears to need a new experience, gain the child's attention and introduce the book. To illustrate, say:
   "Eva, look what I have. I went to the library and checked out a new book on turtles. I know how much you enjoy watching the turtles at the pond. Let's sit and read this book together."

2. Get comfortable and snuggle close. This will allow the toddler to easily see the photographs and enjoy the physical contact.

3. Read the book to the toddler. Connect labels and descriptive words to the photographs by pointing at them while speaking.

4. Pause often to encourage the toddler to converse about the pictures.

5. Reinforce utterances, words, or phrases produced by the toddler; for example:
   "Wow, Eva, you really know a lot about turtles. They are a green color."

6. Provide new information or vocabulary in small amounts; connect to past experiences whenever possible. For example, state:
   "This is a red-eared slider turtle. It lives in a pond, just like the painted turtle we saw yesterday on our walk."

7. Continue to read the book as long as the toddler expresses interest.

Highlighting Development

Very young children enjoy being read to. They will come to value books for a variety of uses. "They discover that books can provide information, comfort, and joy in their lives" (Puckett & Black, 2001, p. 384). For example, toddlers enjoy reading about how other young children cope with being separated from important adults or learning about a favorite animal. At this age they are able to show empathy for characters. In fact, they may even pretend to cry or look sad if one of the characters in the book is upset or crying.

VARIATIONS:

♡ Provide nonfiction magazines on the topic.

♡ Create a picture file on the topic. If you laminate the pictures, toddlers will be able to "read" the photographs independently.

ADDITIONAL INFORMATION:

♡ Observe the toddlers closely to assess their interests as the basis for planning future experiences. To do this, ask yourself questions such as:

What are their topics of conversation?
What are their play themes?
What books do they select independently?

♡ It will be difficult to find a nonfiction book written for the toddler's language abilities. Selecting a book with photographs will provide the toddler with realistic representations of the topic of interest. You will need to read the text or picture captions so that you are accurately describing what everyone is viewing.

25 to 30 months

Dogs, Dogs, Dogs... and a Cat?

Child's Developmental Goals

✓ To practice expressive language skills by describing and labeling a photograph

✓ To practice using gestures as well as words to communicate

MATERIALS:

❑ Instant camera and film
❑ Poster board
❑ Pen
❑ Transparent packing tape
❑ Stapler
❑ Basket

PREPARATION:

♡ Take photographs of at least six different dogs and two different cats. If possible, select animals that are familiar to the child. Prepare the poster board by laying it horizontally in front of you. Cut a third of the bottom of the poster board off. Then, make a pocket by placing that piece on the bottom of the existing board and securing with the tape.

♡ Now divide the large pocket that is taped to the bottom of the sheet into six smaller pockets to accommodate the individual photographs. Measure the photographs to estimate the size of the pockets. Use the stapler to divide the six pockets in the bottom strip. Then, cover each staple on the back of the poster board with transparent tape to increase safety and security.

♡ Print the title "Dogs, dogs, and more dogs" on the poster board. After this, mount one photograph of a dog on the top of the poster board and place the rest of the photographs in a basket.

♡ Make the game accessible to the toddler by securing the poster board to the refrigerator, propping it against a wall, placing it on a bulletin board, or laying it flat on a child-size table or coffee table. Place the basket of photographs beside the poster board.

NURTURING STRATEGIES:

1. When the child selects the activity, observe his behavior. Try to determine how she is using the materials.

2. If this is primarily a fine motor activity, encourage this line of play to continue. Comment on the toddler's behavior by saying, for example: *"Dylan, you are putting the pictures in the pockets!"*

3. Eventually, engage the child in sorting the pictures and labeling his work. Asking questions, while pointing to the pictures, can facilitate such behaviors. For example, ask: *"Are all pictures in the pockets pictures of dogs?"* *"How did you decide which pictures to put in the pockets?"*

4. Expand on the toddler's words, if necessary, or verbally label his gestures.

5. Continue to sort the pictures as long as the toddler is interested.

☼ Highlighting Development

Toddlers are action categorizers during their play (Berk, 1999). By 18 months, toddlers spontaneously and correctly categorize objects into two classes such as dogs and cats or circles and squares. As discussed earlier, this is roughly the same time that toddlers show a language explosion, or a sharp increase in vocabulary, enabling them to label objects. Language development seems to facilitate as well as build on toddlers' ability to categorize a group of items (Berk, 1999).

VARIATIONS:

♡ Take two photographs of the same animal from different angles and see if the toddler can match the two perspectives.

♡ Increase the number of animals in the matching game to increase the challenge.

♡ To simplify the task, take six different pictures of the same dog for the toddler to sort.

♡ If animals are unavailable, cut pictures of them from magazines.

ADDITIONAL INFORMATION:

♡ Adults can help to facilitate language and categorizing skills by verbally describing and labeling objects. Another useful technique is to pause when describing an object, allowing the toddler to fill in the missing condition/label.

25 to 30 months

Lifting Flaps

Child's Developmental Goals

✓ To develop receptive language skills through reading

✓ To practice expressive language skills

✓ To build vocabulary

MATERIALS:

❑ Book, *The Cat in the Hat's Great Big Flap Book,* by Dr. Seuss

PREPARATION:

♡ Attractively display the book at the toddler's eye level.

NURTURING STRATEGIES:

1. When a toddler selects the book, observe the behaviors displayed.
2. Allow the toddler plenty of time to explore/read the book independently.
3. If the child initiates contact or asks you to do the reading, enthusiastically accept.
4. Make reading the story as interactive as possible by asking open-ended questions. Use this technique to draw on the toddler's past knowledge as well. Moreover, make sure the toddler, not you, lifts the book flaps.
5. Provide support and encouragement for language expressed by the toddler.

☼ Highlighting Development

Support for young children's understanding of reading and writing is important during the toddler years. During these early years, children learn many literacy-related concepts while being read to one-to-one or in a small group. Some of these concepts are:

♡ Books are pleasurable.
♡ Books are handled in particular ways.
♡ Pictures in books are symbols.
♡ Books and pictures communicate meaning (McGee & Richgils, 2000, pp. 34–35).

VARIATIONS:

♡ Provide other books with flaps.
♡ Make your own flap books about the toddler's day or favorite subject.

ADDITIONAL INFORMATION:

♡ Books with flaps are very popular with toddlers. Flap books appeal to their understanding of object permanence and their emerging sense of autonomy.
♡ This flap book is enjoyed best when the toddler has had experience with the Dr. Seuss stories referred to in the text. You may wish to introduce those stories first and/or make them available with the flap book.
♡ Reinforcing the flap with clear, strong tape (such as that used for packing) before giving the book to the toddlers will minimize ripping.

25 to 30 months

Secret Pocket

Child's Developmental Goals

✓ To increase receptive language skills

✓ To increase expressive language skills

MATERIALS:

❑ Several objects, small enough to fit inside your pocket

PREPARATION:

♡ Put one or two of the objects into your pocket. Place other items in a convenient location that the toddlers cannot reach.

NURTURING STRATEGIES:

1. If a toddler appears to be searching for a new experience, tell the child you have a game to play. Introduce the game by saying:
   "I have something in my pocket. What do you think it is? Let's see if you can guess what it is."
2. Provide a clue to help the toddler guess. Say, for example:
   "I'm going to give you a clue. Megan, the object in my pocket rolls. What could it be?"
3. Wait to encourage the toddler to guess. If the toddler does not guess after waiting 10 seconds, elaborate on the first clue or supply another clue. Whenever possible, connect your clue to experiences in the child's life. To illustrate, say:
   "I saw you rolling this in the grass when we were outdoors."
4. If the toddler guesses, provide feedback about the accuracy of the guess. Avoid labeling the answer as wrong; instead focus on the part that is correct. Comments include:
   "A car does roll. I have something else in my pocket that rolls."

5. If the toddler guesses the object, show her the item and enthusiastically say:
   "You did it! What a great guess! You used the hints to figure out what I hid."
6. Repeat the game as many times as the toddler desires.

☀ Highlighting Development

Between 18 months and 4 years, sentences produced by young children become longer and more complete or adult-like (Charlesworth, 2000). However, two-year-olds vary a great deal in their expressive capabilities. The developmental range varies from a holophrastic stage (one word represents an entire sentence or idea), to telegraphic speech (sentences only contain essential components), to adult-like speech (sentences contain subjects, verbs, prepositions, noun markers, etc.).

VARIATIONS:

♡ Sew a large pocket onto a child-size apron. Encourage the toddlers to hide objects and have you guess.

♡ Increase the challenge by selecting objects that are less familiar to the children, such as a large paper clip.

♡ Use large and small objects to reinforce these concepts.

♡ Because toddlers are typically able to match three to four colors, use objects of different colors.

 Never leave children unattended with the objects for this activity. If the object easily hides in your pocket, it could be a choking hazard for toddlers. Remove the toy from the area or from the toddlers' reach as soon as the game is finished.

Sequencing Pictures

Child's Developmental Goals

✓ To describe photographs

✓ To increase use of time words, such as *before* and *after*

MATERIALS:

❑ Camera and film

❑ Basket

PREPARATION:

♡ Obtain photographs of a daily routine (e.g., eating breakfast, getting dressed, or playing outdoors). Place them in the basket on a child-size table or coffee table.

NURTURING STRATEGIES:

1. When a toddler selects this activity, sit near the child, being as unobtrusive as possible. Note if he is speaking to himself. If he is, record the words as an anecdotal record.

2. After a while, involve the toddler in a natural conversation about his work. Do so by commenting: *"It looks like you are lining up the pictures. How did you decide what order to put them in?"*

3. Expanding on the toddler's words or gestures will help to motivate him, because young children talk more when they know others understand them. To illustrate, if the toddler says the word *eat*, while pointing to the photograph, you should expand his language by reframing the word and incorporating it into a complete sentence. For example, you could say: *"Eat. You are eating breakfast cereal in this picture."*

4. Ask questions to help the toddler think about the daily routine. Alter the level of directedness needed depending upon the toddler's behaviors/skills. For example, if the toddler is focusing exclusively on the content of the photographs, you may need to encourage him to sequence them by asking: *"Deon, which picture shows you playing outdoors?"* [Pause.] *"That's right. I'm going to put that picture after the one of you eating breakfast. We always play outdoors after breakfast."* On the other hand, if the toddler is attempting to sequence the cards, say: *"You can do it. What do you do every day after lunch?"* [Pause.] *"That's right! You take a nap. Do you see a picture of your crib?"*

5. When the toddler finishes with the photographs, encourage him to clean up by putting them back in the basket.

☼ Highlighting Development

Children often talk to themselves while working. Piaget and Vygotsky differ in their interpretations of this behavior. Piaget believed that the children are unaware that they can be heard, so the speech is egocentric and serves no real development function. Vygotsky, on the other hand, felt that children use private speech as a way to regulate or guide their own behavior. Thus, private speech is an important tool for thought (Charlesworth, 2000).

VARIATION:

♡ Use several photos that sequence one daily event, such as washing hands or going to the toilet.

ADDITIONAL INFORMATION:

♡ The toddlers will probably become very excited when they see themselves, friends, and/or significant others in the photographs.

♡ Increase or decrease the number of photographs for sequencing, depending on the toddlers' abilities.

25 to 30 months

Stroller Talk

Child's Developmental Goals

✓ To use expressive language to communicate thoughts

✓ To engage in a conversation

MATERIALS:

❑ Stroller

PREPARATION:

♡ Secure the toddler in the stroller using the safety restraints.

♡ If you will be traveling for more than 20 minutes, consider packing a small snack and beverage.

NURTURING STRATEGIES:

1. Begin pushing the stroller. Take clues for your behavior from the toddler. If she is excited and talking, join in the conversation. If, on the other hand, she is quiet and attentive to her surroundings, do the same.

2. After a while of enjoying the quiet, initiate a conversation with the toddler. A great question to begin with is:

   "Cynthia, you are really quiet. What are you thinking about?"

3. Elaborate on the toddler's response, if necessary. For example, if the child says "fish," reply:

   "Yes, Mr. Gross does have a fish sculpture in his flower garden."

4. Connect the conversation to the toddler's past experiences whenever possible. Allow the toddler to change the topic if something else of interest comes into view.

Highlighting Development

A period of rapid language development occurs during early childhood. Children progress from uttering sounds to producing sentences containing compete thoughts. Researchers have found that young children can add new words to their vocabulary through a process called fast mapping (Berk, 1999). During fast mapping, toddlers connect a new word to an underlying concept after only a brief encounter. When a term is fast mapped, children have to work to refine their understanding of its exact meaning. Consequently, fast mapping does not capture all of the word's meanings. Rather, understanding the meanings of words happens over many years.

VARIATIONS:

♡ Increase the number of children on your walk.

♡ Take the children to a grocery store, bakery, or library for new things to look at and talk about.

ADDITIONAL INFORMATION:

♡ Overcorrecting young children's pronunciation or grammatical errors often discourages toddlers from trying out new words or creating new sentences; therefore, adults must exercise restraint (Berk, 1999).

 Check your planned route in advance for safety hazards, such as no sidewalk, and modify it as necessary.

 Make sure stroller is in good repair to protect the toddler's safety.

25 to 30 months

We're Off to See . . .

Child's Developmental Goals

✓ To build vocabulary
✓ To have a new experience

MATERIALS:

❑ The materials you select will depend on the outing you plan. For example, if your experience is outside during the summer, pack sunscreen and sunglasses.

PREPARATION:

♡ Make necessary arrangements for your outing. If the outing is part of an early childhood program, follow the stated protocol to protect the health and safety of the toddlers.

NURTURING STRATEGIES:

1. Explain to the toddler where you are going.
2. Engage in conversation to see what the toddler thinks you will do and see there. Gently clarify any misconceptions. Use this conversation to assess the toddler's prior knowledge of the subject.
3. Use this information to guide your conversations while on the outing. For example, reinforce what the toddler already knows and expand on it by introducing new information.
4. Encourage the toddler to engage in conversation while on the outing. Ask open-ended questions to facilitate this process.
5. Review what was learned after the outing.

☀ Highlighting Development

Adults promote and support language development by providing an environment rich in social and informational experiences (Charlesworth, 2000). This gives children many opportunities for both receptive and expressive language experiences. To make the most of these experiences, adults need to engage children in authentic dialog, that is, a dialog in which "children and adults talk to each other about interesting, relevant matters" (Trawick-Smith, 1994, p. 10).

VARIATION:

♡ Take photographs during the outing to review the event or to spark conversation afterwards.

ADDITIONAL INFORMATION:

♡ Toddlers are notoriously curious. They are interested in the world about them, particularly people and objects. Toddlers have had limited exposure to the greater world. At this stage, their understanding of the world comes primarily from their family, pictures, storybooks, and television. First-hand experiences in the neighborhood or community allow toddlers to gather information that helps them develop, clarify, and expand knowledge and concepts. During this process, they will be building their language skills as well.

25 to 30 months

Listening to a Book on Tape

Child's Developmental Goals

✓ To continue developing expressive language skills

✓ To hear native language patterns

MATERIALS:

- ❑ Blank cassette tape
- ❑ Cassette tape recorder that is powered by batteries
- ❑ Green and red circles
- ❑ Book, *Quick as a Cricket,* by Audrey Wood
- ❑ Canvas bag

PREPARATION:

♡ Place all materials in the canvas bag. Encourage adults, preferably the parents or guardians of the toddlers, to record their reading of the story. If necessary, show the adult how to use the cassette recorder. Pass the canvas bag around to a number of adults. Be sure to keep track of the name and language spoken in the order recorded on the tape.

♡ Once the recording is complete, punch out the tabs on the cassette so that it cannot be taped over. Adhere the red circle on the "stop" button and the green circle on the "play" button. Gather the tape player, cassette, and book.

NURTURING STRATEGIES:

1. Gather a small group of toddlers and introduce the experience. While holding up the book, say, for example:
   "This tape contains voices of people reading this story."
   "Pay close attention because all of the readings sound different. See if you can tell me how they are different."
2. Press "play" and turn the pages of the book to accompany the story.
3. To engage them in a brief conversation ask the toddlers:
   "Did you recognize who was reading that story?"
4. Direct their attention back to the tape by saying:
   "Let's listen to the story again."
5. Repeat steps 2 and 3.
6. Have the toddlers compare the two readings of the book by asking open-ended questions.
7. Tell them that you will leave the tape, book, and tape player out for them to use. Explain to the toddlers how to work the tape player. For example, say:
   "Push the green dot to start the tape player and the red dot to stop it."

☀ Highlighting Development

Children need to be immersed in their native language. Some children hear their native language spoken while at child care. Others hear their native language only in their home environment. In 1997, it was estimated that 6 million school-age children in America speak a language other than English at home. Studies indicate that providing experiences in both languages spoken by a child results in greater development in both languages. Furthermore, it shows children that their heritage is valued and respected (see, for example, Berk, 1999).

VARIATIONS:

♡ Have toddlers select their favorite books, then record adults reading the books.

♡ Tape the children's voices, then play them back.

ADDITIONAL INFORMATION:

♡ Tape recordings of stories should be used to supplement daily reading not replace it.

♡ Two-year-olds are gathering information about race, ethnicity, and linguistic patterns of themselves and others. Like adults, young children are sometimes uncomfortable around people who are different than them. This feeling might cause them to laugh at the voices on the tape. See *Anti-Biased Curriculum, Tools for Empowering Young Children* (Derman-Sparks & the A.B.C. Task Force, 1988) for suggestions on how to deal with this behavior.

Reading "Hickory, Dickory, Dock"

Child's Developmental Goals

✓ To develop expressive language skills

✓ To view written words

✓ To develop an appreciation for the printed word

✓ To develop visual memory skills

MATERIALS:

❑ Poster board

❑ Markers

❑ 18-inch to 20-inch strip of Velcro™, cut into 1-inch pieces

❑ Glue

PREPARATION:

♡ Write words to the nursery rhyme (see Appendix F) on poster board, leaving blanks for the time struck and the actions performed by the mouse.

♡ Adhere Velcro strips to the board in the blanks.

♡ Cut five small pieces of poster board for the numbers and five for the actions.

♡ Write each number and action on a separate piece of poster board.

♡ Adhere Velcro strips to the back of each.

NURTURING STRATEGIES:

1. Introduce the activity to the toddler. To illustrate, say: *"This board has the rhyme 'Hickory, Dickory, Dock' written on it, but some words are missing. Let's fill them in."*

2. Hand the number cards to the toddler. Encourage the toddler to stick a number to the board.

3. Recite the nursery rhyme verse that corresponds to the number provided by the toddler. Put up action card before you say the words.

4. Encourage the toddler to remove the number and action cards and select another number card.

5. Do not be concerned about progressing in order from 1 to 5 when reciting the nursery rhyme. Follow the child's lead as long as she is interested in participating.

☀ Highlighting Development

Just as young children need to be spoken to in order to learn to talk, they need to see and hear written language to develop ideas about how to read and write (Puckett & Black, 2001). Frequent and varied experiences with printed media foster literacy development.

VARIATION:

♡ Chant rhymes slowly as a way to help the children relax before naptime

ADDITIONAL INFORMATION:

♡ Listen to children. Toddlers' vocabulary skills are rapidly increasing. As a result, they need myriad opportunities to solidify their concepts (Seefeldt & Barbour, 1994). Toddlers need daily experience with literacy activities such as listening, speaking, reading, and writing.

25 to 30 months

Cognitive Development

TWENTY-FIVE to THIRTY MONTHS

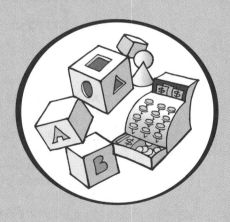

Math Blocks

Child's Developmental Goals

✓ To use blocks for measuring

✓ To count blocks

MATERIALS:

❑ Set of unit (wooden) blocks

❑ Shelf to store blocks

PREPARATION:

♡ Select an area that can be constantly supervised and that is large enough for block play.

♡ Clear this area and place shelf with unit blocks there.

NURTURING STRATEGIES:

1. When a toddler selects the block area, observe the child's behavior. Note how the toddler is using the blocks.

2. Engage the toddler in conversation about the structure, using open-ended questions.

3. During the conversation with the toddler, use mathematical terms such as *estimating* or *comparing*. For example, ask:

   "Porter, I noticed that you used two small blocks here and one larger block here. How did you know to use two small blocks?"

   "Oh, so you compared the lengths of the blocks. You had to use two to equal one."

4. When the child finishes working, assist him in deciding if the structure should be preserved. If yes, decide on the appropriate way to preserve it. For example, the toddler could sketch his work, take a photograph of it, or make a sign asking for it to be saved if space permits.

5. If the child does not wish to save his work, assist him with returning the blocks to the shelves. Focus the child's attention to counting the blocks. To illustrate, say:

   "You pick up the small blocks and hand them to me. I'll put them on the shelf. Hey, I have an idea. I'll count the blocks that you hand to me. I wonder how many you used in building your structure?"

   Count the blocks as the child hands them to you.

6. Thank the child for cleaning up the area. Comments include:

   "It is very responsible of you to clean up the toys you played with."

   "Thanks, now someone else can build with the blocks."

☼ Highlighting Development

Around two years of age, children generally understand that objects, people, and events possess certain characteristics and can hold complex images—or schemata—in their mind. These abilities set the stage for learning more advanced concepts about their world. In other words, the children are ready to transition from the sensorimotor stage of cognitive development to the preoperational stage (Puckett & Black, 2001).

VARIATION:

♡ Add items such as vehicles, road signs, or animals to encourage creative play.

ADDITIONAL INFORMATION:

♡ Toddlers need plenty of space for block play, because they tend to build large, horizontal structures. Sitting on the floor in the block area may result in the toddlers, especially females, spending a greater amount of time in the area.

♡ Blocks are important learning tools for young children. When playing with blocks toddlers are in constant motion: reaching, stretching, lifting, carrying, stacking, and changing body positions. As they interact with blocks they strengthen their muscles and improve their eye-hand coordination skills. They also develop balance, weight, and measurement concepts.

25 to 30 months

Grocery Shopping

Child's Developmental Goals

✓ To substitute one object for another

✓ To represent ideas through play

MATERIALS:

❑ Advertisements/coupons

❑ Shopping bags

❑ 2 shopping carts

❑ 2 cash registers

❑ Shelves and baskets for storing food

❑ Purses/wallets

❑ Dress-up clothes

❑ Many empty food containers (e.g., cardboard boxes, plastic containers, or frozen food bags stuffed with paper and taped shut)

❑ Plastic fruits and vegetables, if available.

PREPARATION:

♡ Create an entrance to the store with a sign, grocery carts, and weekly advertisements/coupons.

♡ Set up store area so that food is grouped like in a natural grocery store. Label several areas.

♡ Place the cash registers on a table or shelf to create checkout lanes.

♡ Create a home area where the toddlers can dress up and write grocery lists before going to the store.

NURTURING STRATEGIES:

1. When a toddler selects the experience, observe her from afar; allow time to explore the materials.

2. If the child is engaging in functional play (e.g., pushing an empty grocery cart), prompt make-believe play by asking a question, such as:
   "Nerida, you have a shopping cart. What are you going to buy at the store?"

3. If a toddler is engaging in make-believe play, provide support for the play. Be cautious not to disrupt the flow of play or to take over the play.

4. Encourage the toddler to engage in conversation while playing with the material by asking open-ended questions. This will allow you to better understand what the child is thinking.

5. Make cleaning up the area part of the play. For example, say:
   "The grocer needs help restocking the shelves. Do you want to replenish the fruits or vegetables?"

☀ Highlighting Development

Preoperational children continue to develop in their ability to use mental symbols. They use gestures and language, typically expressed through play, to represent their thoughts. They also use one object to represent another. For example, they can use a banana as a telephone. Thus, they need to be provided a variety of materials that can be used in multiple ways.

VARIATION:

♡ Take a field trip to a grocery. Then have children help set up the dramatic play area.

ADDITIONAL INFORMATION:

♡ Dramatic play themes/props should reflect the lives of the young children. They cannot yet act out or pretend about something if they lack personal experience.

♡ Communicating with families about frequent experiences such as a train ride to visit grandparents may help young children to select themes/props.

♡ Asking close–ended questions can be disruptive to make-believe play. Close–ended questions, or single-answer questions, are those that require few decision-making skills; most often they require a yes or no answer. For example, asking a child to verbally label an object or its color, or count a group of objects creates interference. Instead, ask an open-ended question such as: "What items are you going to buy at the store?"

 Make sure all of the food containers are clean by washing them in hot, soapy water.

25 to 30 months

Preparing Frozen Bananas

Child's Developmental Goals

✓ To experience transformations
✓ To follow directions

MATERIALS:

- Half banana for each child
- Popsicle™ sticks for each banana
- Corn syrup
- Knife
- Wheat germ
- Wax paper
- 3 metal pie pans
- Cookie sheet
- Finely chopped peanuts
- Permanent markers
- Recipe board including pictures and words

PREPARATION:

♡ Print the following recipe on a large piece of tag board. If desired, draw a picture of each of the five steps on the recipe chart. Hang the chart where the children can easily view it.

RECIPE
1. Remove the peel from the banana.
2. Insert stick into banana.
3. Dip the banana in corn syrup.
4. Roll the banana in wheat germ and/or nuts.
5. Place on cookie sheet.
6. Freeze.

♡ To prevent browning, cut each banana in half before peeling.

♡ Pour a small amount of corn syrup, wheat germ, and nuts in the bottom of the three different pie pans.

♡ Cover cookie sheet with wax paper.

♡ Clean and sanitize child-size table, then place all material there.

♡ Write each child's name on their Popsicle stick for easy identification later.

NURTURING STRATEGIES:

1. Assist each toddler, as necessary, with washing hands.
2. Introduce the experience by saying, for example:
   "We love to eat bananas. I have found a new way to make and enjoy them. Have you ever eaten a frozen banana?"
   Pause for response. Then say:
   "I need your help to make frozen bananas. Here is the recipe for making them. Let's read it together."
3. Assist the children in completing the tasks. To promote independence, provide more verbal assistance than hands-on assistance whenever possible. Further-

more, ask questions to prompt recall. For example, say: *"Dhani, what should you do with this Popsicle stick?"* *"What should you do next?"*

4. Refer to the recipe board for guidance.
5. Ask open-ended questions throughout the activity to spark conversation with the toddler. Questions include: *"Where did the banana go, Dhani? I can only see nuts."*
6. Once the banana is coated and placed on the tray, explain that the last step involves putting the banana in the freezer. Discuss how it will take a long time for the banana to freeze and that he won't be able to eat it until the afternoon snack. Then have the toddler wash his hands.
7. When frozen, serve the banana for snack. Explain that you will read the names written on the sticks to know who made the banana.

☀ Highlighting Development

Good nutrition and healthy eating habits that are developed during the toddler years build the foundation for future good health. A balanced diet ensures that nutritional needs for growth are met and aids in a child's ability to learn (Thompson, 1999). However, a healthy diet for toddlers is not the same as that for adults. Toddlers need to eat three meals with snacks in between because they have smaller stomachs. Furthermore, the amount of food required for each serving is about one-third to one-half of an adult serving.

VARIATIONS:

♡ Roll bananas in peanut butter that has been mixed with small amount of milk.

♡ Find other fruits to eat frozen on hot days, such as blueberries or grapes cut in half.

ADDITIONAL INFORMATION:

♡ Children who learn to make healthy food choices develop life-long habits. The Food Guide Pyramid for young children was developed by the U.S. Department of Agriculture (USDA) as a model for planning meals and snacks for children two to six years old. According to this guide, toddlers need six servings from the grain food group, three servings of vegetables, two servings of fruit, two servings of meat, and two servings of milk daily.

 Check children's records to ensure that there are no food allergies before introducing this experience.

Locating Something Bigger . . . Something Smaller

Child's Developmental Goals

✓ To increase understanding of size differences
✓ To create or modify schema for comparing objects

MATERIALS:

❑ Large object
❑ Small object (large enough so that it is not a choking hazard)

PREPARATION:

♡ Place chosen objects in a convenient and accessible location.

NURTURING STRATEGIES:

1. If you notice a toddler who is not engaged with materials, retrieve the two objects.
2. Gain the toddler's attention by saying her name and inviting her to play a game.
3. Explain the purpose of the game. While holding up the larger object, say:
   "Mackenzie, look at this teddy bear. Isn't it big? Can you find something in the room that is smaller than this bear? Go look."
4. Provide encouragement and support for this challenging task.
5. If necessary, model how to play the game. Describe your actions and thought processes. For example, say:
   "This block is kind of big. I'm going to compare it to the bear to see which is bigger. Yes! The bear is bigger."
6. If the toddler is still interested in the game after finding several items, show her the small item and encourage her to find bigger items.

☀ Highlighting Development

Toddlers spend a great deal of time creating schemas about how the world works. These schema allow them to compare and contrast items along one dimension. Observe toddlers as they seek to understand the concept of size. They are also adding other size concepts such as *big, small, large,* and *tiny* to their vocabulary.

VARIATIONS:

♡ While toileting or changing the toddler's diaper, play this as a word game.
♡ Increase the challenge by having the toddler find items that are smaller than the small object you chose.

ADDITIONAL INFORMATION:

♡ Toddlers at this stage of development can follow two-step directions. They can also provide answers to where questions or place questions that deal with familiar information related to their immediate environment.
♡ Early mathematical experiences should focus on exploration and discovery. Toddlers develop these concepts by using hands-on, minds-on materials and discovering their relationships such as in this activity. In addition to size, other basic mathematical concepts that can be introduced to toddlers include color, shape, classification, space, volume, time, and temperature.

25 to 30 months

Rocking Baby

Child's Developmental Goals

✓ To imitate an action viewed or experienced at an earlier time

✓ To represent understanding of a bedtime routine

MATERIALS:

- ❑ 2 large boot boxes
- ❑ 2 baby dolls
- ❑ 4 baby blankets
- ❑ 2 small pillows, if available

PREPARATION:

♡ Make a bed in the box for the baby.

♡ Fold one blanket as bedding, then place pillow on top.

♡ Place the baby doll in the bed and cover with other blanket. Repeat for second doll.

♡ Place both the dolls and beds in the dramatic play area.

NURTURING STRATEGIES:

1. When you see a toddler playing with the doll, observe his behavior. What do you notice?

2. Use your knowledge of the child, his family, and his behavior to guide your actions. Facilitate his play, if necessary, through the use of the second doll.

3. Model, for example, rocking and soothing the baby by gently patting the doll and singing a lullaby. Label your behaviors verbally. For example, say:
"What a sleepy baby. I'll rock you to sleep and sing your favorite song."

4. Without interrupting the child's play, engage the child in conversation about his behavior. Comments include:
"What a beautiful song. It helped your baby fall right to sleep. Is this a song your grandfather sings to you at night?"
"You rock the baby gently. He'll be asleep in no time."

☀ Highlighting Development

Cognitive development is tied to social interactions. Young children learn from observing and imitating others. Research has found that learning can be enhanced when an adult labels an action while performing it (Hay, Murray, Cecire, & Nash, 1985). While hanging up a coat, an adult might say, "I'm putting the coat on the hook." This strategy of combining modeling with verbal cues, as opposed to using one strategy or another, appears to be more effective in supporting the recall and imitation of behaviors.

VARIATION:

♡ Encourage two children to play together.

ADDITIONAL INFORMATION:

♡ Young children are greatly influenced by other people. Through modeling, they learn new behaviors as well as a context for those behaviors (Fabes & Martin, 2001).

What's for Snack?

Child's Developmental Goals

✓ To read the snack poster

✓ To practice following directions

MATERIALS:

❑ Poster board

❑ Marker

❑ Photographs or pictures of snack items

❑ All snack items on a tray

PREPARATION:

♡ Create a poster that depicts what will be served for snack. Use graphics from magazines, pictures, drawings, and photographs to assist the children with "reading."

♡ If the children are able to have more than one of a particular item, represent the amount they are able to have with the appropriate number of pictures.

♡ Display the poster in a prominent location near the eating area.

NURTURING STRATEGIES:

1. Just before snack time, sanitize a child-size table. Assist the toddlers as necessary with washing their hands.

2. Place tray of snack items on the table. Encourage the toddlers to help, as appropriate, with passing out snack materials such as cups and napkins.

3. Direct the toddlers' attention to the poster.

4. Encourage them to look at the pictures to assist them with reading and understanding the poster. Provide clues, if necessary.

5. Provide positive reinforcement for reading the snack poster. Comments include:
   "You read the poster to know what was for snack."
   "We counted the pictures to know how many crackers to take from the basket."

6. Provide encouragement and support for this challenging task.

☀ Highlighting Development

"The early childhood years—from birth through age eight—are the most important period for literacy development" (Neuman, Copple, & Bredekamp, 2000, p. 3). Adults can use specific strategies or approaches to support this type of learning. To enhance children's awareness that print conveys meaning, for example, comment on signs and notes in the environment by saying, "Look at the snack menu to see how may crackers you can have."

VARIATIONS:

♡ Make a menu for lunch.

♡ In dramatic play, encourage the children to make their own menus using photographs or pictures of favorite foods.

ADDITIONAL INFORMATION:

♡ With practice, the toddlers will eventually be able to independently serve themselves snack, thus promoting autonomy. To assist them in this process, provide unbreakable, lightweight serving dishes, pitchers, and glasses.

25 to 30 months

Ice Tubs

Child's Developmental Goals

✓ To show ownership of an object

✓ To discuss how the medium feels

MATERIALS:

❑ Large plastic container or quilt box for every two children

❑ Ice cubes or crushed ice

❑ ½-cup measuring cup for each child

❑ Small plastic bowl for each child

PREPARATION:

♡ Divide the ice between the plastic containers, if more than one is used. Place two measuring cups and two bowls in each container.

NURTURING STRATEGIES:

1. If two toddlers select the activity, encourage them to play in the same tub. Say, for example:
   "There are enough room and toys for both of you."

2. Assist the toddlers in equally dividing the toys in the tub to reduce potential conflict. Define the toys as being for one child or the other.

3. Encourage the toddlers to touch the ice. Talk about how the ice feels using words such as *cold, slippery,* or *hard.*

4. Describe the child's actions with the tools by saying:
   "You're using the measuring cup to fill up the bowl with ice."
   "You're scooping the ice with your hands."

5. Provide positive reinforcement for sharing the tools. Comments to make include:
   "Each of you has a measuring cup."
   "You're both playing in the ice."

☀ Highlighting Development

Children at this age lack an understanding of others' feelings, including those of their playmates, siblings, and pets. Often they become very physical and engage in hitting, grabbing, or pushing. You need to be to be aware of these behaviors and respond immediately to any physical aggressiveness. For example, you might say, "Your friend Johnny does not like to be hit. Touch him gently on the arm to get his attention."

VARIATION:

♡ Use tongs or large spoons to pick up the ice cubes.

ADDITIONAL INFORMATION:

♡ Toddlers have to be able to show and experience ownership of materials before they will be able to share them.

♡ Toddlers will often want to eat the ice. For sanitation purposes, provide additional crushed ice in cups that can be eaten.

 Observe carefully to reduce a potential choking hazard.

25 to 30 months

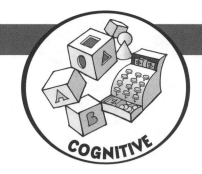

COGNITIVE

Measuring

Child's Developmental Goals

✓ To begin to understand part and whole relationships

✓ To count when filling a cup

MATERIALS:

- ❑ At least two of each of the following measuring cups: ¼-, ½-, and 1-cup
- ❑ Water table or quilt boxes
- ❑ Towels
- ❑ Smock for each child

PREPARATION:

♡ Sanitize water table, move to desired location and fill with 2 to 3 inches of water.

♡ Place towels on the floor to prevent slipping.

♡ Place measuring cups in the water.

NURTURING STRATEGIES:

1. Assist the toddler, if necessary, with washing hands.

2. As the toddler is putting on his smock, introduce the experience by saying, for example:
   "I noticed you measuring sand yesterday. Today, you can measure water with the different size cups."

3. Observe the child working. Note the toddler's use of materials.

4. Describe the toddler's behavior with the measuring cups. Statements include:
   "Diego, you are pouring the water from one cup to another. You are transferring the water."
   "It took four little cups of water to fill up the largest cup."

5. Encourage the toddler to count the number of cups of water that fit inside the largest measuring cup.

6. To spark thinking about quantity and whole-part relationships, ask the toddler to explain a problem he may be facing with the cups. Ask, for example:
   "Why does the little cup overflow every time you pour in water from the big cup?"

☀ Highlighting Development

Through play, toddlers build understanding of concepts such as size, shape, number, classification, comparisons, space, parts and wholes, weight, length, temperature, and time (Charlesworth & Lind, 1999). To promote the development of these concepts, adults must provide a variety of materials and extended periods of time for active learning through exploration. This time of exploration is vital since active learning is the path that promotes optimal brain development (Shore, 1997).

VARIATION:

♡ Use various sizes of measuring spoons with smaller amounts of water.

ADDITIONAL INFORMATION:

♡ The number of measuring cups provided depends on the number of children who can easily engage in the experience at one time. It is best to provide one set of measuring cups for each child who can interact at the same time.

♡ Children acquire concepts through constructive play experiences that activate their senses and engage their minds (Cromwell, 2000).

 Constant supervision is needed to protect children from water hazards. No child should ever be left unattended at a water table or near a water source.

25 to 30 months

Watering Plants

COGNITIVE

Child's Developmental Goals

✓ To experience cause and effect

MATERIALS:
- ❑ Plastic milk jug for each child (gallon or half-gallon size)
- ❑ Hammer
- ❑ Nail
- ❑ Water source (spout or hose)

PREPARATION:
- ♡ To make a watering can, poke holes in the bottom of each milk jug using the hammer and nail.
- ♡ Place near water source.

NURTURING STRATEGIES:
1. When the children notice the "watering cans," fill them with water and introduce the activity. For example, you might say:
   "It hasn't rained in several days. Will you water the plants for me? They need water to be healthy."
2. Describe the children's behavior with the watering cans. Statements include:
   "The ground is soaking up all of the water."
   "You made a puddle in the flower bed."
3. Redirect the children's behavior to maintain a safe, outdoor play area. For example, suggest that the toddlers water the grass instead of the sidewalk because someone might slip on the wet concrete.
4. Refill the watering cans as often as necessary to sustain the toddlers' interest in the experience.

☀ Highlighting Development

Toddlers' thinking capacities reflect a movement toward reasonable and sometimes rational behavior. Their increased verbal abilities allow them not only to express their ideas better but also to understand situations and ideas better. By the middle of the third year of life, toddlers' behavior can be guided by capitalizing on their developing thought and language capabilities (White, 1995).

VARIATIONS:
- ♡ Teach the toddlers how to fill their own watering cans.
- ♡ Fill watering cans with sand and sift it through the holes by shaking.
- ♡ Provide the children with large paintbrushes and bucket of water. They will enjoy "painting" outdoor buildings and sidewalks.

ADDITIONAL INFORMATION:
- ♡ Plan to introduce this experience on a warm day.
- ♡ Experienced teachers recommend providing water and sand experiences, either indoors or outdoors, on a daily basis. Water and sand are nonstructured materials that children find satisfying. By sifting sand or water through their fingers or pouring it back and forth between containers, they release tension (Isenberg, 1993).

25 to 30 months

Counting Cars

Child's Developmental Goals

✓ To develop skills for counting a group of objects

✓ To develop an understanding of the use of numbers

MATERIALS:

❑ Basket

❑ 10 plastic cars

❑ Child–size table or coffee table

PREPARATION:

♡ Clear an area on the child–size table or coffee table.

♡ Place the cars in the basket on the table.

NURTURING STRATEGIES:

1. When a child engages with the materials, observe the toddler's behavior. Determine if the toddler is engaged in functional play.

2. Provide support and encouragement for the functional play. For example, state:
   "Phoebe, you are pushing the cars. They are going fast."

3. If appropriate, model counting the cars. However, take care not to disrupt the flow of play. To illustrate, say: "Five cars: 1, 2, 3, 4, 5 (touch each car while saying the number) are lined up waiting to go to the circus."

4. Note if the child spontaneously imitates your counting of the cars. If the toddler does this, you may consider documenting the behavior with an anecdotal record.

5. Encourage the toddler to count the cars while returning them to the basket at the end of the experience.

☼ Highlighting Development

When provided with frequent and varied experiences, young children begin to acquire a nominal sense of numbers; an understanding that numeral labels represent amounts. Hence, they can verbally apply a number label to an object or group of objects. This is the very beginning of mathematical understanding. At this point, children will use verbal labels inconsistently or in no apparent order.

VARIATIONS:

♡ Find other objects to count.

♡ Counting other objects during cleanup time is a natural thing to do.

ADDITIONAL INFORMATION:

♡ Avoid pushing the toddler to count items. Model applying labels, but encourage free exploration of the materials.

♡ Reciting finger plays, nursery rhymes, and singing counting songs all assist in this development as well (See Appendices F and G).

♡ There are two types of counting used by young children: rote and rational. Rote counting is the process of reciting numbers in order from memory; rational counting involves attaching a numeral to each object in a series or group, which is the type of learning supported in this experience. Listen. Often beginning learners make mistakes by either counting an object twice or failing to count one or more objects. Adults should consider this as normal behavior and need not correct the child. With repeated experiences, children will learn rational counting skills.

25 to 30 months

Social
Development

TWENTY-FIVE to
THIRTY MONTHS

Bluebird

SOCIAL

Child's Developmental Goals

✓ To participate in a small group activity

✓ To sing a song with others

MATERIALS:

None

PREPARATION:

♡ Write words to song on a note card for yourself or on a poster board for everyone to view if this song is unfamiliar.

♡ Clear a large floor space of any obstacles to prevent possible injury and allow for optimal movement.

NURTURING STRATEGIES:

1. Gather a small group of toddlers in the cleared space and introduce the activity. Explain that everyone who wants to fly like a bird in and out of a window will get a chance.

2. Have the children stand up, hold hands and take one or two steps backwards to make the circle bigger. Demonstrate and then assist one toddler with pretending to be a bird by "flying" and weaving between the other children.

3. Set a limit so that the toddler will know when his turn is over. State, for example:
   "Each person will get to fly while we sing two times. I will let you know when your turn is almost over."

4. Lead singing the song.

   Bluebird, bluebird
   In and out my window
   Bluebird, bluebird
   In and out my window
   Bluebird, bluebird
   Won't you fly with me?

5. After the first singing of the song, pause briefly to tell the child that his turn is almost over and then it will be someone else's turn. For example, say: *"Matthew, you can fly for one more song and then it will be Faith's turn."*

6. Encourage the toddlers to sing along with you.

7. Repeat the game for any children who want to participate.

☀ Highlighting Development

Group games are often too complicated for toddlers, because they lack the cognitive ability to understand rules or how to coordinate their actions with one another. However, they revel in playing games that allow them to practice and refine gross motor skills. Thus, the focus for children at this stage of development should remain on movement skills and sharing space rather than following a particular set of rules.

VARIATIONS:

♡ Sing other movement songs such as "London Bridge."

♡ Alter the color of the bird for a bit of variety.

ADDITIONAL INFORMATION:

♡ A child's capacity for developing pro-social behaviors, including turn-taking, increases with age. By three years of age, young children are less egocentric and territorial, thus more able to engage in simple games.

25 to 30 months

Oops!

Child's Developmental Goals

✔ To begin to consider another's perspective

✔ To see the effect of their behavior on others

MATERIALS:

None

PREPARATION:

None

NURTURING STRATEGIES:

1. Carefully observe the toddlers and anticipate situations that might need your assistance. For example, one toddler is building with blocks in the middle of the carpet and another toddler is pushing a grocery cart.

2. When possible, be proactive rather than reactive in your guidance approach. In this situation, you may wish to redirect the toddler with the cart to avoid knocking over a block structure. It is much easier to push the cart elsewhere than to move the block structure. When redirecting the pushing behavior, focus on possible outcomes for both children. Comment, for example:

   "Jodelle, push your cart over here. You can go around the shoe store. Booker would be upset if you accidentally knocked over her block structure."

3. If an accident does occur, move to the children and stoop down to their level. Explain to Booker that it was an accident. Say, for example:

   "Jodelle did not mean to knock over your blocks. It was an accident. Let's tell her how you feel."

4. Gain the other toddler's attention and help the first child explain his feelings. Expand on Booker's comments whenever necessary.

5. In a warm and caring way, explain to Jodelle how she needs to use her toys carefully to keep from interrupting another child's work.

☼ Highlighting Development

A sense of morality grows out of social relationships (Damon, 1988). In the early years, adults externally control a child's morality by using positive guidance techniques that involve discussing the effects of the child's behavior on others. This technique has been shown to support moral development. On the other hand, punitive or guilt-inducing techniques tend to impede moral development (Berk, 1999).

VARIATION:

♡ Describe the child's reaction if she is unable to do so.

ADDITIONAL INFORMATION:

♡ If working in an early childhood setting, you may want to write newsletter articles for parents/guardians on the type of positive guidance strategies. Marion (1999) is an excellent resource for assisting you in this process.

♡ Utilizing positive guidance strategies contributes greatly to creating a caring community of learners (Bredekamp & Copple, 1997). Such an environment fosters consideration and contribution to each person's well-being in a group.

25 to 30 months

What Do You Do?

SOCIAL

Child's Developmental Goals

✓ To begin to understand that men and women can do similar jobs

✓ To continue developing their sense of gender identity

MATERIALS:

❑ Two photographs of familiar people, if possible, who have the same occupation but are different genders such as male and female firefighter

❑ Photo album or three-ring binder

❑ Colored paper

❑ Marker

PREPARATION:

♡ Mount each photograph on a piece of colored paper. Write a caption for each photograph being sure to highlight the name of the person in the picture and his/her occupation. Place the mounted pictures in the photo album or three-ring binder. Then, place the book in a convenient location for the toddlers.

NURTURING STRATEGIES:

1. Observe the toddler once the book is selected.
2. Engage the toddler in a conversation about the pictures by pointing to them and asking questions such as:
   "Who is in this picture?"
   "What job does Malcolm's mom do? Look at her uniform." Pause for a response.
3. Elaborate and/or recast the child's response, if necessary. For example, if the toddler says "policeman" say:
   "Yes, Malcolm's mom is a police officer. She keeps us safe."
4. Encourage the toddler to find the other gender police officer. When the second photograph is located, discuss similarities and differences between the photographs.

5. Continue as long as the toddler is interested.
6. Conclude the experience by commenting:
   "These pictures were fun to look at. We learned that men and women can have the same job."

☀ Highlighting Development

At this stage of development, toddlers are in search of a sense of self. By viewing themselves as separate and different from their primary caregiver, toddlers begin to develop gender identity. This process takes many years, and some argue that there is no end to this process. During toddlerhood, young children can identify themselves and others as boys or girls. To do this, they rely on visual clues. They can easily become confused by appearances such as males with longer hair. It is not until the end of the preschool period that children realize that gender is constant or nonchanging. Until that time, they believe, for example, that little boys can grow up to be mommies, if they want.

VARIATION:

♡ Use paper or wooden dolls that can "dress" in different unrelated uniforms.

ADDITIONAL INFORMATION:

♡ Adopt gender-neutral language when speaking with young children. Contrary to popular belief, they do not think male or female when they hear "fireman or policeman." In their concrete interpretation of the terms, they think "man." Words or phrases such as firefighter, police officer, mail carrier, flight attendant, and hair stylist eliminate such gender bias.

♡ By age two and a half, most children have learned basic stereotypes about the sexes. They think that girls cry a lot and have long hair. On the other hand, boys hit people more and are stronger than girls.

London Bridge

Child's Developmental Goals

✓ To participate in a game
✓ To sing a song with others

MATERIALS:

None

PREPARATION:

♡ Write words to sing on a note card for yourself or on a poster board for everyone to view if this is not a familiar song.
♡ Clear a large space of any obstacles.

NURTURING STRATEGIES:

1. Gather at least two toddlers who are good friends in the cleared space and introduce the activity. Explain that both of them will be able to be the bridge and both of them will be able to walk. Comment also about how they will be taking turns.
2. Sing the song through one time.

   London Bridge is falling down
   Falling down, falling down.
   London Bridge is falling down
   My fair lady.

   Take the key and lock her up
   Lock her up, lock her up.
   Take the key and lock her up,
   My fair lady.

3. Take the hands of one child and form the bridge. Encourage the other toddler to walk under the bridge while everyone sings.
4. When you get to the "lock her up" part, drop your arms around the walking toddler and gently rock back and forth.

5. Comment on the toddlers' enthusiasm and how fun the game is to play.
6. Switch roles and begin again. Encourage the toddlers to sing along.
7. Whenever possible, invite other interested toddlers to join the experience.

☀ Highlighting Development

Young children need time to form relationships with peers. Toddlers who are around age mates on a regular basis, such as at a play group, library story hour, or a child care program are more likely to build true peer relationships that are evidenced by reciprocal play and positive emotion (Ross, Conant, Cheyne, & Alevizos, 1992).

VARIATIONS:

♡ Sing other movement songs such as "Ring Around the Rosie" (see Appendix F).
♡ Have the toddlers be the bridge that you walk through.

ADDITIONAL INFORMATION:

♡ After infancy, there is a gradual shift in the importance of friendships. At this stage of development, toddlers' social relationships are broadening to include peers. However, the ability to form friendships is not innate. Toddlers must be taught to respect and act pro-socially by using positive behaviors. Gradually, they learn that acting in a positive manner elicits positive responses, and therefore, opportunities for friendships with others.

25 to 30 months

Save Some for . . .

SOCIAL

Child's Developmental Goals

✓ To develop concern for the welfare of others

✓ To act in a caring manner

MATERIALS:

❑ Snack items on a tray

PREPARATION:

♡ Clean a child-size table or coffee table.

♡ Place the snack tray on it.

NURTURING STRATEGIES:

1. Assist the toddlers as needed with washing hands.
2. Invite them to join you at the table and find a seat.
3. Enlist their help in distributing napkins, cups, etc.
4. Allow the children to serve themselves snack with guidance. For example, say:
   "Today we have cheese and crackers. You can have four crackers and two pieces of cheese to start with."
5. Engage the children in meaningful conversations. Topics might include discussing their day, either past events or ones to come shortly, or specific projects they worked on.
6. When the children want seconds of snack, involve them in problem solving. Say, for example:
   "Before we have seconds, we need to think about Evita. She is still asleep. What can we do to make sure she gets snack?"
7. Guide them to consider Evita's point of view. Label her possible emotional reactions to waking up hungry and not having any snack.
8. Encourage the toddlers to set aside a serving of snack.
9. Provide positive reinforcement for helping Evita.
10. Set new limits on serving size and repeat steps 4 and 5.

☀ Highlighting Development

According to Charlesworth (2000), toddlers are pre-moral: They are just beginning to learn about right and wrong. Figuring out which kinds of acts fall into each category is complex and takes much trial and error. Thus, it often appears that their values are specific to a situation. For example, just because they have learned to be nice to their sister does not mean they will be nice to a neighbor.

VARIATION:

♡ Encourage the toddlers to make get-well cards for a sick relative or friend.

ADDITIONAL INFORMATION:

♡ Toddlers learn the cognitive skills, values, and norms of their culture through active participation with others. This activity focuses on developing a moral consciousness that unfolds in stages. The initial sense of right and wrong at this stage is concrete with the child anticipating the personal consequences of her act. In other words, the child asks, "What will happen to me if I eat all of the cheesecake?" At a later stage, the child will learn to think of how another person will feel.

♡ Research has shown that toddlers respond emotionally and physically to moral transgressions but often pay little attention to conventional transgressions. Thus, even toddlers demonstrate concern when they or others are harmed or toys are taken without permission (Smetana, 1984, cited in Charlesworth, 2000).

25 to 30 months

SOCIAL

Singing on the Stage

Child's Developmental Goals

✓ To interact with other children

✓ To share a space with another child

MATERIALS:

❑ Large hollow blocks

❑ Transparent adhesive tape

PREPARATION:

♡ Clear a corner of the room.

♡ Build a platform out of the blocks and secure in place with the tape.

NURTURING STRATEGIES:

1. Observe the toddlers' behaviors after they select the stage. Note what they do spontaneously or without your guidance.
2. Prevent inappropriate behavior by suggesting they sing a song. Encourage the toddlers to select the song to be sung. To illustrate, say:
   "This is a stage. People sing from stages. What songs would you like to sing?"
3. Record the children's suggestions, if necessary, so that they do not forget a suggestion.
4. Singing along with the children will denote the value of this experience.
5. If necessary, redirect inappropriate behavior by providing alternative activities. Use comments such as:
   "It is not safe to jump from the stage. Too many friends are close-by. Someone might accidentally get hurt. You can jump over by the climber. That would be safer for everyone—including you!"
   Reinforce the last statement nonverbally with a smile and a gentle squeeze.

☼ Highlighting Development

Children's patterns of behavior have been related to the way in which they are treated by their parents. Baumrind (1967) classified parental control into three groups: authoritarian, authoritative, and permissive. Children of authoritative parents were more likely to be self-reliant, cheerful, cooperative with peers, and so on. Parents, like teachers, can learn positive guidance strategies, which parallel behaviors of the authoritative parenting style (see, for example, Marion, 1999).

VARIATION:

♡ Have the toddlers act out a favorite nursery rhyme or book on the stage.

ADDITIONAL INFORMATION:

♡ All areas of development are interrelated—physical, language and communication, cognitive, social, and emotional. Moreover, the primary focus of socialization in any culture is language. Therefore, it is important for children to develop competence in social communication, which is the ability to convey a message intended to others (Fabes & Martin, 2001). To promote this development, children need a supportive yet challenging environment with excellent role models.

 Construct the platform only one block high. Building higher may be a safety hazard, especially if a toddler would fall.

25 to 30 months

Eggs in a Basket

SOCIAL

Child's Developmental Goals

✓ To play a game with a friend

✓ To interact with another toddler

MATERIALS:

❑ Plastic eggs

❑ 2 or 3 baskets, depending on the number of toddlers

PREPARATION:

♡ Check the eggs to ensure that there are no cracks, which could pinch the children's fingers, scratch, or cut their skin.

♡ Hide the eggs in different locations in the outdoor area where they are easily accessible.

NURTURING STRATEGIES:

1. When a toddler selects a basket, introduce the activity enthusiastically by saying:
   "I saw a chicken out here earlier. I wonder if she left some eggs for us. Can you help me look?"

2. Explain the purpose of the basket, if necessary.

3. At your first opportunity, invite another child to join in the egg hunt. Select this child based on your knowledge of the children's friendships.

4. If a child is becoming frustrated and needs assistance with finding an egg to put in the basket, encourage the other toddler to help. Say, for example:
   "Nassef is frustrated because he cannot find an egg. Can you help him find one?"

5. Provide positive reinforcement for helping. Comments to make include:
   "Nicholas, you were a good friend to Nassef. You helped him to find an egg."
   "You helped Nassef feel better by showing him where to find an egg."

6. Discuss with the toddlers whether the eggs they found came from a real chicken. Clarify and/or reinforce their construction of the concept of make believe depending on the toddlers' current level of understanding.

☀ Highlighting Development

Although they lack the ability to verbally communicate the importance of friends or friendships, older toddlers clearly demonstrate this understanding through their behavior. Watch them. Toddlers will greet a friend with more excitement, engage in more laughter, and talk more to each other than do non-friends (Berk, 1999).

VARIATIONS:

♡ Hide other toys or objects for the toddlers to find.

♡ Encourage the toddlers to hide the eggs and then find them again.

♡ Play the game indoors.

ADDITIONAL INFORMATION:

♡ Increase or decrease the challenge for this experience by using your knowledge of the toddlers' level of understanding about object permanence.

♡ According to Fogel (2001), at this stage of development children are showing a tendency to engage in social play. In the past, they engaged in pretend sequences on their own. Now they are increasing their rates of verbalizations to their peers as well as social interactions.

25 to 30 months

SOCIAL

Sand Roads

Child's Developmental Goals

✓ To engage in parallel play

✓ To demonstrate interest in another child

MATERIALS:

❑ Water table

❑ 8 to 10 plastic cars

❑ Road signs

❑ Clean, sifted sand

❑ Water

PREPARATION:

♡ Clean the water table and fill with 3 to 4 inches of sand.

♡ Place cars and signs in the sand.

♡ If necessary, dampen the sand with water.

NURTURING STRATEGIES:

1. When a toddler selects the activity, observe his behavior noting how the toys are being used.

2. If necessary, invite another child to play in the sand table. To illustrate, say:
   "Ming-Na, would you like to play with the cars in the sand table? These are the cars you built yesterday."

3. When the two toddlers are working at the sand table, observe their behavior. Ask yourself if they are looking at each other and if they are imitating each other's behavior.

4. Comment on the fact that the toddlers are sharing the sand. If applicable, comment on sharing the signs and cars. State, for example:
   "Ming-Na and Caleb, you are both using the sand table. I see that each of you has two cars."

5. Encourage the toddlers to attend to each other's behavior. Comments to make include:
   "Caleb, look at how Ming-Na is making a road. The car drives better on a road."

☀ Highlighting Development

Toddlers are very interested in other children at this stage of development. Unfortunately, they lack important social skills such as the ability to coordinate their actions with another or to share materials. Observe them. Toddlers engage in parallel play. When this type of play occurs, the toddlers play independently but in the same area with similar materials. They will demonstrate interest in each other while playing by observing, making eye contact, and imitating the play behaviors of the children around them.

VARIATIONS:

♡ Use wet sand instead of dry sand to provide a new experience.

♡ Add people to further encourage pretend play.

ADDITIONAL INFORMATION:

♡ Adults play an important role in promoting children's play by showing respect and acting as a facilitator. They can stimulate the children's natural curiosity and active engagement by describing the children's actions or the properties of play objects and asking open-ended questions. In addition to verbally responding, adults can support play by observing and modifying the environment by adding or removing props as necessary.

25 to 30 months

Riding the Horsey

SOCIAL

Child's Developmental Goals

✔ To engage in pretend play

✔ To use a baby doll as the object of their play

MATERIALS:

❑ 2 or 3 baby dolls

❑ Rocking horse

PREPARATION:

♡ Clean an area for the rocking horses.

♡ Place the stuffed animals near the horses, but not too close to cause a safety hazard.

NURTURING STRATEGIES:

1. When a toddler selects a rocking horse, observe the child's abilities.

2. Model giving a baby doll a ride on the other horse. Connect your actions with words by saying:
   "Charlie likes to ride the horse. Hear him say 'whee'?"

3. If the child does not imitate your behavior, allow him time to rock for a while. Then, suggest giving one of the babies a ride. While pointing to the baby doll, say:
   "I think that Charlie would like to ride the horse too. Can he ride with you?" Whenever possible, encourage another toddler to give the doll a ride on the horse or offer for Charlie to share his horse with the toddler.

☀ Highlighting Development

Given their ability to think using symbols, toddlers start to engage in pretend play. In the beginning, their pretend play is self-directed (Berk, 1999). For example, toddlers pretend to feed themselves, go to sleep, or even take a bath. After this stage, they will begin to incorporate pretend objects. To illustrate, instead of feeding themselves, they would feed a doll or stuffed animal. It is not until after toddlerhood that they, typically, become a "detached participant" who assists a doll with feeding itself or one doll with feeding another (Berk, 1999, p. 325).

VARIATION:

♡ Provide cars and stuffed animals.

ADDITIONAL INFORMATION:

♡ Children between 25 and 36 months of age can typically be expected to use a rocking horse for three minutes without falling off (Charlesworth, 2000).

♡ In dramatic play, children try out many roles drawn from daily life. They may be a mommy, daddy, or even baby. They may wash the car, cook dinner, go to a birthday party, or vacuum the rug. Through this type of play, concept development grows as the children engage in practicing their understanding of the world (Gonzalez–Mena, 2001).

25 to 30 months

SOCIAL

Mailing Letters to . . .

Child's Developmental Goals

✓ To communicate with another child

✓ To increase understanding of the purpose of writing

✓ To begin developing an appreciation for print

MATERIALS:

❑ Box for each child (small boxes used by bakeries for cookies are perfect because the lid is attached and they are sturdy)

❑ Photo of each child

❑ Paper

❑ Washable, nontoxic, felt-tip markers

❑ Envelopes

PREPARATION:

♡ Label a box for each child with her or his photograph and printed name.

♡ Display the boxes so that toddlers can easily access them.

♡ Provide paper, markers, and envelopes in a writing area on a child-size table.

NURTURING STRATEGIES:

1. Introduce the mailboxes to the children. To illustrate, say:

   "These boxes are here to collect mail. If you want to write a letter to someone, write it. Then, place it in the box with her or his picture. That way your friend will get the letter you wrote."

2. Once a toddler has completed her letter, you may need to provide assistance in locating the appropriate mailbox. To do this, focus the child's attention on the photographs. When the correct mailbox has been selected, point out the written name also. To illustrate, say:

   "You found Tama's mailbox. Here is her photograph and here is her name. Look at the letters. Here is a T."

3. Keep an informal tabulation regarding who is sending and receiving mail. If a child has not received any mail from a friend, you can encourage someone to write him/her a letter or write a letter to the child yourself.

☀ Highlighting Development

A print-rich environment should be a part of a child's world from birth. However, awareness of print takes many years to develop. As young children experience people around them reading and writing, they come to understand that the printed word can be used for many purposes—to regulate actions, to communicate information, to interact with others, and to seek information—to name just a few (see McGee and Richgils, 2000).

VARIATION:

♡ Create real postcards and take a walking field trip to mail them to important others.

♡ Create a pen pal system with children in other classrooms within your building.

ADDITIONAL INFORMATION:

♡ Mailing and receiving latters can provide meaningful opportunities for literacy development. When writing or identifying a child's name, focus on the first letter.

♡ To encourage pre-writing, children need special space devoted to this purpose. The area should include a variety of tools and paper for exploration. To sustain their interest, this area must remain neat and orderly and contain properly functioning tools. Therefore, the children should assume responsibility for caring for the felt-tip markers to prevent them from drying out. Teach them how to replace the caps. When necessary, provide reminders.

25 to 30 months

Emotional
Development

TWENTY-FIVE to
THIRTY MONTHS

Sitting on the Potty

Child's Developmental Goals

✓ To experience a sense of satisfaction

✓ To gain a sense of accomplishment

✓ To practice self-help skills

MATERIALS:
❑ Regular diapering supplies

PREPARATION:
♡ Arrange supplies on or near the changing table.

NURTURING STRATEGIES:
1. When it is time to diaper the toddler, provide him with a warning about the upcoming change. To illustrate, say:
   "It will be your turn to sit on the potty next, Mac."
2. Provide verbal reminders, as necessary, of the steps in using the potty.
3. Encourage the toddler to pull down his pants and remove his diaper before sitting on the toilet.
4. Engage the toddler in conversation.
5. When the child is finished, move the toddler to the changing table and replace the diaper.
6. Provide support for completing the next two steps of the diapering routine. Say, for example:
   "Pull up your pants Mac. Then wash your hands."
7. Finish the diapering procedures.

VARIATION:
♡ If facilities are available, encourage two toddlers to use the restroom at the same time. Children can be models for each other, so pair a toddler who is almost toilet-trained with a child who is just beginning the process.

Highlighting Development

Learning to use the toilet independently is a complicated task. There are many steps to remember in a relatively set sequence. To promote autonomy and a sense of accomplishment, it is necessary to divide the task into small steps. Between 25 and 30 months of age, toddlers should be able to remove their pants and then pull them back up when finished. Likewise, they should also be able to wash their hands with minimal assistance.

ADDITIONAL INFORMATION:
♡ In a child care program, you may need to provide suggestions to parents or guardians about appropriate clothing for toddlers who are learning to use the toilet independently. Bib overalls, for example, are attractive, but they inhibit young children's ability to undress independently. Sweatpants or other pants with elastic waists are much easier for them to remove.

♡ According to Leach (1992), for young children, becoming clean is far easier than becoming dry. Typically, toddlers will follow a predictable pattern with toilet training. Bowel control usually emerges first followed by the daytime control of the bladder. Finally, nighttime control of the bladder is obtained.

♡ Carefully observe the toddler for toileting cues. Typically, a child will communicate using the same words or gestures whenever needing to use the toilet.

25 to 30 months

EMOTIONAL

My Turn

Child's Developmental Goals

✓ To express emotions appropriately

✓ To take turns

MATERIALS:

❑ 2 toddler swings in outside play area

PREPARATION:

♡ Check that the swings are in good repair and free of any safety hazards.

NURTURING STRATEGIES:

1. When a toddler chooses to swing, provide assistance as needed.
2. Converse or sing with the toddler while pushing the swing.
3. If available, invite another toddler to swing. Involve that child in the conversation or singing.
4. When a third toddler asks to swing, tell him that he can have a turn next. For example, say:
   "Erica, you can swing when either Ida or Santiago is finished."
5. If the toddler becomes upset with having to wait, label the emotion she may be feeling. Use comments such as:
   "It is frustrating to have to wait."
   "You're sad because you wanted to swing."
6. Encourage the toddler to select another area in which to play until it is her turn. This is often a difficult task for toddlers. Therefore, be prepared for the toddler to remain in the area. Set any limits to keep the toddler safe. Say, for example:
   "Erica, please stand in the grass and sing with us. I don't want you to get hit with the swing."

7. If the child does choose another area, politely interrupt her play when it is her turn. Give her a choice of continuing her play or joining the others at the swings. This step is important in maintaining a trustful relationship with the toddler.

☀ Highlighting Development

Learning to express and regulate emotions appropriately has been found to be predictive of later development, whereas a lack of such skill has been associated with pathological disorders (Charlesworth, 2000). Carefully observe toddlers in your care. If you notice a lack of a particular skill, take the time to teach and promote further development. It will pay off in the long run.

VARIATION:

♡ Incorporate literacy skills by posting a notepad near the swings. When a child wants a turn, write the toddler's name on the waiting list.

ADDITIONAL INFORMATION:

♡ Learning to take turns is a high-level skill. Children must trust that you will follow through with what you say. Therefore, do not make promises you cannot keep, because outdoor play space must often be shared. Keep a close eye on the time before promising a child a turn. It may not be possible.

25 to 30 months

Serving Myself Juice

EMOTIONAL

Child's Developmental Goals

✓ To experience sense of accomplishment
✓ To perform a task independently

MATERIALS:

❑ 2 to 3 small, child-size plastic pitchers
❑ Unbreakable glass for each toddler
❑ Snack items
❑ Tray
❑ Juice

PREPARATION:

♡ Pour approximately 4 inches of juice into each pitcher.
♡ Keep extra beverages handy to refill pitchers when necessary.
♡ Place all snack items on a tray.

NURTURING STRATEGIES:

1. Clean and sanitize the child-size table. Remind the toddlers to wash their hands before snack. Set tray with snack items on the table.
2. Assist the toddlers with passing out snack. Encourage them to pour their own juice. Comments might include: "Sydney Ray, please pour your juice and then pass the pitcher to Wade. He would like some juice also."
3. Provide physical and verbal assistance, as needed, with pouring the juice. The main assistance needed might be your holding the cup still while the toddler pours liquid into it.
4. Ask open-ended questions throughout the snack to spark conversations with the toddlers.

☀ Highlighting Development

By 30 months, toddlers should possess sufficient eye-hand coordination skills to pour water from one container to another with minimal spilling (Charlesworth, 2000). Thus, they should be given small pitchers of liquids from which to pour beverages at snack and mealtimes. Serving themselves will not only promote physical development but also their sense of autonomy.

VARIATIONS:

♡ On hot days, make ice water and cups accessible while playing outside. Encourage toddlers to serve themselves when thirsty. This will add to their sense of autonomy and help prevent dehydration.

ADDITIONAL INFORMATION:

♡ Children at this age are learning to coordinate their movements. With age and experience, they will become increasingly more efficient with self-help routines such as eating, dressing, and brushing teeth. Toddlers should possess sufficient skills so they no longer need spillproof cups. Help them pour small amounts of liquids into their cups to reduce cleanup if an accident occurs.

25 to 30 months

Bye, Bye Window

Child's Developmental Goals

✓ To cope with separation distress
✓ To express feelings appropriately

MATERIALS:

❏ Large hollow blocks
❏ Strong, adhesive tape

PREPARATION:

♡ Arrange large hollow blocks into steps and a platform under a window, facing the parking lot.
♡ Measure to ensure that a toddler can easily see out of the window when standing on the blocks.
♡ Secure the blocks with tape to prevent movement.

NURTURING STRATEGIES:

1. When a toddler becomes upset with the departure of a significant other, provide support and comfort. Label the emotion being displayed by the toddler. Say, for example:
   "Ruby, you are mad that dad left. You wanted to leave with him."
   "What a sad face. You will miss mom while she's at work."
2. Encourage the toddler to go to the Bye, Bye Window and wave good-bye.
3. Accompany the toddler to the window, if she desires.
4. Provide positive reinforcement for using positive coping skills to deal with strong emotions. Comments to make include:
   "It hurts when dad leaves. Watching him from the window helped you to calm down."
   "You used the Bye, Bye Window to help you feel less sad."

☀ Highlighting Development

Often toddlers still experience separation distress when a parent or significant adult leaves them. Such behavior can be expected to last up to three years of age. Children who receive a verbal explanation for the leave-taking tend to protest less and show less stress (Field, Gewirtz, Cohen, Garcia, Greenberg, & Collins, 1984). Hence, parents need to know the importance of saying good-bye and of the normalcy of such protests by toddlers.

VARIATIONS:

♡ If windows are low enough, arrange a few chairs for the children to sit in and wave good-bye.
♡ Encourage toddlers to help each other when coping with separation distress.

ADDITIONAL INFORMATION:

♡ Toddlers need to learn that others can be trusted. As a result, help create a positive environment by explaining to parents/guardians the importance of saying and waving good-bye to their toddlers as part of the separation process. Sneaking out of the room damages the child's confidence in the parents/guardians. It can also increase the children's anxiety and create a sense of abandonment.

⊘ CAUTION If the platform needs to be greater than two blocks high, consider having a carpenter build a sturdy platform with stairs and a railing to prevent falls.

25 to 30 months

Welcoming a New Friend

Child's Developmental Goals

✓ To develop pro-social behaviors such as helping someone

✓ To begin considering someone else's perspective

MATERIALS:

None

PREPARATION:

None

NURTURING STRATEGIES:

1. Tell the toddler that a new child will be visiting your home or classroom, whichever the case may be.
2. Engage the toddler in a conversation about how it feels to visit someplace new. Utilize descriptive words such as *excited, scary, nervous, confused,* and so on. Whenever possible, connect your conversation to the toddler's past experiences.
3. Tell the toddler the visitor's name.
4. Encourage the toddler to consider things he could do to help the visitor feel better. Comments to make include:
   "Urian, could you show him your favorite toy?"
   "Maybe you should show him where the bathroom is."
5. When the visitor arrives, greet him by bending to his level and calling him by name. Provide the child time to take in his surroundings before introducing him to Urian.
6. After the visitor leaves, provide positive reinforcement about at least one thing the toddler did to help the visitor. Comment, for example:
   "Urian, I think that Zu-Wang felt much better after you showed him the slide."
   "Our visitor seemed less nervous after you shared animal crackers with him."

Highlighting Development

Piaget's theory suggests that toddlers and young preschoolers are very egocentric, meaning they have difficulty taking another person's perspective. Research on emotional development, specifically pro-social behaviors, is causing this notion to be reconsidered. Toddlers spend a great deal of time studying other people's reactions, which suggests they understand, to a limited degree, that others have feelings or reactions, which may differ from their own. In terms of friendships, they think primarily about their side of the relationship. That is, what others can do for them.

VARIATION:

♡ Help the toddler identify how it feels to meet someone new. Focus on his emotional reactions to the situation.

ADDITIONAL INFORMATION:

♡ Meeting new people and entering new environments can be scary for anyone—adults included. Discussing how you feel can be an important model for the toddlers.

♡ According to Kostelnik, et al. (2002), young children define friendship in terms of proximity. They call those peers with whom they play most often or engage in similar activities their friends. They will also value friendships for possessions. For example, a child might say, "He is my friend; he has a fire truck."

EMOTIONAL

Recovering from a Tantrum

Child's Developmental Goals

✓ To regain control after a tantrum

✓ To use an adult for emotional support

MATERIALS:

None

PREPARATION:

None

NURTURING STRATEGIES:

1. When you see a child throwing a tantrum, clear the area as quickly as possible to prevent injuries.
2. Speak to the child in a calm and loving voice about what behaviors you are observing. State, for example:
   "Amy, I can see that you are very, very upset. You are crying and kicking your feet."
3. Avoid attempting to physically assist or restrain the toddler. This could result in injury to the child or yourself.
4. However, provide verbal support. Say, for example:
   "It is very upsetting to be so out of control. It can even be scary. I can help you calm down."
5. Discuss strategies such as deep breathing or counting to three as a way to regain self-control.
6. When the child begins to regain control, express your desire to provide physical comfort. Offer to hold the child on your lap and read a book or rock in a rocking chair.
7. After the "hot" emotional moment has passed and the child is calm, discuss the event focusing on teaching strategies for dealing with strong emotions.

☀ Highlighting Development

During the second and third year of life, toddlers become very skilled at throwing tantrums. The physical signs of these intense physical and emotional responses may include screaming, crying, and flinging the arms and/or legs. With adult guidance and support, they can also become skilled at recovering from them (Philadelphia Child Guidance Center, 1994). Toddlers dislike the feeling of having "lost control" that accompanies a tantrum. Oftentimes, tantrums are an outward expression of toddlers' struggle between dependence and independence.

VARIATION:

♡ Closely observe children who are prone to tantrums. Try to figure out what "sets them off." Then, work to prevent tantrums by helping the child to cope effectively with the triggering event(s).

ADDITIONAL INFORMATION:

♡ Never shame the toddler for having a tantrum, which is a natural part of toddlerhood for many children. Focus, however, on teaching skills for dealing with strong emotions to reduce the frequency of tantrums.

♡ Toddlers may have tantrums when they do not receive immediate gratification for their wants. According to Kostelnik, et al. (2002), there are four reasons why tantrums often occur:
   1. The child may be fatigued.
   2. The child may be subject to unrealistic adult demands.
   3. The child received little attention for positive behavior.
   4. The child is subject to unpredictable rule enforcement.

25 to 30 months

Helping with the Bags

EMOTIONAL

Child's Developmental Goals

✓ To respond to another person's signal for help

✓ To demonstrate helpful behavior

MATERIALS:

❏ Grocery bags filled from a trip to the grocery store

PREPARATION:

None

NURTURING STRATEGIES:

1. Signal the toddlers to assist with carrying the bags of grocery to the kitchen. To illustrate, say:
   "Wow! Rosie bought lots of good food at the grocery store. I need to carry all of the bags to the kitchen. They sure look heavy. I don't know if I can do it myself."

2. If no one responds to your signal, be more direct and ask one or two toddlers for help. Try to pick toddlers who are not deeply engaged in play. Say, for example:
   "Hunter and Angat, please help carry these bags to the kitchen."

3. Comment on the toddlers' helping behaviors. Discuss, for example, if everyone is carrying separate bags ("We divided the task") or if some are working together to move one bag ("You are helping each other to finish the task").

4. Thank the children for their assistance. Avoid showering them with too much praise because it refocuses their internal motivation for helping on external rewards.

☼ Highlighting Development

When treated respectfully and caringly by adults, toddlers spontaneously show sympathy towards others. They will provide comfort and help those in pain or distress. Oftentimes, toddlers will offer their favorite comfort item, such as a blanket or stuffed animal, to another in distress. This gesture is representative of the sentiment, "It helps me feel better, so it will help you."

VARIATION:

♡ Enlist the children's help with rearranging the furniture in the room, moving boxes, or packing away toys at the end of the week.

ADDITIONAL INFORMATION:

♡ Children must learn their cultural display rules in order to be successfully integrated into society. Imitation, feedback, and direction are important teaching strategies that adults provide. Feedback is instrumental for toddlers to understand how, when, and where to express their emotions. This may be in the form of an adult tone serving as a social reward for appropriate behavior; likewise, it could be ignoring or frowning at inappropriate behavior. Adults can provide a social award for appropriate behavior by using supportive words with accompanying positive tone of voice. Examples include statements such as:
  "Look at Hunter. He is being helpful by carrying Jeffrey's coat."
  "Randy did a good job of hanging up his coat."
  "You should not laugh at children who fall down. It hurts their feelings."

♡ Avoid reinforcing gender stereotypes by requesting help from girls and boys.

25 to 30 months

Dealing with Anger

Child's Developmental Goals

✓ To build vocabulary associated with emotions

✓ To increase understanding of emotions

✓ To discuss nonaggressive strategies for expressing anger

MATERIALS:

❑ Book, *I Was So Mad,* by Mercer Mayer

PREPARATION:

♡ Review the book.

NURTURING STRATEGIES:

1. Gather either one toddler or a small group of toddlers in a comfortable location.
2. Introduce the book by showing the cover and reading the title, author, and illustration. Engage the children's attention by asking what they think the story might be about.
3. Read the story slowly while showing the illustrations to the toddlers.
4. Review the events in the story that made the character mad.
5. Provide positive reinforcement for remembering events. Comments to make include:
   "What a good memory. The frogs were on the first page of the book."
   "You were really paying attention to the story."
6. Discuss reasons for the main character being so angry in the story. Highlight, for example, the fact that he wasn't able to do what he wanted. Ask the toddlers how they feel when they are in that situation. Whenever possible, provide recent examples to help them recall their feelings.
7. Conclude the experience by asking the toddlers for other ways to deal with anger.

☀ Highlighting Development

Young children feel emotions and express emotions; however, they have yet to reach a level of cognitive development where they understand emotions (Marion, 1997). Adults must devote a great deal of time and energy over many years (up through adolescence) to help children understand emotions. When working with young children, it is essential that adults recognize that this is a long road that often is marked by potholes and curves. The first step in dealing with anger is to acquaint toddlers with the vocabulary used to described this emotion.

VARIATIONS:

♡ Record, on large paper, things that make the toddlers angry.

♡ Find other stories to read about anger.

♡ Have the toddlers demonstrate how they act when angry.

ADDITIONAL INFORMATION:

♡ Books are an effective medium for communicating concepts related to emotional expression. Well-chosen books can convey societal and cultural rules regarding emotional expression. Print media can showcase particular situations and how emotions can be demonstrated, as well as what behaviors are acceptable or unacceptable in different situations.

25 to 30 months

Rainy Day Play

EMOTIONAL

Child's Developmental Goals

✓ To label feelings
✓ To counterbalance fear with feelings of self-efficacy

MATERIALS:

❑ Flashlight for each child
❑ Clear, heavy adhesive tape

PREPARATION:

♡ Tape the opening of each flashlight to prevent the batteries from being removed, for safety purposes.

NURTURING STRATEGIES:

1. During free play exploration, introduce the flashlights:
   "Flashlights provide light. They are useful on dark, rainy days like today. I'm going to turn off some of the big lights so that our flashlights are easier to see."
2. Turn off lights. Be sure to keep some blinds or curtains open. This will permit some natural light into the room, thus allowing toddlers to work on other projects.
3. Encourage the toddlers to explore the room using the flashlights.
4. Discuss how the flashlight can help you feel less afraid of the dark. Connect the discussion to other ways for reducing fear of the dark. For example, say:
   "I use a night light when I go to sleep at night. Do you?"
   Continue the activity as long as the toddlers remain interested.

☀ Highlighting Development

Young children live in a world that is far more frightening and emotionally challenging than adults can comprehend. It is important for healthy emotional development that their fears are dealt with in a compassionate and respectful manner. Avoid belittling, laughing, or dismissing a child's fear. Instead, help the child to talk about feelings and develop positive coping skills (Philadelphia Child Guidance Center, 1994).

VARIATIONS:

♡ Have children draw how they are feeling as a way to exercise self-control.
♡ Keep a flashlight accessible during naptime for a toddler who is fearful of the dark.

ADDITIONAL INFORMATION:

♡ Being calm and patient with a toddler experiencing a fearful reaction can have a soothing effect. Between the ages of 24 and 30 months, common fears include specific loud noises, flushing toilets, nightmares, darkness, changes in the environment (moved furniture), and bad weather.

25 to 30 months

Helping Out

Child's Developmental Goals

✓ To perform a task with minimal assistance

✓ To experience a sense of accomplishment

MATERIALS:

☐ Clear plastic container with a screw-on lid.

☐ Paper

☐ Scissors

☐ Tape

☐ Pen

PREPARATION:

♡ Create a Job Jar label and adhere it to container.

♡ Write simple tasks that often need to be completed throughout the day on slips of paper, then fold and place the slips inside the jar.

NURTURING STRATEGIES:

1. When you notice a child wandering and not engaged with an activity, encourage that child to select a job from the Job Jar.

2. Help the child by reading the card. Ask the child questions about the task. Use comments such as: *"Giselle, is the laundry folded? How do you know?"*

3. Make sure that the child understands the task before encouraging her to do it independently. When the child is ready, support her efforts by saying, for example: *"Put all of the towels in the drawer."*

4. Supervise from a distance, being sure to provide ample space and time for the child to complete the task.

5. Comment on the importance of the child's work to the functioning of the classroom. For instance, state: *"No one would know where the clean towels are if you hadn't put them in the drawer."*

☀ Highlighting Development

Erikson (1950) believed that the defining task for toddlers was to achieve autonomy. Even the language used by young children—"Me do it," "Mommy, me," "Mine"—reflects their need to be independent. However, toddlers vacillate between contradictory needs for dependence and independence. At one point, they want to do it all by themselves, and in the next moment they need the comfort and security of a trusted adult.

VARIATIONS:

♡ Put visual representations on the slips so the child can "read" the task card independently.

♡ Have a chart with words and pictures which shows the job assignment for the week.

ADDITIONAL INFORMATION:

♡ Teachers in early childhood programs need to encourage parents to create a Job Jar at home. Provide suggestions such as matching socks or stacking plastic cups that toddlers can accomplish.

25 to 30 months

Physical Development

THIRTY-ONE to
THIRTY-SIX MONTHS

Riding Trikes

Child's Developmental Goals

✓ To improve full-body coordination

✓ To practice steering the tricycle

MATERIALS:

❑ 2 or 3 tricycles

❑ Helmet for each tricycle

PREPARATION:

♡ Inspect the tricycles to make sure they are in good repair.

♡ Hang a helmet on the handlebars of each tricycle.

♡ Designate a "parking lot" and place the tricycles there.

NURTURING STRATEGIES:

1. When a toddler selects a tricycle, assist with securing the helmet.
2. Gently remind the toddler of any limits before he begins to ride.
3. Encourage the toddler to steer the tricycle, as well as peddle. Say, for example:
   "Use your hands to move the handle bars. Turn the handle bars so you stay in the path."
4. Reinforce the toddler's efforts at riding the tricycle. Comments to make include:
   "Jar, you practiced steering the tricycle today. You were able to stay on the path!"
   "You worked hard at steering and pedaling the tricycle."
5. Record your observations of the toddler's physical skills in the form of an anecdotal record. If more than one toddler is present, create a panel with photographs to document the learning.

☼ Highlighting Development

Most toddlers are able to successfully peddle a tricycle with their feet by three years of age (Berk, 1999). There is great variability in steering skills, however. Some toddlers are able to pedal and steer a tricycle with great coordination while others must concentrate exclusively on not falling off of the tricycle. Although most of these differing abilities can be explained by the individual toddler's gross motor skills, the types of toys provided must be examined. Some riding toys have steering wheels that serve no purpose in actually directing the toys' motion. Thus, toddlers learn that steering is not important. When presented with a tricycle, for example, that requires pedaling and steering, they must learn to coordinate both actions.

VARIATION:

♡ Provide other riding toys such as cars.

ADDITIONAL INFORMATION:

♡ When choosing a tricycle, carefully consider the design to prevent children from tipping over. The best-engineered tricycles have large wheels and are built low to the ground.

 To promote the safety of the children, carefully select a protective environment for using the tricycles. For example, make sure the tricycles are behind a fence away from traffic dangers. Then, set limits to guide behavior and require the toddlers to wear helmets. In addition, if more than one toddler is present, set limits on the direction toddlers should ride to prevent head-on collisions.

I'm a Real Sculptor

Child's Developmental Goals

✓ To increase strength of wrists, hands, and fingers

✓ To increase eye-hand coordination

✓ To increase visual perceptual skills

MATERIALS:

❑ Nontoxic potter's clay

❑ Slip

❑ Canvas or work board

❑ Wire for cutting clay

PREPARATION:

♡ Clear a child-size table and cover with canvas.

♡ Place clay and wire in the center of the table.

♡ Prepare slip in a bowl that can be easily passed between toddlers and set on table.

NURTURING STRATEGIES:

1. Introduce the concept of sculpting several days before providing the clay. Ways to do this include taking a field trip to a studio or inviting an artist to visit the toddlers.

2. When a toddler selects the activity, move the clay closer to the child. Assist her, as necessary, with using the wire to cut a piece of clay.

3. Communicate with the toddler about the texture and consistency of the clay. Questions to spark discussion include:
   "Emma, how does the clay feel in your hands?"
   "How can you flatten the clay since it is stiff?"

4. Allow the toddler uninterrupted time to explore the clay.

5. If the toddler attempts to adhere one piece of clay to another, remind her about the slip, while moving it closer to the toddler. Refer to your field trip or visitor, as appropriate. To illustrate, say:
   "Do you remember how the sculptor showed us to put two pieces of clay together?"
   Continue the discussion providing information as appropriate.

6. If more than one child is working, encourage them to pass the bowl of slip around the table. In addition, invite all toddlers to participate in the conversation. Whenever possible, prompt the toddlers to share information (instead of relying on you).

7. Provide positive reinforcement by focusing on the process the children are undertaking rather than the final product.

☀ Highlighting Development

Remarkable advances in the development of fine motor skills occur during early childhood. Observe them. Toddlers gradually gain greater and greater control of their wrists, hands, and fingers. Moreover, they gradually gain muscular strength. As a result, they no longer have to exclusively use soft, homemade clay. Now, a firmer model clay that is used by older children or nontoxic sculpting clay used by adults can be introduced.

VARIATION:

♡ After the children are skilled at manipulating the clay, slowly introduce additional tools.

ADDITIONAL INFORMATION:

♡ You may need to spend time experimenting with the clay and slip in order to best assist/guide the toddlers. At first, the toddlers probably will lack the necessary strength and technique for cutting the clay with the wire. However, it will not take them long to acquire these skills.

♡ Children's reactions to play dough will vary by age. Typical responses of two-year-olds include feeling, squeezing, rolling, pounding, pinching, and tearing (Schirrmacher, 2001). For young children, working with clay is a multisensory experience. Clay has a distinct texture, smell, and color.

Balloon Toss

PHYSICAL

Child's Developmental Goals

✓ To practice catching skills

✓ To improve full-body coordination

✓ To improve eye-hand coordination skills

MATERIALS:

❑ 2 or 3 balloons, depending on the number of toddlers

PREPARATION:

♡ Blow up the balloons and firmly secure with a knot.

♡ Clear an open, outdoor, grassy area, if available, of any obstacles.

NURTURING STRATEGIES:

1. Observe the toddler's behavior with the balloons.
2. Suggest a different way to use the balloon. For example, if the toddler is kicking it, suggest he toss the balloon to you.
3. Encourage the toddler to catch it when you toss it back to him. Comment, for example:
   "My turn to toss. You catch it, Grant."
4. If the toddler is having difficulty with throwing or catching, provide plenty of time to practice those skills. In addition, provide verbal support. Use comments such as:
   "What a great attempt. You held out your arms to catch the ball, Grant."
   "Keep trying. You'll get it!"
5. Continue to throw and catch the balloon as long as the toddler seems interested.

☀ Highlighting Development

During early childhood, gender differences may become apparent in the development of the toddlers' physical skills. Biologically, there appears to be little support for these gender differences. Environmentally, these differences are often attributed to the way adults socialize them. Boys are usually encouraged to be more active, adventuresome, and participate in more rough-and-tumble play (Trawick-Smith, 2000). Thus, it is important to facilitate optimal physical development for children, regardless of gender.

VARIATIONS:

♡ To promote social development, encourage two toddlers to toss the balloon back and forth.

♡ Substitute other large, lightweight balls for the balloons.

ADDITIONAL INFORMATION:

♡ Gross motor development typically precedes fine motor development. Watch the children as they throw the balloons. At this stage, they move their whole body in a rather distorted posture. As the children continue developing, they will gradually be able to coordinate their bodies in a smooth sequence while throwing a balloon or other object.

🚸 **CAUTION** Broken balloons can be a serious choking hazard. Therefore, provide constant supervision when the children are engaged in the experience. Setting clear, positive limits about the use of the balloon can reduce hazards. State, for example,
   "The balloon is for tossing and catching."
   "Use your hands to hold the balloon."

Sketching

Child's Developmental Goals

✓ To refine fine motor skills in the wrist, hands, and fingers

✓ To develop eye-hand coordination skills

✓ To practice grasping a writing tool

✓ To practice making marks with a writing tool

MATERIALS:

❑ Small- and large-diameter pencils for every child

❑ Container for the pencils

❑ A clipboard for every child

❑ Typing or copier paper

PREPARATION:

♡ Put two to three pieces of paper on each clipboard.

NURTURING STRATEGIES:

1. Introduce the activity to a small group of toddlers. To illustrate, say:
   "We've been studying trees for three months now. I noticed the magnolia tree in the yard is blooming. Let's go outside and sketch it. I have a clipboard and pencil for each of you."

2. Accompany the children outside and find a comfortable place to sit to observe the tree.

3. Engage the children in conversation about the tree. Assist the toddlers in describing the tree's leaves, trunk, and so on.

4. Allow the children ample time to sketch uninterrupted. Reserve comments until a child initiates conversation with you.

5. When the children indicate they are finished, record any words they might use to describe their work.

☼ Highlighting Development

Most children will be able to grip a small-diameter pencil in their hand by 36 months of age. There is controversy surrounding the type of pencil to provide children with at this age. It has often been assumed that very young children work best with large-diameter pencils or crayons. However, Carlson and Cunningham (1990) found that some children handle large-diameter pencils better while other children perform better with small-diameter pencils. Therefore, to encourage toddlers to write or draw provide a variety of different sizes and types of tools, thus allowing the children to select the tool they are most comfortable using.

VARIATION:

♡ Take a walk around the neighborhood and find interesting buildings, statues, and/or homes to sketch.

ADDITIONAL INFORMATION:

♡ Children are now becoming aware of colors and their preferences for certain ones. To minimize conflict, provide identically colored tools.

♡ Some children at this stage of development will hold the tool with an overhand grip. Other children will hold it like a hammer between the hands. Observe. When children hold the tools in this manner, you will find that neither the wrists nor fingers move (Herr, 2001).

♡ Children's first drawings are random scribbles. When they are able to hold drawing tools with their fingers, their scribbles will become smaller and more controlled.

Marble Painting

Child's Developmental Goals

✓ To refine small muscle skills

✓ To develop eye-hand coordination skills

MATERIALS:

- ❑ Construction paper
- ❑ Metal bread pans
- ❑ Masking tape
- ❑ 2 cans of paint
- ❑ Damp sponge
- ❑ Large marbles for each child
- ❑ Nonbreakable paint containers
- ❑ Spoon for each marble
- ❑ Smock for each child

PREPARATION:

♡ Cut construction paper to fit inside the bottom of the bread pans. Using masking tape, secure paper in place.

♡ Mix paint to desired thickness by using liquid soap to help facilitate cleanup.

♡ If more than one child is participating, divide each color of paint equally between containers for easy access.

♡ Place one bread pan for each child at a child–size table. Make sure both colors of paint are easily accessible.

♡ Put a smock over the back of each chair.

NURTURING STRATEGIES:

1. When a child chooses the activity, introduce it while the child is putting on the smock. To illustrate, say: *"Elita, do you remember when we painted with the golf balls? This time we're going to use marbles."*

2. If necessary, provide more details about how to use the spoon to scoop up the marble and place it on the paper.

3. Set clear, positive limits on behavior. State, for example:
   "Place the spoon back in the paint container when you are finished with it."
   "Sit in the chair or stand by the table when making your picture."

4. Describe the child's behavior when shaking the pan. Comments to make include:
   "You are shaking the pan fast, Elita."
   "You are moving your entire body from side to side when shaking the pan."

5. Encourage the toddler to use marbles dipped in both colors of paint. Share the toddler's enthusiasm when a new color is produced.

6. Assist the toddler with using the sponge to wipe a spill or dirty hands.

☼ Highlighting Development

Fine motor development is basic for the eventual mastery of handwriting skills. Some prerequisite skills include: thumb–finger coordination, eye-hand coordination, small muscle (wrist and fingers) development, ability to hold a writing tool, and the ability to make basic strokes (Lamme, 1979, cited in Charlesworth, 2000). None of these skills can be directly taught. Rather, they must be developed through play. The adult's role is to provide the necessary materials to foster the development of such skills.

VARIATION:

♡ Use other round objects to paint with such as a ping-pong ball or empty spool of thread.

ADDITIONAL INFORMATION:

♡ Record the child's name in the upper left-hand corner or on the back of the artwork. Use numerals to record the date completed. Consider saving the artwork for the child's portfolio.

 Supervise this activity carefully. Moreover, do not introduce this experience if a toddler still has a tendency to put objects in her mouth.

Transferring Cards

Child's Developmental Goals

✓ To improve fine motor skills

✓ To enhance eye-hand coordination

MATERIALS:

❑ Deck of cards

❑ Plastic container (such as one for peanut butter)

PREPARATION:

♡ Select a jar with a mouth wide enough to insert the cards.

♡ Wash the jar carefully in hot, soapy water.

♡ Check the jar for sharp edges. If any sharp edges are discovered, either sand them smooth or cover them with masking tape.

♡ Place the deck of cards inside the jar and display the container on a child-size shelf.

NURTURING STRATEGIES:

1. When a child selects the materials, observe his behavior. Note what the child does with the cards.

2. Describe the child's behavior with the materials. Provide specific feedback on how the toddler is using his hands. Use comments such as:

   "Paco, you are picking up the cards with your finger and thumb."

   "What precision. You are laying the cards on top of each other."

3. If child does not see the connection between the materials, suggest a way to use both. For example, say:

   "Will the cards fit inside the container?"

4. Providing positive reinforcement while the toddler is working may increase the time the child spends at the activity.

5. Document the child's abilities in the form of an anecdotal record.

☀ Highlighting Development

By five years of age, girls tend to be ahead of boys in the development of fine motor skills (Berk, 1999). Close this gender gap by introducing, encouraging, and supporting boys in fine motor activities as much as, if not more than, girls. In play and activity, the fine motor skills developed at this stage are important. These skills provide the foundation for later skills necessary for cutting, writing, and so on.

VARIATION:

♡ Increase the challenge by having the toddler return the deck of cards to its original box.

ADDITIONAL INFORMATION:

♡ Set up the child's environment to promote the development of fine motor skills. Children at this age delight in exploring. They enjoy dumping, refilling, taking things apart, and putting them back together again. Provide toddlers with puzzles, peg boards, lacing cards, snap beads, and building blocks.

Up, Up, Up

Child's Developmental Goals

✓ To practice walking up stairs

✓ To practice walking down stairs

MATERIALS:

❏ Commercially produced stairs with railing, if available.

PREPARATION:

♡ If a commercial staircase is available, select an area of the room that can be easily supervised. Clear this area and put the staircase there. Without this equipment, carpeted stairs can be used if constantly supervised.

NURTURING STRATEGIES:

1. When a child selects the stairs, observe carefully.
2. If necessary, move closer to the child to provide physical assistance and/or guidance.
3. Verbally describe the toddler's abilities. Comments to make include:
    "Aisha, you are walking up the stairs with your left foot . . . now your right foot . . . now the left."
    "You're holding onto the rail. That helps to keep you safe."
4. Walking up steps tends to develop before walking down. Therefore, provide support and encouragement for walking down the steps. Set and maintain positive limits as necessary to promote safety. State, for example:
    "Jump from the bottom step."

☀ Highlighting Development

By the end of the third year, toddlers should be skilled at walking up small flights of stairs (Charlesworth, 2000). They will alternate feet so that one foot is on a step at a time. Of course, toddlers who have daily experience with walking up and down steps at home and/or school will typically be more skilled than children who do not have such opportunities.

VARIATION:

♡ Locate an interesting set of steps within the community and take a field trip to explore them.

ADDITIONAL INFORMATION:

♡ Major motor achievements occur during the third year of life. Watch. During this stage, children begin engaging in what is called exercise play. This involves playful locomotor movements such as running, chasing, and climbing. This play is vigorous and beneficial because it promotes skill, strength, fitness, and endurance.

 Never leave a child unattended on any stairs.

Trying a New Food

Child's Developmental Goals

✔ To try a new food
✔ To converse about healthy foods

MATERIALS:

❏ Lunch food and supplies

PREPARATION:

♡ Prepare a regular lunch.

NURTURING STRATEGIES:

1. Assist the toddlers with washing hands, as necessary.
2. Encourage the toddlers to help prepare the table for lunch by distributing cups, napkins, utensils, etc.
3. When the table is set, sit at the table with the children. Then begin serving the food "family style."
4. Discuss what is on the menu for today. Highlight the new food by saying, for example:
   "Today we are having burritos, salad, and beans. These are a new kind of bean. They are not mashed like the refried pinto beans we usually eat. These are called black beans."
5. Engage the children in meaningful conversation about the black beans. Ask, for example:
   "Has anyone eaten black beans before?"
6. Weave into the conversation, as naturally as possible, concepts about eating healthy. Discuss, for example, how healthy foods give us energy to run and play.
7. After the meal, encourage the toddlers to clean the table.

VARIATION:

♡ If in an early childhood program, involve the parents in preparing and serving foods that reflect their culture or heritage.

☀ Highlighting Development

It is important for adults to help young children to follow their internal guides for preferences, appetite, and satiation. Therefore, when a new food is introduced, encourage the toddler to try it, but if the child refuses or rejects it, do not force the issue (Gerber & Johnson, 1998). However, try introducing it again at another time. Offering new foods when the toddler is hungry, thirsty, or with others who enjoy the food might increase the child's willingness to try it. Toddlers are like adults. They will have days when their appetite wanes. When this happens, do not force them to eat. Rather, allow them to eat when they are hungry by providing healthy snacks.

ADDITIONAL INFORMATION:

♡ Eating family style is important for toddlers. Serving themselves not only promotes fine motor skills but it enhances autonomy.
♡ Setting the table is a routine that provides toddlers experiences in counting and spatial relationships. To assist them in learning to set the table, use a permanent, felt-tip marker to trace the position of eating utensils, plates, and cup onto a plastic placemat.
♡ Toddlers can also be expected to participate in cleanup after finishing a meal. To facilitate this process, place a utility cart and garbage can near the eating area. After the meal, the toddlers can throw their napkins and other disposable items directly into the trash. They should also be able to scrape food scraps from their plates into the garbage can and place their plates on the utility cart.

Putting the Cassette Inside

Child's Developmental Goals

✓ To improve fine motor coordination skills

✓ To continue developing eye–hand coordination skills

MATERIALS:

❑ Old audiocassette tapes

❑ Cassette holders

❑ Basket

PREPARATION:

♡ Remove all of the tape from the cassettes.

♡ Place all of the cassettes and holders in the basket.

♡ Place the basket where it is easily accessible.

NURTURING STRATEGIES:

1. If you notice a toddler needs something to do, direct his attention to the basket. Introduce the activity by saying, for example:
   "Samuel, can you match every tape with a plastic case?"

2. Observe the toddler's ability to complete this task. Although it seems easy for adults, it can be frustrating. Provide verbal assistance whenever possible. Refrain from providing physical assistance or modeling unless it is absolutely necessary.

3. Encourage the toddler to check his work. Questions or comments include:
   "Will the case close? Try it and see."
   "See if it is right. Test to see if the case will close."

4. Provide positive reinforcement for the process as well as the final outcome. To illustrate, say:
   "Samuel, you did a good job. You figured out. You needed to turn the tape a different direction."
   "You matched every tape with a case. You really worked hard."

5. When the toddler is finished, encourage him to return all of the cassettes and holders to the basket.

☀ Highlighting Development

During the first three years of life, infants and toddlers change their approach to playing with small objects. Infants and young toddlers focus on exploring objects with their hands and mouth to learn as much as possible about them. Older toddlers, in contrast, spend most of their time using objects for practicing simple skills. Older toddlers put objects through openings, manipulate simple locks, and build things up, just to knock them down and begin again (White, 1995).

VARIATION:

♡ Use videocassettes and plastic covers instead of the audiocassette tapes.

ADDITIONAL INFORMATION:

♡ Purchase cassettes at a garage sale or recycle ones you no longer listen to. However, after this activity be sure to keep out of reach the cassettes that you want to listen to. The toddlers might accidentally ruin the tape when playing.

♡ In order for young children to become motorically competent, they must be able to coordinate and integrate all body functions. Coordination of the hands and eyes is one of the most important (Weiser, 1991). Although caregivers cannot teach coordination, they can provide an interesting environment with many opportunities for exploration and practice.

 Remove the tape from the cassette before giving it to the toddlers to prevent strangulation and other safety hazards.

Follow the Leader

Child's Developmental Goals

✔ To imitate another child's physical movement

✔ To play a simple game with rules

✔ To improve visual–perceptual skills

MATERIALS:

None

PREPARATION:

None

NURTURING STRATEGIES:

1. If you notice two children performing similar behaviors, which often occurs naturally during play, describe the toddlers' behavior by saying, for example:

   "Kaya and Lisa appear to be playing a game. Whatever Kaya does, Lisa does the same. Kaya is the leader. I wonder what he'll do next."

2. If the toddler is having difficulty imitating the behaviors, assess to decide why. Vary your response accordingly. For example, if the follower is not as physically skilled, encourage the leader to slow down her behavior.

3. If necessary, encourage the toddlers to switch roles.

4. If possible, invite even more toddlers to join the game.

5. Provide positive reinforcement for both the physical skills demonstrated and the social skills it took to accomplish the task.

6. If in an early childhood program, take photographs to document the physical and social skills developed during simple games. Parents/guardians may not be aware of the benefits.

☀ Highlighting Development

Games that involve several children contain rules and are social in nature. Toddlers can typically play simple games that require few rules. They especially enjoy games that allow them to practice newly developed skills such as running and jumping. During the third year of life, toddlers are also able to enjoy simple games because of the emergence of the ability to lead and follow peers (White, 1995). Socially competent toddlers can easily and comfortably assume both roles and, thus, engage in true socializing with peers.

VARIATION:

♡ Have an adult lead the game at first.

ADDITIONAL INFORMATION:

♡ Gradually, as children develop social skills, they become interested in playing games. With toddlers, games usually involve simple turn taking. As children mature, games will become more complex.

Language and Communication Development

THIRTY-ONE to THIRTY-SIX MONTHS

Once There Was a Toddler . . .

Child's Developmental Goals

✓ To increase receptive language skills

✓ To build vocabulary

MATERIALS:

None

PREPARATION:

None

NURTURING STRATEGIES:

1. When a toddler needs a new activity, invite him to listen to a story. To illustrate, say:
   "Ilya, I have a very special story to tell you. Let's sit together on the couch."
2. Get comfortable and snuggle close.
3. Give your stories a ritual beginning and ending. Begin your story by saying, for example:
   "Once there was a toddler . . ."
4. Speak in a natural voice. Trust yourself to use your voice as a tool to add inflection, drama, or suspense as necessary.
5. End your story using your ritual ending. For example, say:
   "And tomorrow will be a new day."

VARIATIONS:

♡ Encourage the toddlers to actively participate in the development of the story by asking questions or giving the children a choice between two outcomes.

♡ Tell a story when a toddler is relaxing for naptime or bedtime.

☀ Highlighting Development

Storytelling is an important activity for stimulating a lifelong love of literature. It supports cognitive development (imagination), language development (receptive language skills), social development (positive interactions with an important other), and emotional development (increases understanding about feelings; Philadelphia Child Guidance Center, 1994). Furthermore, it is good for the adult–child relationship because it allows time to focus exclusively on the child.

ADDITIONAL INFORMATION:

♡ Choosing the right topic for your story is important. Use your knowledge of the child's needs, interests, and abilities. For example, tell stories about your and your toddlers' days, even when you are separated, or about how another child deals with being afraid of the dark.

♡ Choose a good time for storytelling. Avoid telling a story if time is limited or rushed. A good story needs time to develop. Moreover, you want to maintain a positive atmosphere for storytelling.

♡ Adults often avoid storytelling because it makes them nervous. "What if I say a sentence wrong?" or "What if I use a word wrong?" are things they may worry about. Relax. Begin with a simple story about the toddler's day. Trust in your ability to use the right language.

Waking the Animals

Child's Developmental Goals

✓ To verbally label an object

✓ To actively participate in reading a book by identifying symbols

MATERIALS:

❑ Book, *Inside a Barn in the Country,* by Alyssa Satin Capucilli

PREPARATION:

♡ Place the book in library area with other reading materials.

NURTURING STRATEGIES:

1. When a toddler selects the book, allow her time to explore it independently.
2. Offer to read the story with the toddler.
3. Arrange yourself and the toddler so that there is close physical contact (e.g., have the toddler sit on your lap).
4. Read the title, author, and illustrator of the book. Ask the toddler to create a hypothesis about the content of the book, by saying, for example:
   "Look at this picture. What do you think this story is about?"
   Pause. Respond to comment by saying:
   "Let's read the book and find out!"
5. Begin reading the story. Pausing and pointing to the pictures in the text line may encourage the toddler to fill in the appropriate animal name. Also, encourage the child to make the animal sounds at the appropriate times.
6. Provide positive reinforcement either verbally or nonverbally for the toddler's participation when reading the story.

☀ Highlighting Development

Quality children's literature is a necessity for enhancing literacy development. Every toddler classroom and home should contain a library including picture books, predictable books, and big books (Cecil, 1999). Picture books use pictures, illustrations, and text to tell the story. A special type of picture book is the rebus book that provides pictures or symbols within the lines of texts. Young children feel especially empowered because they can read these books at very young ages.

VARIATIONS:

♡ Make available other rebus books for the toddlers to read independently.

♡ Read the story to a small group of toddlers, if possible.

ADDITIONAL INFORMATION:

♡ Utilize your local library as a resource. Librarians are knowledgeable professionals who can assist with selecting or suggesting books that reflect the children's needs and interests. See also Appendix B.

♡ Select the books based on your knowledge of the toddlers' interests and experiential backgrounds. Toddlers enjoy repetition and typically like to read favorite stories over and over again. Some books quickly become favorites. When you observe this, make sure they are available for a sustained period of time (days, weeks, and months, if necessary).

Finger Puppets

Child's Developmental Goals

✓ To practice using private speech to guide behavior

✓ To practice expressive language skills

MATERIALS:

❑ 2 commercially produced finger puppets for each toddler or adult-size, white cloth work gloves and markers

❑ Basket of plastic cars or wooden blocks

PREPARATION:

♡ If necessary, cut the fingers off of the glove and draw a face on each of the tips using a permanent, felt-tip marker.

♡ Place the finger puppets and basket of toys where they are easily accessible for the toddlers.

NURTURING STRATEGIES:

1. When a toddler selects the puppets or basket of toys, observe the child's behavior. Note how the toddler is using the materials and if he is using private speech.

2. Using the information gathered in Step 1 to direct your behavior, join the toddler with the materials.

3. Model private speech by describing what you are doing. For example, while placing the finger puppets on your fingers, say:
   "It is tough to get these on. I have to pull with my finger and thumb. There, I did it."

4. Have the finger puppets play with toys from the basket. After a few minutes, create a problem for them to solve. For example, have one puppet say to the other:
   "I was using that. Give it back."
   Then model a positive way for solving the problem.

5. Return to observing the toddler. Ask yourself if the toddler's behavior has changed and, if so, how.

6. Record your observations on an anecdotal record form.

☼ Highlighting Development

According to Vygotsky, private speech serves an important developmental function: self-regulation of behavior. Private speech is the process of individuals speaking to themselves when problem solving. Gradually this process will become internalized as a means to help guide thinking. Adults can assist young children in problem solving by supplying the necessary vocabulary, phrases, and strategies that children can use during private speech. For example, you can help a child with matching markers with caps by saying "blue marker, blue cap, push together and snap." Later when the child is working independently to clean up the markers, do not be surprised to hear him echo your words.

VARIATION:

♡ Provide people puppets that cover the entire hand. Encourage the toddlers to involve the puppets in their make-believe play.

ADDITIONAL INFORMATION:

♡ Toddlers at this stage of development should easily be able to place a finger puppet on one finger. Once the puppet is placed on a pointer finger, it may be more challenging to put on the second puppet, as they are unable to use this finger. Consequently, you may have to help with this process.

♡ The word *puppet* comes from the Latin word that means "doll". Puppets are wonderful tools for toddlers. Listen. Puppets often encourage quiet children to talk. Through playing with puppets young children openly express their emotions. The puppets allow them to do or say things that they typically would not.

Singing "B-I-N-G-O"

Child's Developmental Goals

✓ To hear phonemes

✓ To practice expressive language skills

MATERIALS:

❑ Cardboard book, *Bingo,* by Rosemary Wells

PREPARATION:

None

NURTURING STRATEGIES:

1. Gather a small group of toddlers in a comfortable location.
2. Introduce the book to the children by showing the cover and reading the title and author's name. Encourage the toddlers to comment on what they think the book is about.
3. Read the story slowly while showing the illustrations.
4. The last page of text provides additional ways for singing the song (Ringo, Singo, etc.). Encourage the toddlers to sing along with you. Try the verses suggested by the author.
5. If the toddlers are interested in singing additional verses, choose different letters of the alphabet and continue!

☼ Highlighting Development

By their third birthdays, toddlers are skilled at using the individual sounds of the language or phonemes because they are fluent listeners and speakers by this age. However, knowledge of phonemes is unconscious. That is, toddlers use the sounds of the language without thinking about each individual phoneme or combination of phonemes to create words. Conscious awareness (or phonemic awareness) is essential in learning how to read and write (McGee and Richgils, 2000).

VARIATION:

♡ Sing the song while transitioning from one location to another.

ADDITIONAL INFORMATION:

♡ Few young children spontaneously acquire phonemic awareness. Adults must plan activities or interactions to their attention to phonemes (Neuman, Copple, & Bredekamp, 2000).

♡ Young children can learn from an environment in which they are surrounded by sounds of their native language. Reading and singing to young children will promote the development of spoken language. Through reading aloud, children also learn the connection between the spoken and written language.

Our Favorite Songs Book

Child's Developmental Goals

✓ To read illustrations in a book

✓ To sing a song

MATERIALS:

❑ Three-ring binder

❑ Plastic sleeves to hold the paper

❑ 8½ × 11–inch colored paper (typing or copier)

❑ Marker

PREPARATION:

♡ Print the words to a favorite song on each side of the paper. Begin by placing the title of the song at the top of the page. To assist with visual discrimination skills, place a picture that depicts the song beside the title.

♡ Place one piece of paper in each plastic sleeve and then place the sleeve in a three-ring binder.

♡ Decorate the front of the binder and title it "Our Favorite Songs." Display the book where it will attract the toddlers' attention.

NURTURING STRATEGIES:

1. When a toddler selects the book, observe her behavior.

2. If possible, make eye contact with the toddler and invite yourself to read the book by saying: *"Vina, may I read this book with you?"*

3. If the toddler indicates "no," either verbally or nonverbally, respect the child's desire. Then say: *"Maybe I can read it when you're finished."*

4. If the child says "yes" or indicates her approval through body language, say: *"Great! I've been waiting all morning to read this book."*

5. Make sure everyone is comfortable and snuggling close, if desired.

6. Read the title of the book and then encourage the toddler to read the book to you. For example, have her turn the pages and tell you about each song. Encourage her to "read" the pictures beside the title.

7. If necessary, provide hints about the song. Hints can be verbal or a quick humming of the tune.

8. Of course, sing the songs with great enthusiasm!

9. Discuss which song is the toddler's favorite and why.

☀ Highlighting Development

To become proficient at almost any skill, young children need multiple opportunities to practice. It is no different with early literacy skills. Toddlers need to listen, speak, read, and write in meaningful ways.

VARIATIONS:

♡ Instead of you picking the toddlers' favorite songs, have them choose. You will probably be surprised at the variety of songs they know and like.

♡ Make a "My Favorite Songs" book for each toddler. Encourage them to read each other's books and compare/contrast songs.

ADDITIONAL INFORMATION:

♡ With experience and maturity, toddlers' use and understanding of language becomes increasingly more sophisticated. Listen. Many now are using three or more words in their sentences. To convey meaning, their sentences are in an agent-action-recipient order (e.g., "I kiss Momma").

Retelling the Story: Goodnight Moon

Child's Developmental Goals

✓ To demonstrate auditory memory skills by retelling a story

✓ To continue developing expressive language skills

MATERIALS:

❑ Board book, *Goodnight Moon,* by Margaret Wise Brown

PREPARATION:

♡ Display the book so that it will attract the toddlers' attention.

NURTURING STRATEGIES:

1. When a toddler selects the book, observe the child's behavior.
2. Ask the toddler if he will read the book to you. If he appears hesitant, you could offer to read the story to him first. If that is the case, read the story following strategies outlined in Appendix A.
3. Pay close attention to the toddler's book-handling skills. Observe if the child is holding the book right side up, turning pages in the correct directions and one-by-one, and reading the pictures. Furthermore, note the child's knowledge of the text. For example, does he mention key components of the story, such as the moon, brush, or kittens?
4. Provide responses to the toddler's questions (or raised intonation) or comments when the toddler pauses. He is inviting you to participate in the experience just as you have done with him.
5. Thank the child for reading to you and provide positive reinforcement. Use comments such as: *"Wow, Josh, you read every page of the book. You are an excellent reader."*
   "Thanks for reading to me."
6. Record your anecdotal record of the toddler as soon as possible to minimize forgotten details.

☼ Highlighting Development

By the end of their third year of life, most toddlers use adverbs and adjectives frequently (approximately 17 percent of the time) during free speech (Charlesworth, 2000). They will naturally include in conversations words such as *small, large, happy, sad, hot, cold, soft, hard, fast,* and *slow*.

VARIATIONS:

♡ Provide props or a flannel board for retelling the story.

♡ Tell the story and encourage the child to listen and place the props on the flannel board in the sequence the story is told.

ADDITIONAL INFORMATION:

♡ Having children retell stories can be a way to assess their understanding (factual and comprehensive) of the text. It also helps you to assess their auditory memory skills and level of spoken language competence (McGee & Richgils, 2000). Children should have numerous opportunities to have the story read to them before being asked to retell it.

♡ Introduce a few new books every week, but be sure favorites are available to be read over and over again.

♡ Note that children at this stage of development talk about the characters and events in the storybooks and may relate them to their own experiences.

Lunch Count

Child's Developmental Goals

✓ To increase expressive language skills

✓ To connect a written label with a photograph

MATERIALS:

❑ Photograph of each toddler
❑ Velcro, cut in 1-inch pieces
❑ Sentence strip
❑ Poster board
❑ Lunch count form

PREPARATION:

♡ Mount each photograph on the poster board and label with the name of the classroom.

♡ Adhere one side of the Velcro to the poster board under each picture.

♡ Print each toddler's name on a piece of sentence strip. Then, adhere the other side of the Velcro to the back of each sentence strip.

♡ Display the poster board where it is easily accessible, such as on a low bulletin board.

♡ Put the sentence strips on a low shelf near the poster board.

NURTURING STRATEGIES:

1. Greet each child by squatting to the child's eye-level, saying the child's name, and then "hello," "good morning," or "I'm happy to see you today."

2. Assist the toddler with finding the sentence strip with her name on it. Discuss, for example, beginning sounds and letters.

3. Have the toddler place her sentence strip on the poster board, under her picture. Repeat this process for every child who is in your classroom.

4. After arrival time is complete, place any unclaimed sentence strips near the poster, but not on it.

5. During your morning meeting time, refer to the poster board and discuss who is present and who is absent. Assist the toddlers with counting each group. Then, record this information on the lunch count form so the kitchen staff will know how much food to provide at snacks and lunch.

6. Provide positive reinforcement for assisting with providing an accurate lunch count to the kitchen staff and for working together to accomplish a daily chore.

☀ Highlighting Development

Toddlers need an environment containing a variety of interesting materials that promote thinking, talking, drawing, reading, and writing. Furthermore, they need many opportunities to interact, talk, read, draw, and write with other children and adults. To produce the best outcomes, these opportunities must focus on meaningful topics that are worth knowing. In this activity, the goals focus on the promotion of language skills. The activity also focuses on creating a caring community of learners because children are assisting with a meaningful task and learning each other's names.

VARIATION:

♡ Match names and photographs as a class during circle or larger group time.

ADDITIONAL INFORMATION:

♡ Learning to read follows a developmental sequence. One of the first pre-reading tasks children need to learn is that symbols have meaning and make up words, such as their names. As a result, it is important that adults call attention to the printed word and provide a print-rich environment. Include the children's names to identify belongings, cubbies, and artwork. For many children, their first name is the first word they can "read."

I'm the . . . and You're the . . .

Child's Developmental Goals

✓ To communicate with another child

✓ To use expressive language skills to coordinate behaviors

MATERIALS:

☐ Props needed for dramatic play

PREPARATION:

♡ Display all materials in an attractive and inviting manner.

♡ Organize the props by function or purpose to assist the toddlers with cleaning up once finished.

NURTURING STRATEGIES:

1. If one toddler is in the dramatic play area, observe his behavior. Note how the toddler is using the materials.

2. Use this information to invite another toddler to play. Say, for example:
   "Kilian, would you like to help Nyle on his ranch? He needs some help feeding all of the horses."

3. Repeat the toddler's response. If he does not want to join the play, you can provide the needed assistance.

4. Follow the toddler's lead. Your presence in the area may encourage other toddlers to join the area. When this happens remove yourself from the play as soon as possible.

5. Remain in the area to provide guidance and assistance. For example, help the toddlers negotiate roles and responsibilities.

6. Assist also with maintaining the cleanliness of the area to protect the toddlers' safety and to invite new children to the area.

☀ Highlighting Development

Socio-dramatic play typically emerges around 30 months of age. During this type of play, older toddlers combine several complex schema and coordinate their behavior with peers (Berk, 1999). For example, a toddler cares for a baby while shopping in a shoe store. He then asks the salesperson for assistance with finding shoes and paying for the purchase. Toddlers need to be able to clearly articulate their wants, needs, or desires to another person to keep the play episode moving along.

VARIATION:

♡ To increase the challenge, begin to add props that are less realistic. The toddlers will use their imaginations and find uses for them.

ADDITIONAL INFORMATION:

♡ Adults learn to support and guide toddlers as they are learning to coordinate play with peers. Providing appropriate space, materials, and time for dramatic play, both indoors and out, are ways to show children you value this type of play. When guiding play, refrain from dominating or taking over. Rather, expand on the toddlers' behavior by making suggestions, modeling new behaviors, or asking open-ended questions (Miller, 1984). Adults can also help children substitute one object for another. In their play, children at this stage of development can substitute one object, but not two (Kostelnik, et al., 2002).

I'm a Little Teapot

Child's Developmental Goals

✓ To improve receptive language skills

✓ To demonstrate expressive language skills

MATERIALS:

❑ Book, *I'm a Little Teapot,* by Iza Trapani

PREPARATION:

♡ Place the book in an easily accessible location.

NURTURING STRATEGIES:

1. Signal that it is time to clean up the toys by singing a clean-up song. See Appendix G for a list of songs.
2. Model being a responsible member of the community of learners by assisting the toddlers with picking up toys.
3. Gather the children in a group and begin singing the song "I'm a Little Teapot" (see p. 156).
4. Show the cover of the book to the children. Ask them what they think the story will be about.
5. Read/sing the story. Encourage the toddlers to interact with the book by pausing for them to fill in words or by asking questions.
6. Review the story. Start the conversation by asking or stating, for example:
   "What was your favorite part of the story? Tell me about the places the teapot visited."
7. Encourage those who want to hear the story to remain while those not interested can choose something else.

☼ Highlighting Development

Receptive language develops ahead of expressive language even at this stage. By three years of age, children understand approximately 70 percent of the language that they will use in typical conversations throughout their lifetime (White, 1995). Typically, two–year–olds produce around 200 different words. By age six, they possess a vocabulary of around 10,000 words. A child must learn, on average, 5 new words a day to accomplish this (Berk, 1999).

VARIATION:

♡ Read the book, *The Itsy Bitsy Spider,* by Iza Trapani.

ADDITIONAL INFORMATION:

♡ Read/sing the book slowly, allowing the toddlers plenty of time to view the illustrations. They are fabulous!

♡ By this stage of development, children have learned to use language for many purposes. They learn language to tell about the past, solve problems, ask questions, direct the behavior of others, and protect their rights. Children at this age will elaborate on their ideas without being asked.

Name That Tune

Child's Developmental Goals

✓ To improve auditory discrimination skills

MATERIALS:

None

PREPARATION:

None

NURTURING STRATEGIES:

1. When transitioning the toddlers from one location to another, introduce the game by saying, for example: "Listen to this song. Can you guess its name?"
2. Hum or whistle the song.
3. If a child makes a guess, provide positive reinforcement. Say, for example:
   "What a good guess! You are really thinking about songs you know."
4. If necessary, hum or whistle the tune again.
5. When a toddler guesses the song, begin singing it. Encourage the toddlers to sing along with you.
6. If time permits, hum or whistle another song.

☼ Highlighting Development

During the first year of life, infants begin to analyze the internal structure of sentences and words (Berk, 1999). They focus on larger speech units to make sense of what they hear. Gradually, toddlers recognize familiar words when spoken. At this stage of development, they have yet to differentiate each individual sound in their native language. However, involvement with activities that promote auditory discrimination will gradually result in that ability.

VARIATION:

♡ If you play a musical instrument, use it to play the song.

ADDITIONAL INFORMATION:

♡ Choose songs that are very familiar to the toddlers. You want them to remain engaged in the activity while transitioning. Transitions can be very stressful for children and adults alike. Plan for them! Chant nursery rhymes or sing songs (see Appendices F and G) to further develop language skills.

Cognitive Development

THIRTY-ONE to THIRTY-SIX MONTHS

A Balancing Act

COGNITIVE

Child's Developmental Goals

✓ To develop an understanding of the concepts heavy and light

✓ To practice balancing a scale

MATERIALS:

- ❏ Coat hanger
- ❏ Scissors
- ❏ String
- ❏ Objects to wiggle in baskets
- ❏ Hook
- ❏ 2 containers of identical size and weight

PREPARATION:

♡ Punch three holes in each of the containers at equal distance.

♡ Tie string through each hole and then secure the string to the clothes hanger to create the balance.

♡ Secure the hook slightly above the children's eye level and hang the balance in the hook.

♡ Place the container of objects near the balance.

NURTURING STRATEGIES:

1. When a toddler selects the activity, move closer and observe her behavior.

2. Ask questions to obtain an understanding of the child's knowledge base and thinking about the balance. Say, for example:
   "What are the containers for?"
   "What happens when you put the shoe in one container?"

3. Encourage the toddler to experiment with the balance.

4. Describe the results of the toddler's actions. Be sure to use the words *heavy* and *light* to assist the toddler in understanding these concepts. Comment, for example:
   "Amera, the mitten and spool are still lighter than the shoe. The shoe is very heavy."

5. Show your excitement both verbally and nonverbally when the toddler balances the scale. While smiling and clapping, say, for example:
   "You did it! It took lots of patience, but you balanced the weight of the shoe."
   "What a hard worker! You balanced the scale. The mitten weighs as much as three playing cards."

☼ Highlighting Development

According to information processing theory, cognitive growth is characterized by increasing ability to take in, store, use, and retrieve information. From infancy on, young children change in their abilities to organize and manipulate information by becoming more sophisticated in processing information (see, for example, Feldman, 2000). Mere exposure to information will not guarantee that it will be stored or retrieved. Young children often organize information in categories called concepts to help them with processing information and understanding their world. Concepts allow for the meaningful grouping of objects, events, or people that share common properties.

VARIATIONS:

♡ Use a commercial balance scale that can be placed on a child–size table.

♡ Have the toddlers select objects from the environment that are heavier or lighter.

ADDITIONAL INFORMATION:

♡ Understanding concepts such as heavy, light, big, and little occurs through play. Toddlers must be provided repeated opportunities to explore and experiment with a variety of objects in order to construct such knowledge.

Making Fruit Parfaits

Child's Developmental Goals

✓ To practice sequencing by following simple directions

✓ To practice "reading" the recipe board to develop left-to-right progression skills

✓ To associate spoken and written language

MATERIALS:

- ❏ Fruit such as strawberries, apples, blueberries, and bananas
- ❏ 4 ounces (half container) of vanilla yogurt for each toddler
- ❏ Poster board
- ❏ Marker
- ❏ Damp sponge
- ❏ Bowls
- ❏ Plastic parfait cups
- ❏ Plastic knife
- ❏ Napkins
- ❏ Spoons
- ❏ Tray

PREPARATION:

♡ Make and display recipe board using words and pictures/drawings.

♡ Wash your hands and prepare fruit by washing, hulling, peeling, and coring as necessary.

♡ Place each fruit in a separate bowl.

♡ Place all ingredients and tools on a tray.

♡ Clean and sanitize a child-size table or coffee table, then place the tray there.

NURTURING STRATEGIES:

1. Instruct the toddlers to wash their hands before the activity. Provide assistance as necessary.

2. Introduce the activity by enacting prior knowledge. To illustrate, say:
   "Does anyone remember what we had for breakfast yesterday?" [Pause.] *"That's right. We had a bagel and strawberry yogurt. Today, we are going to make a special treat with fruit and yogurt. Let's read the recipe board to see what we need."*

3. While reading the recipe board, point to the illustrations and to the real items to assist the toddlers with connecting words with objects.

4. Encourage each toddler to take a piece of fruit and cut it into smaller pieces to better fit in the parfait cup. Engage in meaningful conversation about the toddler's work.

5. Model the desired behaviors by preparing your own snack.

6. Refer to the recipe board as needed throughout the activity. Encourage the toddler to "read" it to you.

7. Enjoy eating this refreshing snack!

☼ Highlighting Development

Toddlers often have to be reminded of rules or directions over and over again. According to information processing theory, this is because young children do not employ memory, associations, or other strategies to process information (Puckett & Black, 2001). To illustrate, they may not store the information for later retrieval or have a way for retrieving previously stored information. Consequently, they actually do not know the rules. Refer also to the "Making Rules" activity (p. 121).

VARIATIONS:

♡ Mix vanilla yogurt with fresh, squeezed orange juice and dip various types of fruit in it.

♡ Encourage the toddlers to try the yogurt. If they do not care for it, allow them to make the parfait without it.

ADDITIONAL INFORMATION:

♡ Some children will not like the taste of the vanilla yogurt or will prefer one fruit over the other. Encourage them to try everything but do not force them to eat. Allow them to provide suggestions for modifying the recipe to reflect their food preferences.

♡ First cooking experiences should revolve around simple recipes that can be served at snack time.

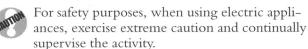 For safety purposes, when using electric appliances, exercise extreme caution and continually supervise the activity.

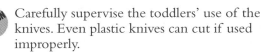 Carefully supervise the toddlers' use of the knives. Even plastic knives can cut if used improperly.

Shadow Fun

Child's Developmental Goals

✓ To investigate shadows

✓ To discuss shadows

MATERIALS:

❑ Thick, outdoor chalk—at least two different colors

PREPARATION:

♡ Select a sunny day to encourage this discussion.
♡ Place the chalk where it is easily accessible.

NURTURING STRATEGIES:

1. Introduce this experience to a toddler who has demonstrated an interest in shadows in the past or is doing so right now. To illustrate, in an excited voice say:
    "Hey, Seth, what is that following you on the ground?"
2. Discuss how the shadow moves. Encourage the toddler to locate the body parts of the shadow and attempt to move them. This helps them to begin connecting an object to a shadow.
3. Initiate a conversational topic about the different sizes of shadows. For example, compare your shadow to that of the toddler's. If available, compare another toddler's shadows. Using such words as *big, bigger,* or *biggest,* as appropriate, may assist with understanding this concept.
4. Encourage the toddler to think about shadows he has viewed in the past. How do they compare?
5. If possible, return to this conversation at a later time during the same day. Trace the toddler's shadow, using one color chalk.

6. Use the second color of chalk to trace the shadows again. Discuss how they have changed. Encourage the toddler to think about why they might by different.

☀ Highlighting Development

Toddlers are very aware of their surroundings. They notice things that we usually overlook. Shadows are intriguing and garner much attention and thought. Like other learning, toddlers must be actively engaged in conversations and exploration to gain a better understanding of shadows. Furthermore, toddlers begin their exploration by using their own bodies as tools for producing shadows.

VARIATIONS:

♡ Introduce objects that can be used for making shadows, such as a small plastic animal or a stick puppet.
♡ Provide a moveable light source such as a flashlight.

ADDITIONAL INFORMATION:

♡ Avoid trying to "teach" toddlers about shadows. The concepts behind shadows are complicated and will take many years to develop. Moreover, several variables need to be considered at one time. Instead, ask many open-ended questions that encourage the toddlers to explore further.
♡ Avoid doing this experience around noon, when the sun will be directly overhead because the shadows will be too small.

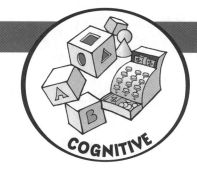

Today I'm Going to . . .

Child's Developmental Goals

✓ To create a plan for the day

✓ To select from a number of options

✓ To review the choice at a later time

MATERIALS:

❏ Photographs of favorite activities
❏ White construction paper
❏ Marker
❏ Glue

PREPARATION:

♡ Cut the construction paper about 1 inch larger than the photographs.
♡ Mount the pictures in the construction paper.
♡ Label each photograph with a short phrase, such as "riding my tricycle" or "building with blocks."

NURTURING STRATEGIES:

1. When it is time to begin the day, show the toddler the photographs. Begin by discussing each photograph and encouraging the toddler to describe what she sees. Point to the photograph to highlight the connection between the spoken and written language.

2. Ask the toddler to look at the pictures and select how she would like to begin her day. Say, for example: *"Mieko, look at the pictures. Pick the activity you'd like to do first today."*

3. Discuss the toddler's selection. Ask, for example: *"What do we need to do so you can ride your tricycle?"*

4. Set up the experience, as necessary, and enjoy it!

5. At a later time, such as lunch, ask the toddler about what she did on her tricycle.

☀ Highlighting Development

Language and cognitive development are intertwined. "As the toddler learns more language, there is more material to process when thinking, and as thought capabilities become more complex, language can be used in more complex ways" (Charlesworth, 2000, p. 298).

VARIATIONS:

♡ Have the toddler select her three favorite activities.
♡ Have the toddler sequence the things she did from the beginning until the end of the day.

ADDITIONAL INFORMATION:

♡ Only provide photographs that are options for the day. If, for example, it is raining, remove outdoor experiences.
♡ Reviewing the event at a later time serves three main functions. First, it promotes visual and auditory memory recall skills. Second, it fosters the development of expressive language skills. Finally, it assists with the development of language concepts, such as past, present, yesterday, today, and first.

Drawing a Flower Arrangement

COGNITIVE

Child's Developmental Goals

✓ To represent ideas using symbols

MATERIALS:
- Fine-tip, nontoxic pens
- Pencils
- White paper
- Containers for materials

PREPARATION:
- Ensure that all pens and pencils are in working order.
- Place all materials neatly in containers for easy access by the children.

NURTURING STRATEGIES:
1. As the child finishes the "Arranging Flowers" activity (see p. 25), suggest that he draw a picture of his arrangement.
2. If necessary, rearrange the sculpture so that it is at eye level in the child's working space.
3. Allow the child time to observe the flower arrangement and select tools.
4. Encourage the child to continue working by commenting on his work. To illustrate, say:
   "Diego, you are drawing the tall stick first."
   "What a detailed evergreen twig. I see lots of points."

 Highlighting Development

Drawing skills follow a predictable developmental sequence. First, children engage in random scribbling, that is, relatively uncontrolled movements of arms and shoulders and the resulting patterns on paper. Gradually, the movement becomes more controlled. In the second stage, controlled scribbling, children label their work (Charlesworth, 2000). For example, after finishing they may say, "It's a crocodile."

VARIATION:
- Provide real flowers in vases for the children to observe and draw or paint.

ADDITIONAL INFORMATION:
- Study the movements of a two-year-old using a drawing tool. They are large, muscular, and random. At this stage, the child enjoys the feeling of a marking tool in his hand. Children are universally similar in their artistic development. They begin with basic strokes such as circles, horizontal lines, and vertical lines. Gradually, using these basic forms they will be able to draw a person with three parts.

Move Like a . . .

Child's Developmental Goals

✓ To enhance mental representation skills

✓ To improve creativity

MATERIALS:

❑ Pictures of animals

PREPARATION:

♡ Clear a large area, preferably carpeted, of obstacles.

♡ Place pictures so they are easily accessible.

NURTURING STRATEGIES:

1. Gather the toddlers in the cleared space and introduce the activity. To begin, say:
   "We are going to move like animals today. I thought we'd do this because I noticed yesterday that Tyrienne was crawling on her belly. Do you know of any animals that crawl on their bellies?"

2. Discuss answers, allowing many to be correct. Remember that most any animal can drag its belly on the ground. However, introducing the idea of "most of the time" or "once in a while" might help the toddlers to distinguish the animals' movement patterns.

3. Set positive limits on behavior. State, for example:
   "In order to keep everyone safe, I need you to try very hard to remember to watch where you are going. This will help keep you and your friends safe."

4. Then, hold up the first picture of an animal. Have the toddlers label it and describe how it moves. Ask the toddlers to move their bodies in that way.

5. Move like the animal in the picture for a minute or so, then show another picture. Announce the change by saying:
   "Now, let's move like a penguin."
   Pause to encourage the toddlers to label the animal. Then, just begin moving. Trying to have a discussion at this point would probably be impossible because the toddlers are excited.

6. Repeat step 5 for each picture. Judge the number of pictures to show based on your observations of the toddlers.

7. End the activity by showing an animal that moves very slowly, such as a turtle or snail, to assist the toddlers with calming down for the next event of the day.

☀ Highlighting Development

Engaging in make-believe play not only requires certain developmental skills, such as the ability to represent objects, thoughts and actions symbolically, it also contributes to the development of cognitive, language, and social skills. Thus, adults should take particular steps to support make-believe play. Some suggestions include providing space, materials, and time for play, supporting play themes without controlling them, and providing many real-word experiences to inspire play (Berk, 1999).

VARIATIONS:

♡ Use a commercially produced song on a cassette or compact disc.

♡ Encourage the toddlers to move like a particular animal when moving from one location to another during transitions.

ADDITIONAL INFORMATION:

♡ To incorporate literacy, chart the toddlers' answers to your questions about types of movements.

♡ Creative movement, like that fostered in this activity, is a special type of make-believe play. The toddlers must pretend to be a particular animal and move in a way consistent with it. In this way, creative movement enriches intellectual development (Hughes, 1999).

Mirror, Mirror

COGNITIVE

Child's Developmental Goals

✓ To exercise visual–perceptual skills

MATERIALS:

☐ 2 nonbreakable, handheld mirrors

PREPARATION:

♡ If necessary, clean the mirrors before placing them in a convenient location.

NURTURING STRATEGIES:

1. Introduce this experience to a toddler when he lacks involvement with other activities. To illustrate, say:
   "I have two mirrors. Let's each look into one and talk about what we can see."
2. Ask the toddler to describe what he sees in the mirror.
3. Model looking beyond your own reflection to see objects or people in the background. Comment, for example:
   "Above my head I can see a flower pot."
4. Introduce the following rhyme:

   Mirror, mirror in my hand
   Find the clock
   So I can stand.

5. Encourage the toddler to use the mirror to find the object spoken of in the rhyme. Say, for example:
   "Franklin, see how I'm using the mirror? Look in the mirror to see the reflection of the clock."
6. Continue the activity as long as the toddler demonstrates interest.

☀ Highlighting Development

Infants are not born with the ability to see objects at the same distance or with the same acuity as adults. Visual acuity improves steadily throughout the first year of life. Once infants have near-adult capabilities, they must begin differentiating and categorizing what they are viewing to make sense of their world (Berk, 1999). Infants and toddlers must make finer and finer distinctions among stimuli. Visual-perceptual skills continue to improve over many years. These skills are necessary for recognizing and discriminating particular letters in order to successfully read and write in early elementary school.

VARIATION:

♡ Allow the toddler to lead the game by selecting items for you to locate with the mirror.

ADDITIONAL INFORMATION:

♡ This activity is best introduced to toddlers on a one-on-one basis.
♡ Select items to find and view with care. Begin with large items and gradually decrease in size. Also, begin with items easily viewed from the child's position. The toddler may lose interest if he has to continually reorient his body.

COGNITIVE

Moving Fast . . . Moving Slow

Child's Developmental Goals

✓ To create or modify a schema

MATERIALS:
❑ Drum

PREPARATION:
♡ Clear a large area, preferably carpeted, for this experience.

NURTURING STRATEGIES:
1. Stand in the cleared area. Gather the toddlers there by slowly and softly playing the drum. When a toddler joins you, avoid talking. Rather, begin moving your body to the music.
2. Whisper any directions to the toddlers. Say, softly, for example:
   "How else can we move our bodies to this music?"
3. Follow the toddlers' suggestions. If you are not sure what the toddler is suggesting, encourage the child to model for everyone.
4. Change the tempo to fast. Alter your behavior to better fit the music. Again, ask the toddlers for suggestions.
5. Alternate the tempo of the music between slow and fast.
6. Ending with a slow tempo will help the toddlers calm down after this activity.
7. Conclude the experience by briefly discussing the concepts of fast and slow. Encourage the toddlers to relate these terms to their previous actions.

☼ Highlighting Development

Toddlers still use the processes of assimilation and accommodation to modify their schemas. You might recall that a schema is an organized way of making sense of an experience. Sometimes, new information can be added to an existing schema (assimilation), whereas at other times schemas have to be adjusted or even created (accommodation) to understand it. Both of these processes require active, thoughtful exploration on the part of a child. Merely telling a child about a new concept is not enough. Toddlers often have to experience things to understand them.

VARIATION:
♡ Make your own or use a commercially prepared tape or compact disc instead of playing the drum.

ADDITIONAL INFORMATION:
♡ Physical movement and dancing activities are wonderful ways to foster the development of concepts such as fast, slow, loud, and soft, as well as spatial relationships. According to White (1995), well-developed toddlers can engage in elaborate, imaginative play, both alone and with others. Furthermore, through these experiences children can explore their bodies as they move.

31 to 36 months

Where Do I Belong?

Child's Developmental Goals

✓ To improve understanding of spatial symbols

✓ To match a part to a whole

MATERIALS:

❑ 2 sets of photographs of simple objects found in a house or classroom setting

❑ Photo album (commercially produced or homemade)

❑ Tape

❑ Resealable plastic bag

❑ Scissors

PREPARATION:

♡ Place one set of photographs in a photo album, making sure to place one photograph on each page.

♡ Cut one object from each photograph in the remaining set. The goal is for the toddler to match this object with the photograph containing it. Select the object to match carefully (see Additional Information).

♡ Tape the plastic bag to the last page or inside the back cover of the album. The bag will hold the matching objects when not in use.

♡ Place the photo album where it is easily accessible.

NURTURING STRATEGIES:

1. When a toddler selects the photo album, observe her behavior. If you notice a toddler needing a new activity, draw attention to the album.

2. If necessary, explain what the photo album is.

3. Engage the toddler in meaningful conversation about the photographs. Encourage the toddler to label and describe objects in the photographs. Ask open-ended questions such as:
   "What is your favorite thing to do in your bedroom?"
   "Leilani, what do you do with the letters on your refrigerator?"

4. Discuss the photographs at the toddler's pace. Stop and linger or skip pages depending on the toddler's interest level.

5. When the toddler discovers the plastic bag, encourage her to remove the objects from the bag.

6. Talk about the pictures. Draw her attention to the fact that you just saw these objects in other pictures.

7. Encourage the toddler to find the picture with the rocking chair in it. If necessary, suggest looking at the photographs in the picture album again.

8. Continue to match the objects to the photographs as long as the toddler is interested.

9. Encourage her to return the objects to the plastic bag before finding something else to do.

☀ Highlighting Development

Within each stage of development, there are new abilities and limitations. According to Piaget (1952), once in the preoperational stage of cognitive development, toddlers are able to solve problems by first thinking them through. Furthermore, they are able to extensively use symbolic representations. They also improve in their ability to understand spatial symbols such as photographs or simple maps. One limitation to preoperational thinking is called centration. This involves the child centering on one aspect of a problem and ignoring other relevant details.

VARIATIONS:

♡ Match photographs or pictures with real items.

♡ Encourage the toddlers to make maps or verbally describe their homes.

ADDITIONAL INFORMATION:

♡ In the beginning, select items for matching that are in the immediate environment. Gradually increase the challenge by selecting more difficult items. The toddler will have to use visual discrimination skills to find the exact match.

Planting and Tending a Garden

Child's Developmental Goals

✓ To begin to understand transformations

✓ To follow simple directions

MATERIALS:

❑ Flower bed or garden
❑ Handheld tools such as hoe, trowel, and rake
❑ Plants or seeds
❑ Watering can

PREPARATION:

♡ Clear the flowerbed or garden to get it ready for planting.
♡ Fill the watering can. Make sure the toddler is able to lift it.
♡ Gather the rest of the tools and items to be planted and place near the flowerbed or garden.

NURTURING STRATEGIES:

1. Before taking the toddler(s) outside, explain that you have a surprise. Using your voice as a tool to communicate enthusiasm, say:
   "I have a surprise! Do you remember what you had in your cereal for breakfast?"
   Pause to encourage answering.
   "It was strawberries. Because we love strawberries, I bought some strawberry plants. We can grow our own strawberries in the garden. Let's go read the directions on how to plant them."
2. Walk with the toddlers to the garden area. Read the directions to the toddlers and discuss the steps in planting the strawberry plants.
3. Assist the toddlers with completing the steps one at a time. However, if more than one toddler is present, encourage each toddler to move at his or her own pace. Avoid trying to have everyone do the same thing at the same time.
4. Provide positive reinforcement for following directions and/or behaving in a helpful manner.
   "Pierre, thank you for handing me the trowel. I needed it for digging a hole."
   "You remembered to pack down the dirt before watering the strawberry plant. Good memory."

5. Over the next weeks and months, periodically direct the toddlers' attention to the strawberry plants. Help them tend to the plants by pulling weeds or providing water, as necessary. Discuss how the plants are growing and changing.

☀ Highlighting Development

Preoperational children often have difficulty understanding transformations. They tend to treat the initial and final states as unrelated events; thus, ignoring the step or steps that occurred between them. For example, masks at Halloween often scare older toddlers. Watching a family member or friend put on the mask does not seem to help reduce the fear. They focus on the familiar face of the person and then the mask. They ignore, or are unable to use, their knowledge of the person under the mask.

VARIATIONS:

♡ Plant bulbs instead of plants or seeds.
♡ Plant a tree to celebrate a special occasion. Create a photo album of the toddlers. Find pictures of them at different ages. Discuss how the toddlers have changed.

ADDITIONAL INFORMATION:

♡ This experience will continue over many days, weeks, and months. Help the toddlers to recognize the change, or transformations, occurring in the seeds/plants by sketching or measuring them on a regular basis, such as once a week. If you measure the plants, display the results on a chart or graph.
♡ The planting activity may turn into a sensory experience. Set aside a special area for this in the beginning.
♡ This experience is probably best done one-on-one or in a small group. The toddlers will need assistance with following the steps in planting the seeds or plants. Moreover, make sure each toddler has the opportunity to plant several different plants.

 Before planting trees, shrubs, or flowers carefully research the varieties to make sure that they are nonpoisonous.

Social Development

THIRTY-ONE to THIRTY-SIX MONTHS

Making Cards

Child's Developmental Goals

✓ To develop an interest in the written form of communication

MATERIALS:

❑ Construction paper, folded in half
❑ Felt-tip, nontoxic, washable markers (fat and thin)
❑ Envelopes
❑ Container for writing tools

PREPARATION:

♡ Place all materials so they are attractive and easily accessible to the toddlers.

NURTURING STRATEGIES:

1. When a toddler selects the materials, observe. Ask yourself questions, such as:
   "Are tools being used? If so, how?"
   "What is the child writing about?"
   "Does the work seem to be for anyone else?"
2. If necessary, move closer to the child as she is working.
3. Gently begin a conversation by asking questions that reflect your observations. Ask, for example:
   "I see that you've put your paper inside the envelope. Naomi, are you going to give this card to someone special?"
4. Label the paper as a card. Ask the toddler if she has ever received a card before. Discuss the purpose of the card and how she felt about receiving it.
5. If appropriate, discuss a friend or relative who is celebrating a birthday in the near future. Suggest making a card for that person. Record the toddler's words about the card for the recipient.
6. When the card is completed, discuss how the child can get it to the other person. If the toddler does not seem to notice the envelope, direct the child's attention to it.
7. Conclude the experience by either mailing the card or getting it ready for someone else to mail.

☀ Highlighting Development

With exposure to print and written materials, toddlers begin to understand that written language is useful and powerful, and serves many different functions. For example, when eating at a restaurant, toddlers understand that a waitperson writes down something when you order and later produces a bill telling something else. They also learn that written language can create interactions with others. To illustrate, an invitation to a birthday party can result in a social event. Writing a letter or a note can also result in future interactions with the person (see, for example, McGee & Richgils, 2000).

VARIATIONS:

♡ In an early childhood program, encourage the toddlers to write a letter when they are sad that their parents/guardians are away.
♡ Have a toddler or group of toddlers send a thank you card to a visitor or leader of a field trip.

ADDITIONAL INFORMATION:

♡ Printing what a child tells you about her card/ illustrations assists with learning about the functions of written language.
♡ Encourage the toddlers to make a card for someone else. However, some toddlers are not ready for this because they are still working on ownership issues. This is developmentally appropriate.

SOCIAL

It's Mine

Child's Developmental Goals

✓ To discuss a problem and possible solutions

✓ To communicate a want or desire verbally

MATERIALS:

None

PREPARATION:

♡ During playtime, observe the toddlers for signs of conflict.

♡ Move quickly to provide guidance before the toddlers become too emotionally upset.

NURTURING STRATEGIES:

1. When you observe a situation that warrants your attention, move swiftly to the children's level.

2. Neutralize the object and identify the problem from your perspective and ask for confirmation from the toddlers. Say, for example:
   "Anoki and Victor, it looks to me like both of you want the red car. Is this the problem you are trying to solve?"

3. Listen to each toddler describe his version of the problem. To assist with perspective taking, encourage each toddler to listen to the other. Expand on the toddlers' statements, if necessary, to ensure that their needs are clearly defined.

4. Generate solutions to the problem. This step is a "brain-storming" step, so validate all suggestions. If necessary, provide possible solutions to model divergent thinking.

5. Select one solution that both toddlers can agree on.

6. Carry out the solution providing support and assistance, as needed.

7. Have the toddlers evaluate the effectiveness of the solution. If it is not working for one child, return to step 5 and select another solution.

☼ Highlighting Development

Researchers have studied children's abilities to solve problems with one solution (convergent problem solving) and with multiple solutions (divergent problem solving) (see Hughes, 1999). Young children who have many experiences with open-ended materials, such as blocks, sand, and dramatic play props, are more original and flexible in their problem-solving approaches when faced with both convergent and divergent problems (see Hughes, 1999, for a review of the literature). Thus, young children need many opportunities to discover that numerous approaches can be applied to any problem and that they have the power to solve problems.

VARIATION:

♡ Have two puppets have a conflict. Invite the toddlers to help them solve the problem.

ADDITIONAL INFORMATION:

♡ Using positive guidance strategies, such as the "no-lose" method of problem solving, assists the toddlers with learning nonviolent ways for resolving conflicts, as well as preserving their dignity (Marion, 1999).

♡ Toddlers are bombarded with messages about how to solve problems. Unfortunately, many of these messages model or discuss the use of violence, force, or other aggressive solutions. Such solutions are damaging to young children's senses of safety and the development of morality and pro-social behaviors.

Puppets Talk to Solve a Problem

Child's Developmental Goals

✓ To solve a problem in a peaceful manner

✓ To increase perspective-taking skills

MATERIALS:

❑ 2 multicultural people puppets

❑ Basket of small toys

❑ 2 empty and sanitized liquid soap containers approximately the same size as the puppets

PREPARATION:

♡ Place the puppets over the top of the sanitized liquid soap containers to display them.

♡ Place the puppets and basket in a convenient location.

NURTURING STRATEGIES:

1. Tell the toddlers that a change in activities is coming by saying, for example:
   "Carmella, in two minutes we are going to clean up. Then we will gather on the rug."

2. After the two minutes have passed, begin singing a clean-up song (see Appendix G). Sing as long as it takes to pick up the toys.

3. Gather your materials and invite the toddlers to sit on the carpet with you.

4. Sing a song to welcome and identify everyone sitting on the carpet.

5. Then, introduce the activity using your voice as a tool to communicate excitement. To illustrate, say:
   "I have invited 2 special people to visit us today. Here come Sonia and Carlos now." Have the puppets greet the children and vice versa.

6. Have the puppets begin to play with the materials in the basket. Using your knowledge of the toddlers, create situations that pose challenges and conflicts. Examples include a block tower falling over because of its structural design; having to share toys, materials, or space; solving problems with violence; and failing to assist with cleanup.

7. Stop the puppets from playing and encourage the toddlers to help them solve the problem.

8. Set a rule that all solutions must be peaceful or nonviolent.

9. If the toddlers seem interested, pose another challenge or problem.

10. Provide positive reinforcement for the content or number of solutions generated.

☼ Highlighting Development

Toddlers tend to display instrumental aggression when a goal is blocked. This type of aggression results from wanting an object, privilege, or space and using aggressive strategies to get it. For example, a child sees another playing with a ball and pushes to gain ownership of the ball. Toddlers may also hit, bite, and shout to acquire a desired outcome. As verbal skills and social skills, such as the ability to compromise and share, increase, acts of instrumental aggression decrease.

VARIATION:

♡ In an early childhood program, make the puppets available for the toddlers' use during free choice time.

ADDITIONAL INFORMATION:

♡ Children who use violent methods of solving problems typically experience a stressful, conflict-ridden family atmosphere (see Berk, 1999). As a result, they lack the ability, when faced with a problem, to generate nonviolent solutions. Furthermore, toddlers in this situation tend to rely on using one or two solutions, regardless of the nature of the problem.

Water Colors

Child's Developmental Goals

✓ To discuss artwork with another

✓ To engage in parallel play

MATERIALS:

❏ Red and blue individual watercolors and tray for each toddler
❏ Watercolor paintbrush for each toddler
❏ Small container for water
❏ Construction paper
❏ Damp sponge

PREPARATION:

♡ Set up workspaces on a child-size table or coffee table by arranging a watercolor tray, brush, water, and piece of paper for each child.

♡ Place a small amount of water on the watercolors so they are ready to use.

NURTURING STRATEGIES:

1. When a child selects the experience, observe his behavior. Note if the child seems to understand how to use this type of paint.

2. Use your observations to guide your behavior. If necessary, ask the toddler questions to guide his discovery of the water. If that does not seem to work, highlight another child's use of the materials. If further assistance is necessary, model the use of the materials while verbally describing your actions.

3. Discuss the process of making a picture. For example, describe the toddler's marks or use of space by saying: *"Radney, you are making red lines. The lines run clear across the page." "I see a blue circle in the center of the paper."*

4. When a toddler discovers the color purple, share in his excitement. Ask him how he made the color purple.

5. If more than one toddler is present, encourage the children to converse while working. However, if a toddler prefers to work in silence or concentrate on his work, be respectful of that desire.

6. Encourage the toddler to describe his work when it is finished. Print his name on the top left corner and then record the toddler's exact words.

7. If possible, discuss the similarities and differences between the toddlers' artwork. For example, say: *"Radney used red to make lines. Liang used red and blue."*

8. Save examples of the children's work to place in their portfolios.

☀ Highlighting Development

In *Picturing Learning,* Karen Ernst (1994) describes how art experiences can be used to assist children with making meaning. Ernst goes on to describe the need to include literature as part of artistic experiences, because painting and making pictures are true forms of expression. Through reading picture books, children learn how illustrations and written language work together to tell a story. Moreover, the children can use books to inspire their own work. Although an individual often creates works of art, many can enjoy them. Toddlers should engage in a sharing time in which they describe their work to an audience of peers or significant others. This time of sharing further connects early literacy, self-expression, and meaning making.

VARIATIONS:

♡ Make this activity a two-day experience. On the first day, provide crayons for drawing; on the second, provide watercolors. Encourage the toddlers to discuss how the two mediums work together.

♡ Read a story that is illustrated with watercolors, highlighting and discussing the pictures with the toddlers.

♡ Use one large piece of paper to make a group picture.

ADDITIONAL INFORMATION:

♡ Keep your expectations appropriate for the toddlers. At this stage of development, they are just beginning to label their work when it is complete. Dictating their descriptions about their artwork will assist in promoting the connections described in Highlighting Development.

31 to 36 months

Shape Game

SOCIAL

Child's Developmental Goals

✓ To play a simple game
✓ To share physical space with another child
✓ To recognize basic shapes

MATERIALS:

❑ 8½ × 11–inch sheets of red, green, blue, and yellow construction paper for each pair of toddlers
❑ Transparent, self-adhesive paper
❑ Scissors

PREPARATION:

♡ Cut the largest possible shapes (triangle, circle, and square) from the construction paper. Leave two colors of construction paper whole to represent rectangles. You should end up with two different colors of each shape. Add shapes, as necessary, so that no shape will have to be shared by more than two toddlers. Prepare one extra of each shape to use when introducing the activity.

♡ Cut sheets of transparent, self-adhesive paper that are larger than the shapes.

♡ Clear a large area of obstacles and lay the shapes on the floor about 2 feet apart. Adhere each shape to the floor with the self-adhesive paper.

NURTURING STRATEGIES:

1. Gather the toddlers in the cleared space and introduce the experience. To begin, say:
   "I have a game for us to play. This game involves shapes. Let's review. I'm going to hold up a shape and you can tell me what it is."

2. Hold up each shape, one by one. Label and discuss each shape.

3. Direct the toddlers' attention to the shape on the floor. Tell them they will be finding a shape to stand on during the game. Also, discuss the importance of having to share the shapes with someone else. Converse about safe ways to move and share the shapes.

4. Begin the game by singing:
   Go stand on a circle, on a circle,
   Go stand on a circle, on a circle,
   Go stand on a circle
   Oh, do it just for me
   Go stand on a circle, on a circle.

5. Repeat the song until you have substituted each shape.

6. Provide verbal and physical support, as necessary, for sharing the space.

7. Provide positive reinforcement on the toddlers' ability to share the shapes and/or to play the game. For example, say:
   "What a fun game. Everyone shared the shapes. Everyone kept their bodies safe while standing on the shapes. That made playing this game fun."

☀ Highlighting Development

Once children have acquired a sense of autonomy and feel secure about separating from parents/guardians, they are ready to tackle the next conflict of initiative versus guilt (Erikson, 1950). This transition often occurs around their third birthdays. Children who possess initiative are spiritual, enterprising, and ambitious. They have a sense of purpose and are eager to learn new skills, try new experiences, and join in activities with peers. Children who feel too much guilt are timid and approach the world in an overly fearful manner. Erikson believed that high levels of guilt result from excessive threatening, criticizing, and punishing by adults.

VARIATIONS:

♡ Play the game focusing on colors instead of shapes.
♡ Substitute other actions such as "pat your feet," "touch your elbow," or "pat your knees."

ADDITIONAL INFORMATION:

♡ Toddlers are not emotionally mature enough for games that have a strong acceptance-rejection theme (Philadelphia Child Guidance Center, 1994). Therefore, they should be encouraged to share and cooperate so that all players can stand on the shapes.

♡ Whereas some toddlers will be able to easily recognize the shapes, given their experiential backgrounds, other toddlers will lack this skill. Refrain from overcorrecting or attempting to "teach" shapes to the toddlers; rather, keep the game moving along.

SOCIAL

Copy Cat

Child's Developmental Goals

✓ To engage in a social interaction

✓ To perform the role of a leader and the role of a follower

MATERIALS:

None

PREPARATION:

♡ If necessary, write the following words to the chart as an index card:

Copy Cat, Copy Cat
Name of the game
Whatever Jen does,
We'll do the same. (Slap thighs to beat while chanting)

♡ Clear an area, preferably carpeted, of obstacles.

NURTURING STRATEGIES:

1. Gather the toddlers in the cleared area and introduce the game. To illustrate, say:
   "I have a game for us to play today. Everyone will have a chance to be the leader. Whatever the leader does, we'll do also. Let's try it."

2. Begin the chant. Model being a leader and then encourage the toddlers to imitate your motions.

3. Play the game and monitor who has been a leader to ensure that every child has an opportunity.

4. Find at least one behavior that every child does, label it, and encourage the other toddlers to do it also. This is particularly important for children who are uncomfortable being in a leadership role. For example, if a child turns her head away from you to avoid eye contact, say:
   "Jen turned her head to look out the window. Let's do it also."

5. Provide positive reinforcement to the entire group of toddlers when the game is complete. Comment, for example:
   "What wonderful leaders. Everyone came up with actions for us to copy."

☼ Highlighting Development

Play, for very young children, is far from being asocial. As early as the first few months of life, infants show interest in each other and by the end of the third year, they are showing the ability to differentiate complementary roles (Hughes, 1999). Such social play involves the ability to communicate effectively with a peer so that one child leads the play and another child follows.

VARIATION:

♡ Play other simple games that allow a child to lead the play such as I Spy or Bee Bee Bumblebee.

ADDITIONAL INFORMATION:

♡ Toddlers gain much of their knowledge through daily interactions with adults who are much more skilled than themselves. Scaffolding is one successful teaching method that adults typically use. This is an informal teaching strategy that helps children extend their current skills to a higher level of competence. To illustrate, the adult may say, "Watch me do it," while demonstrating a new technique. Likewise, the adult might provide a cue by drawing attention to an object. For example, the caregiver may say to a child struggling with a puzzle, "Find the blue piece. The color matches the piece already in the puzzle."

31 to 36 months

Day 1: Making the Car Wash

SOCIAL

Child's Developmental Goals

✓ To cooperate with others

✓ To practice expressive language skills

✓ To improve perspective-taking skills

MATERIALS:

❑ Cardboard box large enough to drive a wheeled vehicle, such as a tricycle, through

❑ Nontoxic, washable, felt-tip markers

❑ Containers to hold markers

PREPARATION:

♡ Place the box and markers within easy access.

NURTURING STRATEGIES:

1. Observe the toddlers playing with the wheeled vehicles. When they appear to need something new, facilitate their play by suggesting the creation of a car wash. Comment, for example:
   "Your cars are dirty. They need a wash. What can you do about that? Why don't you make a car wash to clean them?"

2. Engage the toddlers in a conversation about how to make the car wash. When they begin to discuss the materials needed, tell them about what you have gathered. Avoid being too directive; this is their project. Gather additional materials as needed.

3. Verbally support the toddlers' work as necessary.

4. Provide assistance with problem solving, as necessary. Encourage the toddlers to use expressive language skills to communicate their needs and desires.

5. Assist the toddlers with planning ahead by conversing about how they are going to use the car wash once it is complete. If there is not enough time to play with the car wash immediately, discuss the reasons for this decision.

☀ Highlighting Development

Social construction play, that which results in a final product such as a block structure, requires cooperation and coordination, just like socio-dramatic play (see "Day 2: Washing the Cars"). Children skilled in socio-dramatic play often demonstrate "group productivity," which is the ability to work with other children as a team to construct a specific object. Being a member of a team requires planning, cooperation, and the ability to avoid disagreements or, at least, resolve the conflicts nonaggressively (see Hughes, 1999).

VARIATION:

♡ Provide water, buckets, and towels for actually washing the vehicles.

ADDITIONAL INFORMATION:

♡ Toddlers need to continue play themes from one day to another. This provides the opportunity to begin to understand time concepts, such as yesterday, today, and tomorrow.

♡ Children benefit when they act pro-socially. Helping, sharing, comforting, giving, and cooperating are all examples of pro-social behaviors. These are all acts of kindness and affection that help others and promote friendships.

SOCIAL

Day 2: Washing the Cars

Child's Developmental Goals

✓ To engage in socio-dramatic play
✓ To practice expressive language skills
✓ To improve perspective-taking skills

MATERIALS:

❑ Car wash, constructed the previous day (see "Day 1: Making the Car Wash")
❑ Wheeled vehicles, such as cars or tricycles
❑ Helmets for each vehicle

PREPARATION:

♡ Place the car wash where it is easily accessible to the toddlers.
♡ Inspect the wheeled vehicles to ensure they are in good repair.

NURTURING STRATEGIES:

1. When the toddlers select the tricycles or wheeled vehicles, assist with putting on helmets, as necessary.
2. Remind the toddlers of their conversation about how they wanted to use the car wash. Discuss if this is still their plan or if they have thought of something new.
3. Provide plenty of uninterrupted time for playing with the car wash.
4. Monitor the toddlers' play theme and provide guidance, as necessary, to promote problem-solving and perspective-taking skills.
5. Document this experience and the learning occurring during it by taking photographs of the children while playing.

☀ Highlighting Development

Up to this point, toddlers have engaged in solitary or parallel make-believe play. Now, however, socio-dramatic play is evident. This is organized make-believe play within a social setting that follows rules designed by the children. Socio-dramatic play is the most social form of play and, therefore, has the greatest impact on the social development of young children. In order for young children to engage in this type of play, they must cooperate and coordinate their own behavior with the behavior of others. Thus, young children must verbally communicate their thoughts to others, as well as listen to and take the perspective of their play partners.

VARIATION:

♡ Create a "garage" where the toddlers can repair "broken" tricycles or other wheeled vehicles.

ADDITIONAL INFORMATION:

♡ Planning, doing, and then reviewing are teaching techniques that promote thoughtful and meaningful play by the toddlers. This process also assists with the development of cognitive skills.
♡ Toddlers' play becomes more complex with advances in cognition and expressive language skills. At this stage, they can represent thought with the use of symbols such as words, toys, make-believe actions, and scribbles (Trawick-Smith, 2000).

Bouncing Babies

Child's Developmental Goals

✓ To interact in a caring manner

✓ To engage in pretend play with a doll

MATERIALS:

❏ Baby doll

PREPARATION:

♡ Dress the doll, if necessary, and sit in a location that will attract the toddler's attention.

♡ Write the following words to the song on an index card.

This is the way the baby rides,
The baby rides, the baby rides,
This is the way the baby rides,
So early in the morning.

NURTURING STRATEGIES:

1. When a toddler selects the baby doll, observe his behavior.
2. Join the toddler at his level and discuss what he is doing with the baby. State, for example:
   "You're feeding the baby cabbage. She must be very hungry."
3. If the toddler appears to need a new idea to sustain his play, say:
   "Gosh, your baby is still crying. Maybe she'd like to play a game with you. I know a song that you really liked when you were a baby."
4. Pick up another baby doll, if available, and model singing the song while bouncing the baby on your knee.

5. Encourage the toddler to join in the singing and bouncing.
6. Comment on how singing the song stopped the baby from crying.

☀ Highlighting Development

Research suggests that the availability of play materials early in life is related to later intellectual development. Play materials serve as an incentive for social interactions with adults and other children through functional, constructive, or pretend play. Thus, the structure and makeup of the physical environment seems to be important in supporting cognitive growth. This relationship holds true even when the quality of parent-child interactions is considered (see Hughes, 1999, for a review of this literature).

VARIATIONS:

♡ Substitute the child's name, "mommy," "daddy," and a friend's name, and use a different way to bounce for each new person.

ADDITIONAL INFORMATION:

♡ Children's abilities for developing pro-social behaviors are influenced by the adults in their lives. These adults can create a positive atmosphere by continuously modeling prosocial behaviors, helping children to develop pro-social skills, and providing positive reinforcement for their efforts.

Making Rules

Child's Developmental Goals

✓ To participate in a group discussion

✓ To assist with creating rules

MATERIALS:

❑ Marker

❑ Easel paper

❑ Easel

PREPARATION:

♡ Clear an area, preferably carpeted, that is large enough for the children to sit comfortably.

♡ Place the materials there.

NURTURING STRATEGIES:

1. Gather a small group of toddlers in the selected area. Tell them that a new piece of equipment such as a climber has been installed outdoors.

2. If possible, view the equipment from a window or provide a photograph of it.

3. Ask the toddlers what rules should be set to keep everyone safe when playing on the new climber.

4. Record the toddlers' answers exactly as spoken.

5. Review the list produced as a way to provide positive reinforcement for their suggestions. Say, for example:
   "Nahima thought we should not jump from the climber and Quentin thought we shouldn't run on the climber."

6. Assist the toddlers with framing the limits in a positive manner. Ask questions to elicit even more responses. Refer the children to the equipment or photograph to answer the questions, as necessary. For example, ask:
   "Nahima, where can we jump from?"

7. Post the completed list of rules outdoors, so the toddlers can easily view them.

8. Review the list of rules after a few days to see how they are working. Adjust as needed.

☀ Highlighting Development

The cognitive development perspective of morality regards children as active thinkers about social rules (Berk, 1999). In order for young children to understand and follow rules, they must actively make sense of their experiences in moral situations. When adults highlight that moral rules are important for the protection of the rights and welfare of people, young children begin to believe this as well. However, children need repeated experiences to support this development. Young children need opportunities to work out their ideas about justice and fairness.

VARIATION:

♡ Discussing existing rules and their importance can assist toddlers with actively thinking about them and, hopefully, following them.

ADDITIONAL INFORMATION:

♡ Before forming rules, study child development norms to learn what behaviors and understanding can be expected of toddlers. Toddlers need as few rules as possible to maximize their ability to follow them. Rules should be introduced for the protection of the health and safety of the children. In addition, they should protect property and psychological well-being of others.

♡ Morality is a set of principles or values that helps children to distinguish between right and wrong. As children develop relationships with others, morality becomes an important part of their lives (Fabes & Martin, 2001).

Emotional Development

THIRTY-ONE to THIRTY-SIX MONTHS

Falling Asleep

EMOTIONAL

Child's Developmental Goals

✓ To follow a routine to calm down

✓ To rest or sleep

MATERIALS:

❑ Napping and resting materials for each toddler, such as cot, blanket, and any necessary security items

❑ Materials needed for transition such as tape and tape player

PREPARATION:

♡ Begin the transition to napping by turning down the lights and making cots available.

♡ Turn on soft, soothing music.

NURTURING STRATEGIES:

1. When the toddlers have used the toilet, washed hands, brushed their teeth, and had a drink of water encourage them to gather their special nap items from their cubbies.

2. Help each toddler get comfortable on a cot. Demonstrate respect by following the toddler's preferences for getting comfortable. Some toddlers like to have their backs rubbed while others prefer to be tucked in, kissed "good nap," and left alone.

3. Use your voice as a tool for calming the child. Speak slowly and softly.

4. Avoid power struggles or long discussions about naptime with toddlers. These only serve to increase anxiety and the amount of time needed to calm down.

5. If a child is not ready to sleep, encourage the toddler to rest quietly by choosing and looking at books in the "nap box."

☀ Highlighting Development

Because of their level of physical activity, toddlers need regular sleep and napping patterns to replenish their energy. However, this is often easier to say than do. Toddlers are so busy exploring, playing, and learning that they frequently resist stopping to sleep. Creating naptime and bedtime routines can be very helpful in signaling the child that a transition from waking to sleeping will occur soon (Lindsay, 1998). Observe and listen. To create a successful routine, following the expressed interests of the toddler is important.

VARIATIONS:

♡ Sing each child short lullabies that use the toddler's name.

♡ Read a story about sleeping.

♡ Play soft music or lullabies to help calm the children during naptime.

ADDITIONAL INFORMATION:

♡ Children at this stage sleep from 9 to 13 hours a day. Most toddlers take a nap. Some toddlers may resist falling asleep. Accept this behavior and provide them a quiet space and quiet materials, such as books, for resting. Resting approximately 30 minutes should help them feel and act rested. However, if in an early childhood program be sure to carefully read and follow any state or local guidelines for naptime.

♡ In an early childhood program, enlist the help of parents/guardians to better understand each toddler's naptime preferences.

♡ Whenever possible, schedule quiet activities before naptime, such as listening to a story.

Our Daily Routine

Child's Developmental Goals

✓ To practice predicting the daily schedule

✓ To develop a feeling of security

MATERIALS:

☐ Poster board
☐ Photographs
☐ Basket
☐ Markers
☐ Velcro, cut in 1-inch pieces

PREPARATION:

♡ Take photographs of the toddlers engaging in daily routines, such as playing indoors and outdoors, eating, napping, separating and reuniting with parents/guardians, and/or participating in circle time, classroom meetings, or large groups.

♡ Label the poster board with a title, such as "Our Daily Routine."

♡ Adhere four strips of Velcro to the poster board. Next, place a piece of Velcro on the back of each photograph and put them in the basket.

♡ Prop the poster board against a wall or secure to a refrigerator or bulletin board at the toddlers' eye level.

♡ Set the basket of photographs nearby.

NURTURING STRATEGIES:

1. When a toddler selects the activity, join him by sitting at his level. Observe his behavior.

2. Describe the toddler's behavior. State, for example: *"Romig, you are sticking the pictures to this board."*

3. Engage the toddler in a conversation about his work. Comments to make include:
   "Tell me how you decided which photographs to put on the board."
   "Are these pictures in any order?"

4. Prompt the toddler to think about his day by discussing what he does first, second, etc. Then, connect his words to the photographs by saying: *"You said we eat breakfast first. Here is the picture of you eating pancakes."*

5. Encourage the toddler to put the first picture on the first piece of Velcro on the left-hand side.

6. When the board is completed, "read" the daily schedule back to the toddler. While pointing, say: *"Romig, let's read the daily schedule you made. First, you eat breakfast, then you play outdoors, third, you nap, and finally your grandma comes to pick you up."*

7. Encourage the toddler to make any changes to the schedule.

☼ Highlighting Development

According to Erikson (1950), each developmental crisis, such as trust versus mistrust, autonomy versus shame and doubt, or irritation versus guilt, must be successfully resolved or it impacts the resolution of future crises. Toddlers, like infants, need routines and rituals to help them feel secure. This sense of security assists toddlers with exploring their environment more freely and, later on, willingly attempting new tasks. In other words, children's early experiences can influence their later lives.

VARIATIONS:

♡ To decrease the challenge, use fewer pieces of Velcro on the poster board.

♡ Increase the challenge by providing more than four photographs, thus allowing for different yet equally correct daily routines. This will encourage problem-solving behaviors and increase flexibility of thinking.

ADDITIONAL INFORMATION:

♡ To provide additional protection to the photographs, mount them on pieces of construction paper and laminate before adhering the Velcro.

♡ Sequencing is a challenging but achievable task if the toddlers are asked to order familiar events.

31 to 36 months

My Place Mat

EMOTIONAL

Child's Developmental Goals

✓ To express one's feelings through art
✓ To discuss healthy living habits

MATERIALS:

☐ Construction paper
☐ Transparent lamination or clear self-adhesive paper
☐ Oil pastels
☐ Containers to hold oil pastels
☐ Permanent markers

PREPARATION:

♡ Set up workspaces on a child-size table or coffee table by placing construction paper and oil pastels there.

NURTURING STRATEGIES:

1. When a toddler selects the activity, observe her behavior.
2. Engage in a natural conversation about the toddler's work. Describe, for example, the lines and colors you see.
3. Discuss what this artwork is for. To illustrate, say: *"I noticed that we need to have place mats to protect the table at lunch. I would like to save this artwork. Later, I will make it into a place mat."*
4. Discuss, if the toddler is interested, the steps in making the place mat.
5. Continue the conversation to discuss what you will be having for lunch. You can extend the topic to include favorite foods and reasons for healthy eating.

 Highlighting Development

During this stage of development, toddlers need to feel independent. They learn new skills best when adults realize what they can do and scaffold their learning by adding small steps. Take putting on shoes, for example. If the toddler can locate the shoes, then the next step might be having her untie them. You can help match the shoes to the correct feet and have the toddler put her feet inside, and so on. Encouraging toddlers to be independent by doing what they can do for themselves builds their self-confidence. Toddlers who are confident in their ability to learn are more willing to make choices and are pro-active. They will make things happen in their lives rather than waiting for things to happen to them (Van der Zande, 1995).

VARIATION:

♡ Make place mats that provide outlines of where to place the eating utensils, plates, and cups. That way, the toddlers can set the table independently.

ADDITIONAL INFORMATION:

♡ Children need to acquire a sense of independence and an "I can do it" attitude. To acquire these traits, they need to have adults in their lives who provide predictability and encourage them to create and take risks, as well as to engage in lively and imaginative play with peers (Trawick-Smith, 2000).

Door Painting

Child's Developmental Goals

✓ To express feelings through art

✓ To cope with feelings of frustration in a positive manner

✓ To express feelings in a socially acceptable manner

MATERIALS:

❑ Used storm door made of Plexiglas™

❑ 2 colors of liquid tempera paint

❑ 4 paintbrushes

❑ 2 containers

❑ Damp sponge

❑ Smocks for the maximum number of children who can paint at once.

PREPARATION:

♡ Pour paint into the containers.

♡ Prop the storm door up against a fence or building.

♡ Place paint containers and brushes nearby. Also, keep sponge handy for wiping hands at end of activity.

NURTURING STRATEGIES:

1. Before going outdoors introduce the activity. To illustrate, say:
   "I noticed Rex and Lorenzo were making handprints on the door yesterday. When they touched the glass, it left a mark. I found an old storm door for you to paint on today."

2. Set any limits necessary to protect the children or materials at this time. Use comments such as:
   "Please leave the storm door right where it is."
   "Everyone needs to wear a smock."
   "You may paint the storm door window with your hands or with the paintbrushes."

3. When a toddler selects the experience, provide verbal and/or physical assistance with putting on a smock.

4. Expect that conflict might arise around sharing the two containers of paint. When you see a toddler becoming frustrated, talk the child through the emotion. Comment, for example:
   "Lorenzo, it is frustrating to have to wait. Does Rex know that you want to use the green paint?"
   Pause, and then continue by saying:
   "You need to tell him then."

5. Encouraging the toddlers to problem solve and label their feelings will increase their perspective-taking skills.

☀ Highlighting Development

Toddlers at this stage are continuing to learn about display rules for emotions. These rules help them to learn how, when, and where to display emotions. Display rules also help toddlers to learn more about socially accepted methods of expressing emotions. For example, sensitive adults help children learn display rules for all emotions. Adults, who label and explain emotions, have toddlers who will gradually learn to do the same.

VARIATION:

♡ Use a variety of media on the screen door, such as fingerpaint, mud, shaving cream, or markers.

ADDITIONAL INFORMATION:

♡ Painting outdoors often reduces tension between adults and children because the worry about being messy is greatly reduced.

 To protect the safety of the toddlers, select a storm door made of Plexiglas™. The door will be lightweight and the glass will not shatter, if it was to break.

I Have to Go

Child's Developmental Goals

✓ To communicate when needing to use the toilet

✓ To practice self-help skills

MATERIALS:

None

PREPARATION:

None

NURTURING STRATEGIES:

1. Carefully track the time when a toddler was last reminded to use the toilet and whether the child eliminated.
2. Create a routine for toileting, just as you did for diapering. Always encourage the toddler to use the toilet, but do not attempt to force her because that will usually cause the toddler to resist even more.
3. Discuss with the toddler how to recognize bodily cues.
4. Encourage the toddler to tell you when she needs to eliminate. When the child signals, move quickly as there probably will be little time to spare.
5. Encourage the toddler to assist with the process as much as possible. For example, have the toddler tear off a piece of toilet paper for you, flush the toilet, and then pull up her clothing.
6. Provide verbal and nonverbal reinforcement for becoming more independent. For example, smile while saying:
   "Karmele, thank you for telling me that you had to go potty. You've stayed dry all morning!"

☀ Highlighting Development

One of the major developmental milestones for toddlers is the ability to use a toilet. Controlling elimination depends on muscular maturation, cognitive abilities such as recognizing bodily signals and remembering instructions, emotional readiness, and desire. On average, boys tend to be ready for toileting slightly later than girls. However, most children are able to accomplish staying dry during the day by age three.

ADDITIONAL INFORMATION:

♡ In an early childhood program, frequent communication with parents or guardians is a must when helping toddlers learn to use the toilet. To support learning, all adults must use a consistent approach. Families and cultures differ in what they believe is the "right" way. Open communication can help reduce misunderstanding and increase consistency.

♡ There are several signs to indicate that children are ready to be toilet trained. First, bowel movements occur on a somewhat predictable schedule. Through facial expressions, actions, or comments, the child is signaling that he is ready to have a bowel movement. Then too, during diaper checks, dryness communicates that the child's bladder is capable of storing urine.

"Feelings"

Child's Developmental Goals

✓ To discuss different emotions

✓ To connect behaviors with emotions

MATERIALS:

❑ Felt-tip markers

❑ Poster board

❑ Easel with clean sheet of paper

PREPARATION:

♡ See Appendix G for the song, "Feelings." Print the words to the song on the poster board.

♡ Place the easel in the area where the toddlers will gather.

♡ Clip the poster board to the easel and then a piece of clean paper on top of it.

♡ Place the markers in tray of easel.

NURTURING STRATEGIES:

1. Signal that it is time to pick up the toys by singing a cleanup song. See Appendix G for a list of songs.

2. Model cleanup skills by assisting the toddlers in picking up toys.

3. Gather the children in one area and introduce the topic of emotions. Say, for example:
   "I noticed this morning that some children were happy to come to school while others appeared sad. I was thinking about how people can feel many different emotions."

4. Provide clues to help the toddlers identify different emotions, if necessary. Connect your clue to the toddlers' past experiences whenever possible. To connect feelings with behaviors, discuss how others might know what emotion you are feeling.

5. When the list is complete, uncover the poster board and introduce the song.

6. Slowly sing the song a number of times so that the toddlers can sing along as well as perform the actions.

☀ Highlighting Development

Toddlers can experience many emotions within a very short period of time. One moment they are telling you how much they like you, and the next how much they dislike you. Instead of becoming upset or angry, reassure the toddler that you care for him and that you are sorry that he is feeling upset (Lindsay, 1998). Encourage the toddler to talk about his feelings. Label the emotions and discuss appropriate ways for coping with them.

VARIATION:

♡ Locate other songs to sing about emotions.

ADDITIONAL INFORMATION:

♡ Children's social competence is directly affected by the way they understand their own emotions as well those of others. By nature, the behavior of two-year-olds includes ups and downs and mood swings. Their emotional responses change rapidly. One moment they may appear happy and cheerful and the next they may be angry. Even though they can experience many emotions at a time, they are struggling to understand individual emotions. With maturity, the children learn to understand the succession of emotions that they and others experience.

Decorating a Flower Pot

EMOTIONAL

Child's Developmental Goals

✓ To feel proud about an accomplishment

✓ To add information to their sense of self

MATERIALS:

☐ Glue

☐ Leaves, flower petals

☐ Clay flowerpot for each toddler

☐ Thin paintbrushes

☐ 2 small containers

☐ Newspaper

☐ Masking tape

☐ Damp sponge

PREPARATION:

♡ Cover a child-size table or coffee table with the newspaper and secure it with the tape.

♡ Pour glue into the two containers, place two brushes in each container, and set these on the table.

♡ Place the items for gluing around the table.

♡ Set a flowerpot upside down at each chair or workstation.

NURTURING STRATEGIES:

1. Observe the toddler when the activity is selected.

2. Introduce the experience, if necessary, by saying: *"We needed some new flowerpots to hold the flowers. I thought you could help decorate them by gluing these flower petals and leaves on them."*

3. To decrease the level of difficulty, you may want to suggest that the toddler apply the glue as if it were paint. Moreover, laying the pot on its side may help as well.

4. Allow the toddler time to work uninterrupted.

5. Before the toddler leaves the area, thank her for decorating the flowerpot. Discuss how her behavior is important to the whole community of learners. Say, for example: *"Matsuko, thank you for decorating this pot. It will look wonderful in the room. Everyone will enjoy looking at it. It will really help make this room beautiful!"*

☀ Highlighting Development

During early toddlerhood, young children firmly establish separateness from others. Listen to them and you'll hear them using words such as *me, mine,* or even their own name. This language allows the toddlers to talk about the "I-self"— their own subjective experience of being (Harter, 1998). The next stage in the development of the self is called the "me-self," which is the recognition and evaluation of the self's characteristics (Berk, 1999). Young children, at this stage, begin to develop a sense of who they are— their attributes, abilities, preferences, attitudes, and values. This will be reflected in their language. Listen. They will label themselves and others on the basis of age (*baby, kid*), physical characteristics (*big, strong*), and accomplishments ("I did it").

VARIATION:

♡ After the glue dries, encourage the toddlers to use tempera paint to add another layer of decoration.

ADDITIONAL INFORMATION:

♡ Adults play an important role in helping young children to understand their emotions, develop a sensitivity to the feelings of others, and develop effective ways to cope with the emotions they experience (Kostelnik, et al., 2002).

Lost Basket

Child's Developmental Goals

✓ To develop strategies for coping with strong emotions

✓ To experience a sense of accomplishment

MATERIALS:

❑ Letter

❑ Envelope

❑ Basket

PREPARATION:

♡ Write a letter to a friend and place it inside the envelope.

♡ Place the envelope in the basket.

♡ Put the basket in a convenient location.

NURTURING STRATEGIES:

1. If you notice a toddler who needs an activity, show the child the basket and introduce the experience. To illustrate, say:
   "I have a basket that I'm using to carry a letter to the post office. See, here is the letter I want to mail to a friend. Let's walk to the post office."

2. Begin walking around the room or outdoor area. While walking, sing:
   "A tisket, a tasket, a very pretty basket, I wrote a letter to my friend [hide basket] *and on the way I lost it."*

3. Using your voice as a tool, communicate concern about the lost basket. Encourage the toddler to find the basket.

4. Assist the toddler in dealing with strong emotions, if necessary. If a toddler is upset because he can't find the basket, say, for example:
   "You can do it, Lev. Keep looking. Don't forget to look behind things."
   If the toddler is so excited that he can't concentrate, say, for example:
   "Slow down, Titus. Walk so you can search well for the basket."

5. When the basket is discovered, congratulate the child on the discovery and read the letter to the toddler. Vary your reading of the letter to individualize it for the toddler.

☀ Highlighting Development

Humans have two minds: the emotional mind and the rational mind, or one that feels and one that thinks, respectively. Although thought to be two separate minds, it is now clearer that emotions are crucial, or even indispensable, to effective thought (Goleman, 1995). Having a high emotional IQ means that one can recognize one's own emotions, manage emotions, motivate oneself, recognize the emotions of others, and handle relationships with others. These tasks are well beyond the capabilities of toddlers at this stage, yet the foundations for these skills should be laid.

VARIATIONS:

♡ Have the toddler "write" a letter to put in the basket.

♡ Encourage two toddlers to play the game.

ADDITIONAL INFORMATION:

♡ Emotional awareness is associated with cooperative and friendly behavior. Children who have greater emotional knowledge also have an increased ability to get along with others and, therefore, are inclined to experience success in their social relationships. Consequently, it is important that adults help and support children's development of these emotional skills.

Whispering

Child's Developmental Goals

✓ To use self-talk to control impulsive behavior

✓ To increase perspective-taking skills

MATERIALS:

None

PREPARATION:

None

NURTURING STRATEGIES:

1. When you see a child becoming very excited, move closer to the toddler.
2. State brief, positive limits for the toddler. Say, for example:
   "Inside voice. Please use your inside voice."
3. Encourage the toddler to repeat the limit, and then explain that she can say those words to herself to help remember it.
4. Observe the toddler to see if she is using private speech to guide her behavior. If yes, move away and allow her to resume playing. If no, provide a reminder. If this does not work, attempt a new strategy such as joining in the play and modeling whispering to the child.
5. After the play episode, discuss with the toddler the need to talk softly indoors. Include in your discussion how it hurts others' ears or disrupts their play.
6. Provide positive reinforcement for using an inside voice. Note how this is beneficial to others in the room by saying, for example:
   "Shari, thank you for talking softly. It helped me and Valerie concentrate on the book we were reading."

☀ Highlighting Development

In order to display self-control—the ability to resist the impulse to engage in a socially disapproved behavior—toddlers must be able to think of themselves as separate, autonomous beings who can make decisions (Berk, 1999). This ability develops gradually during early childhood. Research suggests that toddlers with more advanced language skills are more able to control themselves (see Berk, 1999, for a review). These toddlers are able to use strategies such as distraction or self-talk to guide their behavior. For example, they will sing a song to avoid touching a desired object.

VARIATIONS:

♡ Whisper to the children during transitions because it tends to attract the toddlers' attention.

♡ If reasonable for your situation, provide choices such as whispering indoors or playing outdoors.

ADDITIONAL INFORMATION:

♡ Adults play a significant role in the development of toddlers' self-control. Using positive guidance strategies, such as giving advance notice when the toddler needs to stop an enjoyable activity, assists with both self-control and emotional control.

I Hear Thunder

Child's Developmental Goals

✓ To learn coping skills for dealing with the emotion of fear

✓ To express fear appropriately

✓ To talk about fears

MATERIALS:

❑ Poster board

❑ Markers

PREPARATION:

♡ Write the following song lyrics on the poster board.

"I Hear Thunder" (to the tune of "Frere Jacques")
I hear thunder, I hear thunder   (stomp feet)
Listen now, listen now   (put hand to ear)
Pitter-patter raindrops,   (wiggle fingers in air)
Pitter-patter raindrops,
Now it's through, now it's through   (smile)

I see lightning, I see lightning
See it now, see it now   (point)
Pitter-patter raindrops,   (wiggle fingers in air)
Pitter-patter raindrops,
Now it's through, now it's through   (smile)

♡ Display the song at the children's eye level in the area where you will be working.

NURTURING STRATEGIES:

1. When a child expresses anxiety about thunder, lightning, or storms in general, discuss his fear.
2. To improve vocabulary skills, label his reactions with words such as *nervous, anxious,* or *afraid*.
3. In addition, talk about degrees of these feelings. For example, discuss whether storms make him a little anxious or a lot anxious. Encourage the toddler to compare his feelings about storms with another time when he felt anxious. Comment, for example,
   "Salim, are you a little bit anxious or a lot anxious about the storm outside?"
   Pause for an answer, and then continue:

"Do you remember meeting our new neighbors yesterday? That seemed to make you anxious also. Are you more or less anxious now about the storm?"

4. Continue the conversation as long as the toddler wants to talk. Then, introduce the song by saying, for example:
   "I have a new song we can sing about thunder and lightning. Sing along with me when you're ready."
5. Sing the song slowly to help the toddler learn the words and join in. Add the motions during the second singing.
6. Repeat the song at least one more time.
7. Bring closure to the experience by encouraging the toddler to sing the song the next time he is frightened by thunder and lightning.

☼ Highlighting Development

When immersed in emotionally rich environments, toddlers also engage in an expressive style of language usage (Berk, 1999). In other words, toddlers use language for the primary goal of talking about feelings and needs of themselves and others. In such an environment, toddlers seek to communicate how they are feeling with specific words (Philadelphia Child Guidance Center, 1994).

VARIATION:

♡ Sing songs about other fears, such as separation anxiety.

ADDITIONAL INFORMATION:

♡ Emotional development for infants and toddlers occurs in developmental stages. First, there are the four core emotions, including joy, anger, sadness, and fear. In the beginning, these emotions are extremely intense. That is why infants and toddlers typically have strong reactions and outbursts (Kostelnik, et al., 2002). Gradually, they begin to use language to express their emotions. For example, they may say, "I'm mad at you."

References

Baumrind, D. (1967). Child care practices anteceding three patterns of preschool behavior. *Genetic Psychology Monograph, 4* (1, Pt. 2).

Bentzen, W. R. (2001). *Seeing young children: A guide to observing and recording behavior* (4th ed.). Clifton Park, NY: Delmar Learning.

Berk, L. E. (1999). *Infants, children, and adolescents* (3rd ed.). Boston: Allyn & Bacon.

Bredekamp, S., & Copple, C. (Eds.). (1997). *Developmentally appropriate practice in early childhood programs* (Rev. ed.). Washington, DC: National Association for the Education of Young Children.

Carlson, K., & Cunningham, J. L. (1990). Effect of pencil diameter on the graphomotor skill of preschoolers. *Early Childhood Research Quarterly, 5,* 279–293.

Cecil, N. L. (1999). *Striking a balance—Positive practices for early literacy.* Scottsdale, AZ: Holcomb Hathaway.

Charlesworth, R. (2000). *Understanding child development* (5th ed.). Clifton Park, NY: Delmar Learning.

Charlesworth, R. & Lind, K. K. (1999). *Math and science for young children* (3rd ed.). Clifton Park, NY: Delmar Learning.

Damon, W. (1988). *The moral child: Nurturing children's natural moral growth.* New York: Free Press.

Derman-Sparks, L., & the A.B.C. Task Force. (1989). *Anti-bias curriculum: Tools for empowering young children.* Washington, DC: National Association for the Education of Young Children.

Erikson, E. H. (1950). *Childhood and society.* New York: Norton.

Ernst, K. (1994). *Picturing Learning: Artists and writers in the classroom.* Portsmouth, NH: Heinemann.

Fabes, R. & Martin, C. (2001). *Exploring development through childhood.* Boston: Allyn & Bacon.

Feldman, R. S. (2000). *Development across the life span* (2nd ed.). Upper Saddle River, NJ: Prentice Hall.

Field, T., Gewirtz, J. L., Cohen, D., Garcia, R., Greenberg, R., & Collins, K. (1984). Leave-taking and reunions of infants, toddlers, preschoolers, and their parents. *Child Development, 55,* 628–635.

Fogel, A. (2001). *Infancy* (2nd ed.). Belmont, CA: Wadsworth.

Gandini, L., & Goldhaber, J. (2001). Two reflections about documentation. In L. Gandini and C. Pope Edwards (Eds.), *Bambini: The Italian approach to infant/toddler care* (pp. 124–145). New York: Teachers College Press.

Gerber, M., & Johnson, A. (1998). *Your self-confident baby: How to encourage your child's natural abilities—From the very start.* New York: Wiley.

Gonzalez-Mena, J. (2001). *Foundations: Early childhood education in a diverse society* (2nd ed.). Mountain View, CA: Mayfield.

Hay, D. F., Murray, P., Cecire, S., & Nash, A. (1985). Social learning of social behavior in early life. *Child Development, 56,* 43–57.

Helm, J. H., Beneke, S., & Steinheimer, K. (1998). *Windows on learning: Documenting young children's work.* New York: Teachers College Press.

Herr, J. (2001). *Creative learning activities for young children.* Clifton Park, NY: Delmar Learning.

Hughes, F. P. (1999). *Chlidren, play, and development* (3rd ed.). Boston: Allyn & Bacon.

Isenberg, J., & Jalongo, M. (1993). *Creative expression and play in early childhood education.* New York: Merrill.

Kostelnik, M., Stein, L., Whiren, A. P., Soderman, A. K., & Gregory, K. (2002). *Guiding children's social development.* Clifton Park, NY: Delmar Learning.

Kratcoski, A. M., & Katz, K. B. (1998). Conversing with young language learners in the classroom. *Young Children, 53*(3), 30–33.

Lamme, L. L. (1979). Handwriting in early childhood curriculum. *Young Children, 35,* 20–27.

Leach, P. (1992). *Your baby and child: From birth to age five.* New York: Alfred A. Knopf.

Lindsay, J. W. (1998). *The challenge of toddlers* (Rev. ed.). Buena Park, CA: Morning Glory.

Marion, M. (1999). *Guidance of young children* (5th ed.). Upper Saddle River, NJ: Merrill.

McGee, L. A., & Richgils, D. J. (2000). *Literacy's beginnings: Supporting young readers and writers* (3rd ed.). Boston: Allyn & Bacon.

Miller, K. (1984). *More things to do with toddlers and twos.* Chelsea, MA: TelShare Publishing.

Morrison, G. S. (1996). *Early childhood education today.* Upper Saddle River, NJ: Merrill.

Neuman, S. B., Copple, C., & Bredekamp, S. (2000). *Learning to read and write: Developmentally appropriate practices for young children.* Washington, DC: National Association for the Education of Young Children.

Philadelphia Child Guidance Center. (1994). *Your child's emotional health: The early years.* New York: Macmillan.

Piaget, J. (1952). *The origins of intelligence in children.* New York: International Universities Press.

Puckett, M. B., & Black, J. K. (2001). *The young child: Development from prebirth through age eight* (3rd ed.). Upper Saddle River, NJ: Merrill-Prentice Hall.

Ross, H. S., Conant, C., Cheyne, J. A., & Alevizos, E. (1992). Relationships and alliances in the social interactions of kibbutz toddlers. *Social Development, 1,* 1–17.

Schirrmacher, R. (2001). *Art and creative development for young children* (4th ed.). Clifton Park, NY: Delmar Learning.

Seefeldt, C., & Barbour, N. (1994). *Early childhood education.* New York: Macmillan.

Shore, R. (1997). *Rethinking the brain: New insights into early development*. New York: Families and Work Institute.

Thompson, J. (1999). *Toddler care day-by-day*. New York: HarperPerennial.

Trawick–Smith, J. (1994). Authentic dialogue with children: A sociolinguistic perspective on language learning. *Dimensions of Early Childhood, 22,* 9–16.

Trawick–Smith, J. (2000). *Early childhood development* (2nd ed.). Upper Saddle River, NJ: Merrill-Prentice Hall.

Turner, B., & Hammer, T. (1994). *Child development and early education*. Needham Heights, MA: Allyn & Bacon.

Van der Zande, I. (1995). *1, 2, 3 . . . The toddlers years*. Santa Cruz, CA: Santa Cruz Toddler Care Center.

Vygotsky, L. S. (1978). *Mind in society: The development of higher mental processes*. Cambridge, MA: Harvard University Press. (Original works published 1930, 1933, and 1935)

Weiser, M. (1991). *Infant/toddler care and education*. New York: Macmillan Publishing Company.

White, B. L. (1995). *The new first three years of life*. New York: Fireside.

Appendix A

Books for Toddlers

Young children need to be immersed in a literacy-rich environment. A foundation for reading success begins as early as the first few months of life. Exposure to books and caring adults nourishes literacy development. Books and oral language are tools to help toddlers become familiar with language. Young children enjoy handling books and listening to stories. Toddlers enjoy the visual and auditory stimulation of having books read to them over and over again.

Books help very young children by:

♡ Developing visual discrimination skills

♡ Developing visual memory skills

♡ Developing listening skills

♡ Developing auditory memory skills

♡ Presenting new and interesting information

♡ Introducing new vocabulary

♡ Stimulating new thoughts and ideas

♡ Helping children learn book-handling skills such as turning pages and reading text versus pictures

Books that are developmentally appropriate for toddlers are abundant. Some of the best examples feature various physical formats combined with clearly developed concepts or a simple story and distinctive art or photographic work.

Books for toddlers feature scaled-down size and sturdiness. Other features may include interactivity such as touch-and-feel, lift-the-flaps, and detachable or cling-on pieces. Concept development remains paramount, and simple stories predominate. Recently, several picture book stories have been redone in board book format, greatly expanding the availability of quality literature for toddlers.

SELECTING BOOKS

Careful consideration should be given to selecting age-appropriate books for young children. When choosing books, begin by looking for award winners. You can ask the librarian at your local library to give you a list of award-winning picture books; likewise, do not hesitate to ask the salesperson at a local bookstore to provide this information. Chances are they will have a list of these award-winning books or can complete a computer search to obtain this information for you. On-line merchants should also be able to provide you this information.

You should also review the illustrations for size and quality before selecting a picture book. Study them carefully. You will notice a wide variety of illustration types in books for toddlers. There are photographs, watercolors, line drawings, and collages. As you review books, remember that toddlers need to have large, realistic illustrations. Realistic illustrations serve two purposes: They help the young children maintain their interest in the book and they help develop concept formation.

Other questions beside award-winning status and quality of illustrations to ask yourself while evaluating books for young toddlers include:

♡ Is the book developmentally appropriate for the child or group of children?

♡ Does the book have visual appeal?

♡ Are the pages thick, durable, and easy to clean?

♡ Are the illustrations large and brightly colored?

♡ Do the illustrations contain pictures of familiar objects, routines, or people?

♡ Does the story reflect the children's own experiences?

♡ Is the vocabulary appropriate?

For older toddlers, ask yourself the following questions:

♡ Is the story simple and easy to follow?

♡ Does the book contain rhyming or repetitive phrases to entice toddlers to join in the reading?

♡ Does the book accurately depict children and/or people of different races, cultures, and abilities?

TRANSITIONING TO PAPER BOOKS

Older toddlers may be ready to transition to paper books. At first, provide paper copies only when you can constantly supervise their use. Toddlers' fine motor skills can still be somewhat jerky, resulting in torn pages. In addition, until they have been taught how to appropriately handle paper pages, toddlers tend to treat paper books in the same manner as they would cardboard books. With your guidance, they can learn to read a paper book "just like a big kid."

SUGGESTIONS FOR READING TO TODDLERS

There are seven steps to making reading an enjoyable and educational experience for toddlers.

♡ Get comfortable! Sit on a couch, in a rocking chair, or on the floor with your back against a wall. Hold the child in your lap or snuggle close to a small group of children.

♡ Read slowly, allowing plenty of time for children to look at the illustrations. This increases the pleasure and enjoyment derived from books for *everyone* involved.

♡ Ask questions to engage children in conversation. The experience should be as much about speaking skills as listening skills for young children.

♡ Pause to encourage children to read along with you. You will find that toddlers will supply words or phrases. These experiences also serve to reinforce the development of turn-taking skills.

♡ Follow their lead. For example, encourage children to turn the pages. Do not worry if pages are skipped. It is highly likely that whatever you miss now will be covered in future readings of the book.

♡ Encourage children to read the story to you.

♡ Read for as long as children enjoy it. Forcing young children to remain in a situation when they are finished only serves to diminish their "love of books."

♡ Share your enthusiasm for the book through your voice and facial expressions. Children learn to love books when an adult shares their own enjoyment.

CLOTH BOOKS

Animal Play. Dorling Kindersley, 1996.

Briggs, Raymond. *The Snowman.* Random House, 1993.

Cousins, Lucy. My First Cloth Book series. Candlewick Press.
  Flower in the Garden. 1992.
  Hen on the Farm. 1992.
  Kite in the Park. 1992.
  Teddy in the House. 1992.

Harte, Cheryl. *Bunny Rattle.* Random House, 1989. (Has a rattle in it)
  Ducky Squeak. Random House, 1989. (Has a squeaker in it)

Hill, Eric. *Clothes-Spot Cloth Book.* Putnam, 1993.
  Play-Spot Cloth Book. Putnam, 1993.

My First Notebook. Eden International Ltd. (Has a rattle inside and plastic spiral rings.)

Pienkowski, Jan. Jan Pienkowski's First Cloth Book series. Little Simon.
  Animals. 1995.
  Friends. 1995.
  Fun. 1996.
  Play. 1995.

Pienkowski, Jan. *Bronto's Brunch.* Dutton Books, 1995. (Has detachable pieces. Ages 3+)
  Good Night, Moo. Dutton Books, 1995. (Has detachable pieces. Ages 3+)

Potter, Beatrix. Beatrix Potter Cloth Books. Frederick Warne & Co.

My Peter Rabbit Cloth Book. 1994.
  My Tom Kitten Cloth Book. 1994.

Pudgy Pillow Books. Grosset & Dunlap.
  Baby's Animal Sounds. 1989.
  Baby's Little Engine That Could. 1989.
  Barbaresi, Nina. *Baby's Mother Goose.* 1989.
  Ulrich, George. *Baby's Peek A Boo.* 1989.

Tong, Willabel L. Cuddly Cloth Books. Andrews & McMeel.
  Farm Faces. 1996.
  My Pets. 1997.
  My Toys. 1997.
  Zoo Faces. 1997.

Tucker, Sian. My First Cloth Book series. Simon & Schuster.
  Quack, Quack. 1994.
  Rat-A-Tat-Tat. 1994.
  Toot Toot. 1994.
  Yum Yum. 1994.

VINYL COVER AND BATH BOOKS

Bracken, Carolyn. *Baby's First Rattle: A Busy Bubble Book.* Simon & Schuster, 1984.

De Brunhoff, Laurent. *Babar's Bath Book.* Random House, 1992.

Hill, Eric. *Spot's Friends.* Putnam, 1984.
  Spot's Toys. Putnam, 1984.
  Sweet Dreams, Spot. Putnam, 1984.

Hoban, Tana. *Tana Hoban's Red, Blue, Yellow Shoe.* Greenwillow Books, 1994.
  Tana Hoban's What Is It? Greenwillow Books, 1994.

I. M. Tubby. *I'm a Little Airplane.* Simon & Schuster, 1982. (Shape book)
  I'm a Little Choo Choo. Simon & Schuster, 1982. (Shape book)
  I'm a Little Fish. Simon & Schuster, 1981. (Shape book)

My First Duck. Dutton, 1996. (Playskool shape book)

Nicklaus, Carol. *Grover's Tubby.* Random House/ Children's Television Workshop, 1992.

Potter, Beatrix. Beatrix Potter Bath Books series. Frederick Warne & Co.
  Benjamin Bunny. 1994.
  Jemima Puddle-Duck. 1988.
  Mr. Jeremy Fisher. 1989.
  Peter Rabbit. 1989.
  Tom Kitten, Mittens, and Moppet. 1989.

Reichmeier, Betty. *Potty Time.* Random House, 1988.

Smollin, Michael J. *Ernie's Bath Book.* Random House/ Children's Television Workshop, 1982.

Tucker, Sian. Sian Tucker Bath Books series. Simon & Schuster.
  Animal Splash. 1995.
  Splish Splash. 1995.

TOUCH AND FEEL BOOKS

Carter, David A. *Feely Bugs*. Little Simon, 1995.

Chang, Cindy. *Good Morning Puppy*. Price Stern Sloan, 1994.

    Good Night Kitty! Price Stern Sloan, 1994.

Demi, Hitz. *Downy Duckling*. Grosset & Dunlap, 1988.

    Fluffy Bunny. Grosset & Dunlap, 1987.

Hanna, Jack. *Let's Go to the Petting Zoo with Jungle Jack*. Doubleday, 1992.

Hill, Eric. *Spot's Touch and Feel Day*. Putnam, 1997.

Kunhardt, Dorothy. *Pat the Bunny*. Western Publishing, 1968.

Kunhardt, Dorothy & Edith. *Pat the Cat*. Western Publishing, 1984.

    Pat the Puppy. Western Publishing, 1993.

Lodge, J. *Patch and His Favorite Things*. Harcourt Brace, 1996.

    Patch in the Garden. Harcourt Brace, 1996.

Offerman, Lynn. *Puppy Dog's Special Friends*. Joshua Morris Publishing, 1998.

Scarry, Richard. *Richard Scarry's Egg in the Hole Book*. Golden Books, 1997.

Witte, Pat & Eve. *The Touch Me Book*. Golden Books, 1946.

CHUNKY AND CHUBBY BOOKS

Barton, Byron. Chunky Board Book series. HarperCollins.

    Boats. 1994.

    Planes. 1994.

    Trains. 1994.

Bond, Michael. *Paddington at the Seashore*. HarperCollins, 1992.

Brown, Marc. Chunky Flap Book series. Random House.

    Arthur Counts. 1998.

    Arthur's Farm Tales. 1998.

    D.W.'s Color Book. 1997.

    Where Is My Frog? 1991.

    Where's Arthur's Gerbil? 1997.

    Where's My Sneaker? 1991.

Cowley, Rich. *Snap! Snap! Buzz Buzz*. Firefly Books, 1996.

Dunn, Phoebe. *Baby's Animal Friends*. Random House, 1988.

    Farm Animals. Random House, 1984.

Freeman, Don. *Corduroy's Toys*. Viking, 1985.

Fujikawa, Gyo. *Good Night, Sleep Tight! Shhh . . .* Random House, 1990. (Chunky shape)

Hill, Eric. Spot Block Book series. Putnam.

    Spot's Favorite Baby Animals. 1997.

    Spot's Favorite Numbers. 1997.

    Spot's Favorite Words. 1997.

Hirashima, Jean. *ABC*. Random House, 1994. (Chunky shape)

Ingle, Annie. *Zoo Animals*. Random House, 1992.

Loehr, Mallory. *Trucks*. Random House, 1992. (Chunky shape)

Marzollo, Jean. *Do You Know New?* HarperCollins, 1997.

McCue, Lisa. *Little Fuzzytail*. Random House, 1995. (Chunky Peek a Board Book)

Miller, Margaret. Super Chubby Book series. Simon & Schuster.

    At the Shore. 1996.

    Family Time. 1996.

    Happy Days. 1996.

    Let's Play. 1997.

    My Best Friends. 1996.

    Water Play. 1996.

    Wheels Go Round. 1997.

Oxenbury, Helen. *Helen Oxenbury's Little Baby Books*. Candlewick Press, 1996.

    Boxed set includes: *I Can; I Hear; I See; I Touch*.

Pienkowski, Jan. Nursery Board Book series. Simon & Schuster.

    Colors. 1987.   *Sizes*. 1991.

    Faces. 1991.   *Stop Go*. 1992.

    Food. 1991.   *Time*. 1991.

    Homes. 1990.   *Yes No*. 1992.

Ricklen, Neil. Super Chubby Book series. Simon & Schuster.

    Baby Outside. 1996.   *Baby's Good Night*. 1992.

    Baby's 123. 1990.   *Baby's Neighborhood*. 1994.

    Baby's ABC. 1997.   *Baby's Playtime*. 1994.

    Baby's Big & Little. 1996.   *Baby's Toys*. 1997.

    Baby's Clothes. 1997.   *Baby's Zoo*. 1992.

    Baby's Friends. 1997.   *Daddy and Me*. 1997.

    Baby's Home. 1997.   *Mommy and Me*. 1997.

    Baby's Good Morning. 1992.

Ross, Anna. *Knock Knock, Who's There?* Random House/Children's Television Workshop, 1994. (Chunky flap)

Ross, Katharine. *The Little Quiet Book*. Random House, 1989.

Santoro, Christopher. *Open the Barn Door*. Random House, 1993. (Chunky flap)

Scarry, Richard. *Richard Scarry's Lowly Worm Word Book*. Random House, 1981.

    Richard Scarry's Cars and Trucks from A–Z. Random House, 1990. (Chunky shape)

Shappie, Trisha Lee. *Where Is Your Nose?* Scholastic, 1997.

Smollin, Michael. *In & Out, Up & Down*. Random House, Children's Television Network, 1982.

    Ernie & Bert Can . . . Can You? Random House, Children's Television Network, 1982.

Snapshot Chubby Book series. Dorling Kindersley.

    ABC. 1994.

    Colors. 1994.

    My Home. 1995.

    My Toys. 1995.

    Shapes. 1994.

Van Fleet, Matthew. *Fuzzy Yellow Ducklings.* Dial Books, 1995.
Wik, Lars. *Baby's First Words.* Random House, 1985.

BOARD BOOKS

Alborough, Jez. *Ice Cream Bear.* Candlewick Press, 1997.
  It's the Bear. 1994.
  My Friend Bear. 1998.
  Bare Bear. Random House, 1984.
  Running Bear. 1985.
Bang, Molly. *Ten, Nine, Eight.* First Tupelo Board Book edition. Tupelo Books, 1998.
Boynton, Sandra. Boynton Board Book series. Simon & Schuster.
  But Not the Hippopotamus. 1995.
  Blue Hat, Green Hat. 1995.
  Doggies, A Counting and Barking Book. 1995.
  Going to Bed Book. 1995.
  Moo, Baa, La La La. 1995.
  Opposites. 1995.
  Hey! Wake Up! Workman Publishing, 2000.
Brett, Jan. *The Mitten: A Ukrainian Folktale.* Putnam, 1996. (Board book)
Brown, Margaret Wise. First Board Book editions. HarperCollins.
  Child's Good Night Book. Pictures by Jean Charlot. 1996.
  Goodnight Moon. Pictures by Clement Hurd. 1991.
  Runaway Bunny. Pictures by Clement Hurd, 1991.
Carle, Eric. First Board Book editions. HarperCollins.
  Do You Want to Be My Friend? 1995.
  The Mixed-Up Chameleon. 1998.
  The Secret Birthday Message. 1998.
  The Very Quiet Cricket. Putnam, 1997.
  Have You Seen My Cat? First Little Simon Board Book edition. Simon & Schuster, 1996.
  The Very Hungry Caterpillar. First Board Book edition. Philomel Books, 1994.
Carle, Eric. Play-and-Read Books. Cartwheel Books.
  Catch the Ball. 1998.
  Let's Paint a Rainbow. 1998.
  What's for Lunch? 1998.
Carlstrom, Nancy White. Illus. by Bruce Degen. Simon & Schuster. (Board book)
  Bizz Buzz Chug-A-Chug: Jesse Bear's Sounds. 1997.
  Hooray for Blue: Jesse Bear's Colors. 1997.
  I Love You, Mama, Any Time of Year. Jesse Bear Board Book. 1997.
  I Love You, Papa, In All Kinds of Weather. Jesse Bear Board Book. 1997.
  Jesse Bear, What Will You Wear? 1996.
Choosing Colors. Photos by Sandra Lousada. Dutton Children's Books/Playskool, 1995. (Board book)
Cohen, Miriam. *Backpack Baby.* Star Bright Books, 1999.
  Say Hi, Backpack Baby: A Backpack Baby Story. 2000.
Cousins, Lucy. Dutton Children's Books. (Board book)
  Humpty Dumpty and Other Nursery Rhymes. 1996.
  Jack & Jill and Other Nursery Rhymes. 1996.
  Little Miss Muffet and Other Nursery Rhymes. 1997.
  Wee Willie Winkie and Other Nursery Rhymes. 1997.
Day, Alexandra. *Good Dog, Carl.* First Little Simon Board Book edition. Simon & Schuster, 1996.
Degen, Bruce. *Jamberry.* First Board Book edition. HarperCollins, 1995.
dePaola, Tomie. *Strega Nona.* First Little Simon Board Book edition. Simon & Schuster, 1997.
Ehlert, Lois. *Color Farm.* First Board Book edition. HarperCollins, 1997.
  Color Zoo. First Board Book edition. HarperCollins, 1997.
  Eating the Alphabet. First Red Wagon Books. Harcourt Brace, 1996.
Fleming, Denise. *Count!* First Board Book edition. Henry Holt, 1997.
  Mama Cat Has Three Kittens. 1998.
  The Everything Book. 2000.
Hoban, Tana. *Black on White.* Greenwillow Books, 1993.
  Red, Blue, Yellow Shoe. 1986.
  What Is It? 1985.
  White on Black. 1993.
Hooker, Yvonne. Illus. by Carlo A. Michelini. Poke and Look books. Grosset & Dunlap.
  One Green Frog. 1989.
  Wheels Go Round. 1989.
Hopp, Lisa. *Circus of Colors.* Illus. by Chiara Bordoni. Poke and Look book. Grosset & Dunlap, 1997.
Isadora, Rachel. *I Touch.* Greenwillow Books, 1991. (Board book)
Keats, Ezra Jack. *The Snowy Day.* Viking, 1996. (Board book)
Kirk, David. *Miss Spider's Tea Party: The Counting Book.* First Board Book edition. Callaway & Kirk/Scholastic Press, 1997.
Lewison, Wendy. *Nighty Night.* Illus. by Giulia Orecchia. Poke and Look book. Grosset & Dunlap, 1992.
Lundell, Margaretta. *Land of Colors.* Illus. by Nadia Pazzaglia. Poke and Look book. Grosset & Dunlap, 1989.
Lundell, Margo. *What Does Baby See?* Illus. by Roberta Pagnoni. Poke and Look book. Putnam & Grosset, 1990.
Martin, Bill. Illus. by Eric Carle. First Board Book editions. Henry Holt.
  Brown Bear, Brown Bear, What Do You See? 1996.
  Polar Bear, Polar Bear, What Do You Hear? 1997.
Martin, Bill, & Archambault, John. *Chicka Chicka ABC.* Illus. by Lois Ehlert. First Little Simon Board Book edition. Simon & Schuster, 1993.
Marzollo, Jean. *I Spy Little Book.* Illus. by Walter Wick. Scholastic, 1997. (Board book)
  I Spy Little Animals. Photos by Walter Wick. 1998. (Board book)
  Do You Know New? HarperCollins, 1997.
  Mama, Mama. HarperFestival, 1999.

Papa, Papa. 2000.

Pretend You're a Cat. Dial Books, 1990.

McBratney, Sam. *Guess How Much I Love You.* First Board Book edition. Candlewick Press, 1996.

McMullan, Kate. *If You Were My Bunny.* Illus. by David McPhail. First Board Book edition. Cartwheel Books, 1998.

Miller, Margaret. *Baby Faces.* Little Simon, 1998.

What's On My Head? 1998.

Miller, Virginia. *Be Gentle!* Candlewick Press, 1997.

Eat Your Dinner! 1992.

Go to Bed! 1993.

In a Minute! 2000.

On Your Potty! 1998.

Ogden, Betina, illus. *Busy Farmyard.* So Tall board book. Grosset & Dunlap, 1995.

Omerod, Jan. *101 Things to Do With a Baby.* Mulberry Books, 1993.

Opie, Iona Archibald. Illus. by Rosemary Wells. Mother Goose Board Book series. Candlewick Press.

Pussycat, Pussycat and Other Rhymes. 1997.

Humpty Dumpty and Other Rhymes. 1997.

Little Boy Blue and Other Rhymes. 1997.

Wee Willie Winkie and Other Rhymes. 1997.

Oxenbury, Helen. Baby Board Books. Wanderer Books.

Dressing. 1981.

Family. 1981.

Friends. 1981.

Playing. 1981.

Working. 1981.

Pfister, Marcus. Board book. North–South Books.

Hopper. 1998.

Hopper Hunts for Spring. 1998.

The Rainbow Fish. 1996.

Rainbow Fish to the Rescue. 1998.

Pinkney, Andrea & Brian. *Pretty Brown Face.* Harcourt Brace, 1997.

Piper, Watty. *The Little Engine That Could.* Illus. by Christina Ong. Platt & Munk, 1991.

Potter, Beatrix. *The Tale of Peter Rabbit.* Illus. by Florence Graham. Pudgy Pal Board Book. Grosset & Dunlap, 1996.

Pragoff, Fiona. Fiona Pragoff Board Books. Simon & Schuster.

Baby Days. 1995.

Baby Plays. 1995.

Baby Ways. 1994.

It's Fun to Be One. 1994.

It's Fun to Be Two. 1994.

Raffi. First Board Book editions. Crown Publishers.

Baby Beluga. Illus. by Ashley Wolff. 1997.

Wheels on the Bus. Illus. by Sylvie Kantorovitz Wickstrom. 1998.

Rathmann, Peggy. *Good Night, Gorilla.* Board book. Putnam, 1996.

Reasoner, Charles, & Hardt, Vicky. *Alphabite! A Funny Feast from A to Z.* Board book. Price Stern Sloan, 1989.

Rey, H. A. & Margret. Board books. Houghton Mifflin, 1998.

Curious George and the Bunny. 1998.

Curious George's ABC's. 1998.

Curious George's Are You Curious? 1998.

Curious George's Opposites. 1998.

Rosen, Michael. *We're Going on a Bear Hunt.* Illus. by Helen Oxenbury. First Little Simon Board Book edition. Simon & Schuster, 1997.

Seuss, Dr. Bright and Early Board Book series. Random House.

Dr. Seuss's ABC. 1996.

The Foot Book. 1997.

Mr. Brown Can Moo, Can You? 1996.

The Shape of Me and Other Stuff. 1997.

There's a Wocket in My Pocket. 1996.

Snapshot Board Book series. Dorling Kindersley.

All about Baby by Stephen Shott. 1994.

Baby and Friends by Paul Bricknell. 1994.

Good Morning, Baby by Jo Foord, et al. 1994.

Good Night, Baby by Mike Good & Stephen Shott. 1994.

Waddell, Martin. *Owl Babies.* Illus. by Patrick Benson. First Board Book edition. Candlewick Press, 1992.

Wells, Rosemary. *Max's Birthday.* Max Board Book. Dial Books for Young Readers, 1998.

Old MacDonald. Bunny Reads Back Board Book. Scholastic, 1998.

Wilkes, Angela. *My First Word Board Book.* Dorling Kindersley, 1997.

Williams, Sue. *I Went Walking.* Illus. by Julie Vivas. First Red Wagon Books edition. Harcourt Brace, 1996.

Williams, Vera B. *More, More, More Said the Baby.* First Tupelo Board Book edition. William Morrow, 1997.

Wood, Jakki. *Moo Moo, Brown Cow.* Illus. by Rog Bonner. First Red Wagon Board book. Harcourt Brace, 1996.

Ziefert, Harriet. Board Book. Dorling Kindersley.

Food! 1996.

Let's Get Dressed. Illus. by Susan Baum. 1997.

My Clothes. 1996.

Appendix B

Books for Two-Year-Olds

POP-UP BOOKS

Capucilli, Alyssa Satin. *Peekaboo Bunny: Friends in the Snow.* Scholastic, 1995.

Cousins, Lucy. *Maisy's ABC.* Candlewick Press, 1994.

Demarest, Chris L. *Honk!* Bell Books, 1998.

Doyle, Malachy. *Well, a Crocodile Can.* Millbrook Press, 2000.

Leslie, Amanda. *Flappy, Waggy, Wiggly.* Dutton, 1999.

Nagy, Krisztina (Illus.). *Fuzzy Bear's Bedtime.* Piggy Toes Press, 1999.

Nobles, Kristen. *Drive This Book.* Chronicle Books, 2001.
Kiss This Book. Chronicle Books, 2001.

Rowe, Jeanette. *Whose Feet?* Little, Brown, 1998.

MOVEABLE BOOKS

Alexander, Harry. Mop Top Books series. Reader's Digest.
Blue Rabbit. 2000.
Red Dog. 2000.
Yellow Bird. 2000.
Green Cat. 2000.

Cousins, Lucy. *Maisy at the Farm.* Candlewick Press, 1998.

Davenport, Andrew. *Teletubbies: Po's Magic Watering Can.* Scholastic, 2000.

Davis, Billy (Illus.). *Tap the Tambourine!* Scholastic, 2000.

Dr. Seuss. *The Cat In The Hat's Great Big Flap Book.* Random House, 1999.

Maloney, Joan. *Teletubbies: The Boom-Boom Dance.* Scholastic, 2000.

Murphy, Chuck. *Slide 'n Seek Colors.* Simon & Schuster, 2001.

Regan, Dana. *Wheels on the Bus.* Scholastic, 1996.

Touch and Feel Farm. DK Publishing, 1998.

Touch and Feel Home. DK Publishing, 1998.

Watt, Fiona. *That's Not My Bunny.* Usborne, 2000.
That's Not My Kitten. 2000.
That's Not My Teddy. 1999.
That's Not My Train. 2000.

Wells, Rosemary. *Goodnight, Max.* Penguin Putnam, 2000.

CLOTH BOOKS

Cousins, Lucy. *Flower in the Garden.* Candlewick Press, 1992.

Milne, A. A. *Hello, Eeyore.* Dutton Children's Books, 2000.
Hello, Piget. 2000.
Hello, Pooh. 1998.
Hello, Tigger. 1998.

Ross, Anna. Furry Faces series. Random House.
Big Bird. 1999.
Cookie Monster. 1999.
Elmo. 1999.
Ernie. 1999.
Grover. 1999.
Oscar. 1999.

Warne, Frederick. *My Peter Rabbit Cloth Book.* Penguin Books, 1994.

BOARD BOOKS

Albee, Sarah. *Budgie and Pippa Count to Ten.* Simon & Schuster, 1996.
Oreo Cookie Counting Book. 2000.

Alborough, Jed. *Hug.* Candlewick Press, 2000.

Awdry, Rev. W. *Thomas' Busy Day.* Random House, 2000.

Bailey, Debbie. *Hats.* Annick Press, 1991.

Boynton, Sandra. *Moo, Baa, La La.* Simon & Schuster, 1995.

Brown, Margaret Wise. *Goodnight Moon.* Harper & Row, 1947.

Carlstrom, Nancy White. *Jesse Bear's Tra-la Lub.* Alladin, 1994.
Jesse Bear's Tum-tum Tickle. 1994.

dePaola, Tomie. *Tomie's Little Mother Goose.* Putnam & Grosset, 1985.

Dadko, Mary Ann. *Barney's Color Surprise.* Barney Publishing, 1993.

Degen, Bruce. *Jamberry.* Harper & Row, 1983.

Eastman, P. D. *Go Dogs, Go.* Random House, 1961.

Endersby, Frank. *Baby Sitter.* Child's Play, 1986.

Freeman, Don. *Courduroy Goes to the Doctor.* Viking, 1987.
Courduroy's Busy Street. Viking, 1987.
Courduroy's Party. Viking, 1985.

Geddes, Anne. *1-2-3.* Especially Kids, 1995.
Colors. 1995.
Dress Ups. 1995.
Faces. 1995.

George, Emma. *Hop and Play.* Joshua Morris Publishing, 1989.

Greenfield, Eloise. *Honey, I Love.* Crowell, 1978.
Kia Tanisha. HarperCollins, 1997.

Hayward, Linda. *Mine!* Random House, 1988.

Hines, Anna. *What Can You Do in the Rain?* Greenwillow, 1999.
What Can You Do in the Snow? 1999.
What Can You Do in the Sun? 1999.
What Can You Do in the Wind? 1999.

Hughes, Shirley. *Being Together*. Candlewick Press, 1997.

Inkpen, Mick. *Wibbly Pig Likes Bananas*. Penguin Putnam, 1995.

Kenyon, Tony. *Pat-a-cake*. Candlewick Press, 1994.

Martin, Bill. *Polar Bear, Polar Bear*. Henry Holt, 1991.

Martin, Bill Jr. & Archambault, John. *Here Are My Hands*. H. Holt, 1998.

Marzollo, Jean. *Mama, Mama*. HarperCollins, 2000.
   Papa, Papa. 2000.

McGrath, Barbara B. *M & M's Counting Board Book*. Charlesbridge, 1997.

Miller, Virginia. *Go to Bed*. Candlewick Press, 1993.
   On Your Potty. 1994.

Opie, Iona. *Humpty Dumpty and Other Rhymes*. Candlewick Press, 1996.
   Little Boy Blue. 1996.

Oxenbury, Helen. *Tom and Pippa*. Simon & Schuster, 1988.

Pandell, Karen. *Around the House*. DK Publishing, 1993.
   In the Yard. DK Publishing, 1993.
   I Love You, Sun, I Love You, Moon. G. P. Putnam's, 1994.

Pfister, Marcus. *Where Is My Friend?* NorthSouth Books, 1986.

Pinkney, Andrea & Brian. *Pretty Brown Face*. Harcourt Brace, 1997.

Tafuri, Nancy. *This Is the Farmer*. Greenwillow Books, 1994.

Tangvald, Christine & Rondi. *My Two Feet*. Chariot, 1990.
   My Two Hands. 1990.

Waddell, Martin. *Owl Babies*. Candlewick Press, 1992.

Wellington, Monica. *Baby at Home*. Dutton Children's Books, 1997.
   Baby Goes Shopping. 1997.
   Bunny's Rainbow Day. 1999.

Wells, Rosemary. *Bear Went over the Mountain*. Scholastic, 1998.
   BINGO. 1999.
   Itsy Bitsy Spider. 1998.
   Old MacDonald. 1998.
   Max's Bath. Dial Books for Young Readers, 1985.

Williams, Sue. *I Went Walking*. Harcourt Brace, 1989.

Wolff, Ashley (Illus.). *Baby Beluga*. Crown, 1990.

Worth, Bonnie. *Bye-bye, Blankie*. Western Publishing, 1992.

VINYL BOOKS

Hoban, Tana. *Red, Blue, Yellow Shoe*. Greenwillow, 1994.

Warne, Frederick. *Benjamin Bunny*. Penguin Books, 1994.
   Tom Kitten, Mittens, and Moppet. 1989.

Yablonsky, Buster. *Where Is Slippery Soap?* Nikelodeon, 2001.

SCRATCH AND SNIFF

DK Publishing.
   Garden. 1999.
   Food. 1999.
   Party. 1999.

HARDCOVER PICTURE BOOKS

Brandenberg, Alexa. *I Am Me!* Red Wagon Books, 1996.

Burningham, John. *First Steps*. Candlewick Press, 1985.

Capucilli, A. S. *Inside a Barn in the Country*. Scholastic, 1995.

Carlson, Nancy. *I Like Me*. Puffin, 1988.

Carlstrom, Nancy White. *Jesse Bear, What Will You Wear?* Macmillan, 1986.

Cousins, Lucy. *Maisy* (series). Candlewick Press, 2001.

Crews, Donald. *Flying*. Greenwillow, 1986.

Davis, Katie. *Who Hoots?* Harcourt Brace, 2000.

Day, Alexandra. *Carl* (series). Farrar Straus Giroux, 1995.

Falwell, Cathryn. *We Have a Baby*. Clarion, 1993.

Florian, Douglas. *Vegetable Garden*. Voyager, 1991.

Ford, Miela. *Follow the Leader*. Greenwillow, 1996.
   Little Elephant. 1994.

Fox, Mem. *Zoo Looking*. Mondo, 1996.

Frankel, Alona. *Once Upon a Potty* (His/hers versions). Barron's, 1984.

French, Vivian. *Not Again, Anna!* Levinson, 1998.
   Oh No, Anna! Peachtree, 1997.

Gardiner, Lindsey. *Here Come Poppy and Max*. Little, Brown, 2000.

Geddes, Anne. *Down in the Garden (Alphabet Book)*. Cedco, 1997.
   Down in the Garden (Counting Book). 1997.

Ginsburg, Mirra. *Asleep, Asleep*. Greenwillow, 1992.

Hubbell, Patricia. *Pots and Pans*. Harper, 1998.
   Bouncing Time. Harper, 2000.

Jay, Allison. *Picture This*. Dutton, 1999.

Krauss, Ruth. *Carrot Seed*. HarperTrophy, 1945.

LaCome, Julie. *I'm a Jolly Farmer*. Candlewick Press, 1994.

Lavis, Steve. *Cock-a-doodle-doo*. Lodestar Books, 1996.

Lewis, Kevin. *Chugga-chugga Choo-choo*. Hyperion, 1999.

Maccarone, Grace. *Cars! Cars! Cars!* Scholastic, 1995.
   Oink, Moo! How Do You Do? Scholastic, 1995.

Mayer, M. *I was so mad*. A Golden Book, 1983.
   Me Too! 1983.
   When I Get Bigger. 1983.

Paul, Ann W. *Hello Toes! Hello Feet!* DK Ink, 1998.

Rau, Dana Meachen. *A Box Can Be Many Things*. Children's Press, 1997.

Reid, Rob. *Wave Goodbye*. Lee & Low, 1996.

Siddals, Mary McKenna. *I'll Play With You*. Clarion, 2000.

Sis, Peter. *Fire Truck*. Greenwillow, 1998.
   Trucks, Trucks, Trucks. 1999.

Trapani, I. *I'm A Little Teapot*. Whispering Coyote Press, 1996.
   The Itsy Bitsy Spider. 1993.

Whitman, Candace. *Now It Is Morning*. Farrar Straus Giroux, 1999.

Williams, Sue. *I Went Walking*. Harcourt Brace, 1989.

Criteria for Selecting Materials and Equipment for Children

Even though most materials and equipment appear safe, you will find that toddlers have an uncanny ability to find and remove parts. This may pose a threat. Therefore, to reduce safety hazards, you must constantly check and observe.

SAFETY	Yes	No
A. Is it unbreakable?		
B. Is it durable?		
C. Is it washable?		
D. Is it too large to be swallowed?		
E. Is it free of removable parts?		
F. Is it free of sharp edges?		
G. Is it constructed from nontoxic materials?		
H. Is it free of pinching cracks?		
I. Is it suitable for the available space?		
PROMOTES DEVELOPMENT		
A. Is it developmentally appropriate?		
B. Does it challenge the child's development?		
C. Does it complement existing materials or equipment?		
D. Does it teach multiple skills?		
E. Does it involve the child?		
F. Is it nongender biased?		
G. Does it promote a multicultural perspective?		
H. Does it promote nonviolent play?		

Appendix D

Materials and Equipment for Promoting Optimal Development

Materials and equipment play a major role in promoting a or toddler's development, as well as provide enjoyment.

Materials and Equipment to Promote Development for Toddlers

animal, toy
baby lotion
balls
bells
blanket or mat
blocks for building, lightweight
books (black & white and picture books—cardboard, cloth, and/or vinyl)
carpet pieces
cars, large toy
cassettes or compact discs, a variety of music: jazz, lullabies, classical, etc.
couch or sturdy furniture
crayons, large
diaper-changing table
dishes, nonbreakable (e.g., cups, spoons, plates)
doll accessories: blanket, bed, clothes

dolls, multiethnic
doughs and clays
elastic bands
fill and dump toys
glider
high chair
household items (e.g., pots, pans, wooden spoons, metal or plastic bowls, laundry baskets)
infant seat
infant stroller
large beads to string
mirrors (unbreakable)
mobile
musical instruments, child-size
nesting cups
pacifier
pails and shovels
paintbrushes
pictures of infants
pillows

pop-up toys
props to accompany finger plays
puppets
puzzles with large pieces
push and pull toys
rattles, different sizes, shapes, weights, and textures
riding toys
rocking chair
rubber toys
squeeze toys
stacking rings
stroller
stuffed animals
sun catchers
tape or compact disc recorder
teething rings
towels
toy telephones
wheeled toys
wind chimes

in addition . . .
blocks
cardboard boxes
dramatic play items: pots, pans, dishes
dress-up clothes: hats, shoes, scarves, jewelry, purse
drum
hammer and peg toy

masks
nuts and bolts
pencils and washable felt-tip markers
ring toss game
sand toys: scoops, shovels, cans, sifters
simple puzzles
simple shape sorters

snap beads
transportation toys: cars, trucks, boats, trains, airplanes
tricycles
wagon
wheelbarrow
wheeled push toys

Appendix E

Movement Activities for Children from Thirteen to Thirty-Six Months

Movement activities, like music, are valuable for young children. Movement is an important tool for young children to express themselves. They can move to verbal directions or music. For example, you may ask the children to lumber along like an elephant or hop like a bunny. Remember children's responses to movement will vary depending on age.

Through movement activities children can:

♡ Learn vocabulary words such as fast, slow, soft, and loud

♡ Explore their bodies as they move

♡ Practice combining rhythm and movements

♡ Learn how movement is related to space

♡ Express their imaginations (Herr 2001, p. 140)

This appendix contains movement activities designed for young children. To introduce these activities, you should demonstrate the actions for the children, while simultaneously giving the directions.

LISTEN TO THE DRUM

Fast.
Slow.
Heavy.
Soft.
Big.
Small.

MOVING SHAPES

Try to move like something huge and heavy—
    an elephant.
Try to move like something small and heavy—
    a fat frog.
Try to move like something big and light—
    a beach ball.
Try to move like something small and light—
    a butterfly.

PRESENT PANTOMIME

You're going to get a present.
What is the shape of the box?
How big is the box? Feel the box.
Hold it. Unwrap the present.
Take it out. Now put it back.

OCCUPATION PANTOMIME

Show me how a clown acts.
Show me how a truck driver acts.
Show me how a baby acts.
Show me how a mama acts.
Show me how a daddy acts.
Show me how a bus driver acts.

PANTOMIME FEELINGS

Show me how you look when you are happy.
Show me how you feel when you are tired.
Show me how you feel when you get up in the
    morning.
Show me how you feel when you are sad.
Show me how you feel when you are mad.

TO BECOME AWARE OF SPACE

Place your leg in front of you.
Place your leg in back of you.
Lift your leg in front of you.
Reach up high to the ceiling.
Touch the floor.

TO BECOME AWARE OF TIME

Run very fast.
Walk very slowly.
Jump up and down.
Jump slowly.
Jump fast.
Sit down on the floor slowly.
Slowly curl up on the floor as small as possible.

Appendix F

Favorite Finger Plays, Nursery Rhymes, and Chants

Finger plays, nursery rhymes, and chants help toddlers to develop social interaction skills, listening and auditory memory skills, expressive language skills, and concept formation. They also help toddlers become aware of their body parts and see themselves as persons who can do things.

Finger plays use a variety of actions and words together; some involve whole body actions. An example is the finger play "This Little Piggy," which is a favorite for infants. The younger the child, the shorter and simpler the rhyme and the body action need to be. For these children, larger body parts are more suitable. The young child will join you visually and participate in the actions before learning the words. Typically, after repeated exposure, the toddlers will gradually learn some of the words while others may learn the entire finger play. This appendix contains examples of finger plays, nursery rhymes, and chants that children may enjoy. Note that finger plays can be an important technique for teaching "Who am I?"; young children particularly enjoy these activities when their names are included.

ANIMALS

Can you hop like a rabbit?
   (*suit actions to words*)
Can you jump like a frog?
Can you walk like a duck?
Can you run like a dog?
Can you fly like a bird?
Can you swim like a fish?
And be still like a good child?
As still as this?

BODY TALK

When I smile, I tell you that I'm happy.
   (*point to the mouth*)
When I frown I tell you that I am sad.
   (*pull down corners of the mouth*)
When I raise my shoulders and tilt my head I tell you,
   "I don't know."
   (*raise shoulders, tilt head, raise hands, and shake head*)

BRUSHING TEETH

I move the toothbrush back and forth.
   (*pretend to brush teeth*)
I brush all of my teeth.
I swish the water to rinse them and then
   (*puff out cheeks to swish*)
I look at myself and smile.
   (*smile at one another*)

THE CHIMNEY

Here is the chimney,
   (*make hand into a fist with thumb inside*)
Here is the top.
   (*place other hand on top of fist*)

Open the lid.
   (*remove top hand*)
Out Santa will pop.
   (*pop up thumb*)

A CIRCLE

Around in a circle we will go.
Little tiny baby steps make us go very slow.
And then we'll take some great giant steps,
As big as they can be.
Then in a circle we'll stand quietly.

CIRCUS CLOWN

I'd like to be a circus clown
And make a funny face,
   (*make a funny face*)
And have all the people laugh at me
As I jump around the place.
   (*act silly and jump around*)

CLAP YOUR HANDS 1

Clap your hands 1, 2, 3.
   (*suit actions to words*)
Clap your hands just like me.
Roll your hands 1, 2, 3.
Roll your hands just like me.

CLAP YOUR HANDS 2

Clap, clap, clap your hands,
As slowly as you can.
Clap, clap, clap your hands,
As fast as you can.

CLOCKS

*(rest elbows on hips; extend forearms and index fingers up
and move arms sideways slowly and rhythmically)*
Big clocks make a sound like
Tick, Tock, Tick, Tock.
(speak slowly)
Small clocks make a sound like
(move arms faster)
Tick, tock, tick, tock.
And the very tiny clocks make a sound
(move still faster)
Like tick, tick, tock, tock.
Tick, tock, tick, tock, tick, tock.

FIVE LITTLE PUMPKINS

*(hold up five fingers and bend them down one
at a time as verse progresses)*
Five little pumpkins sitting on a gate;
The first one said, "My it's getting late."
The second one said, "There are witches in the air."
The third one said, "But we don't care."
The fourth one said, "Let's run, let's run."
The fifth one said, "It's Halloween fun."
"Wooooooo" went the wind,
(sway hand through the air)
And out went the lights.
(loud clap)
These five little pumpkins ran fast out of sight.
(place hands behind back)

FRIENDS

I like my friends,
So when we are at play,
I try to be very kind
And nice in every way.

GOBBLE, GOBBLE

A turkey is a funny bird,
His head goes wobble, wobble.
(place hands together and move back and forth)
And he knows just one word,
Gobble, gobble, gobble.

GRANDMA'S SPECTACLES

*(bring index finger and thumb together and place against face
as if wearing glasses)*
These are Grandma's spectacles.
This is Grandma's hat.
(bring fingertips together in a peak over head)
This is the way she folds her hands,
(clasp hands together)
And lays them in her lap.
(lay hands in lap)

HERE IS A BALL

Here is a ball,
(touch fingers of both hands to form a ball)
Here is a bigger ball,
(bow the arms with fingers touching to form a second ball)
And here is the biggest ball of all.
(extend arms and do not touch fingers)
Now let us count the balls we made:
One,
Two,
Three
*(repeat making the balls to reinforce the concepts by
showing the increasing size)*

HICKORY, DICKORY, DOCK

Hickory, dickory, dock.
The mouse ran up the clock.
The clock struck one, the mouse ran down,
Hickory, dickory, dock.

I LOOKED INSIDE MY MIRROR

I looked inside my mirror
To see what I could see.
It looks like I am happy today,
Because that smiling face is me.

I LOVE MY FAMILY

Some families are large.
(spread arms out wide)
Some families are small.
(bring arms close together)
But I love my family
(cross arms over chest)
Best of all!

JACK AND JILL

Jack and Jill went up a hill
To fetch a pail of water.
Jack fell down and broke his crown
And Jill fell tumbling after.

JACK-IN-THE-BOX

Jack-in-the-box
Sit so still
(squat or stoop down, placing hands over head as a cover)
Won't you come out?
Yes, I will!
(open hands and jump up)

LITTLE JACK HORNER

Little Jack Horner
Sat in a corner
Eating a Christmas pie.
  (*pretend you're eating*)
He put in his thumb,
  (*point thumb down*)
And pulled out a plum
  (*point thumb up*)
And said, "What a good boy am I!"
  (*say out loud*)

LITTLE MISS MUFFET

Little Miss Muffet
Sat on a tuffet
Eating her curds and whey.
Along came a spider
And sat down beside her
And frightened Miss Muffet away!

RING AROUND THE ROSIE

(*teacher and children hold hands and walk around
  in a circle*)
Ring around the rosie,
A pocket full of posies,
Ashes, ashes,
We all fall down.
  (*everyone falls to the ground*)

THE MONKEY

The monkey claps, claps, claps his hands.
  (*clap hands*)
The monkey claps, claps his hands.
  (*clap hands*)
Monkey see, monkey do,
The monkey does the same as you.
  (*use pointer finger*)

The monkey pats his arm, pats his arm.
  (*pat arm*)
The monkey pats his arm, pats his arm.
  (*pat arm*)
Monkey see, monkey do,
The monkey does the same as you.
  (*use pointer finger*)

The monkey touches his head, touches his head.
  (*touch head*)
The monkey touches his head, touches his head.
  (*touch head*)
Monkey see, monkey do,
The monkey does the same as you.
  (*use pointer finger*)

The monkey gives a big smile, gives a big smile.
  (*smile big*)
The monkey gives a big smile, gives a big smile.
  (*smile big*)

Monkey see, monkey do,
The monkey does the same as you.
  (*use pointer finger*)

The monkey crawls all around, crawls all around.
  (*get down on hands and knees and crawl*)
The monkey crawls all around, crawls all around.
  (*get down on hands and knees and crawl*)
Monkey see, monkey do,
The monkey does the same as you.
  (*use pointer finger*)

THE MUFFIN MAN

Oh, do you know the muffin man,
The muffin man, the muffin man?
Oh, do you know the muffin man
Who lives on Drury Lane?
Yes, I know the muffin man,
The muffin man, the muffin man.
Oh, yes, I know the muffin man
Who lives on Drury Lane.

THE MULBERRY BUSH

(*Since this is a lengthy finger play, begin with just a verse or
two and then gradually individually add the remaining verses
as the toddlers gain proficiency.*)

Here we go 'round the mulberry bush,
The mulberry bush, the mulberry bush.
Here we go 'round the mulberry bush,
So early in the morning.

This is the way we wash our clothes,
Wash our clothes, wash our clothes.
This is the way we wash our clothes,
So early Monday morning.

This is the way we iron our clothes,
Iron our clothes, iron our clothes.
This is the way we iron our clothes,
So early Tuesday morning.

This is the way we scrub our clothes,
Scrub our clothes, scrub our clothes.
This is the way we scrub our clothes,
So early Wednesday morning.

This is the way we mend our clothes,
Mend our clothes, mend our clothes.
This is the way we mend our clothes,
So early Thursday morning.

This is the way we sweep the house,
Sweep the house, sweep the house.
This is the way we sweep the house,
So early Friday morning.

This is the way we bake our bread,
Bake our bread, bake our bread.
This is the way we bake our bread,
So early Saturday morning.

This is the way we go to church,
Go to church, go to church.
This is the way we go to church,
So early Sunday morning.

(The children can join hands with you and skip around in a circle. They can act out the words of the song beginning with the second verse. If church is inappropriate for Sunday, another activity can be substituted such as barbeque, play ball, mow the lawn, etc.)

MY PUPPY

I like to pet my puppy.
   (pet puppy)
He has such nice soft fur.
   (pet puppy)
And if I don't pull his tail
   (pull tail)
He won't say, "Grr!"
   (make face)

MY RABBIT

My rabbit has two big ears
   (hold up index and middle fingers for ears)
And a funny little nose.
   (join the other fingers for a nose)
He likes to nibble carrots
   (separate thumb from other two fingers)
And he hops wherever he goes.
   (move whole hand jerkily)

MY TOOTHBRUSH

I have a little toothbrush.
   (use pointer finger)
I hold it very tight.
   (make hand into fist.)
I brush my teeth each morning,
And then again at night.
   (use pointer finger and pretend to brush)

MY TURTLE

This is my turtle.
   (make fist; extend thumb)
He lives in a shell.
   (hide thumb in fist)
He likes his home very well.
He pokes his head out when he wants to eat.
   (extend thumb)
And pulls it back when he wants to sleep.
   (hide thumb in fist)

OLD KING COLE

Old King Cole was a merry old soul
   (lift elbows up and down)
And a merry old soul was he.
   (nod head)

He called for his pipe.
   (clap two times)
He called for his bowl.
   (clap two times)
And he called for his fiddlers three.
   (clap two times then pretend to play violin)

ONE, TWO, BUCKLE MY SHOE

One, two, buckle my shoe.
   (count on fingers as verse progresses)
Three, four, shut the door.
   (suit actions to words)
Five, six, pick up sticks.
Seven, eight, lay them straight.
Nine, ten, a big tall hen.

OPEN, SHUT THEM

Open, shut them.
   (suit actions to words)
Open, shut them.
Open, shut them.
Give a little clap.
Open, shut them.
Open, shut them.
Put them in your lap.
Creep them, creep them
Right up to your chin.
Open up your little mouth,
But do not put them in.
Open, shut them.
Open, shut them.
Open, shut them.
To your shoulders fly,
Then like little birdies
Let them flutter to the sky.
Falling, falling almost to the ground,
Quickly pick them up again and turn
Them round and round.
Faster, faster, faster.
Slower, slower, slower.
   (repeat first verse)

PAT-A-CAKE

Pat-a-cake, pat-a-cake, baker's man.
Bake me a cake as fast as you can!
   (clap hands together lightly)
Roll it
   (roll hands)
And pat it
   (touch hands together lightly)
And mark it with a *B*
   (write B in the air)
And put it in the oven for baby and me.
   (point to baby and yourself)

POPCORN CHANT I

Popcorn, popcorn
Hot, hot, hot
Popcorn, popcorn
Pop, pop, pop.

POPCORN CHANT 2

Popcorn, popcorn
In a pot
What'll happen when you get hot?
Boom! Pop. Boom! Pop. Pop.
That's what happens when you get hot!

POPCORN CHANT 3

Popcorn, popcorn
In a dish
How many pieces do you wish?
1, 2, 3, 4
Eat those up and have some more!

RAINDROPS

Rain is falling down.
Rain is falling down.
   (*raise arm, flutter fingers to the ground, tapping the floor*)
Pitter–patter
Pitter–patter
Rain is falling down.

READY NOW, LET'S GO

I am a little kitty,
I have to tippy toe.
Come and do it with me.
Ready now, let's go.
   (*take tiny steps*)

I am a little rabbit.
I love to hop, hop, hop.
Come and do it with me.
It's fun we will never stop.
   (*hop around*)

I am a big bird.
I love to fly around using my wings.
Come and do it with me.
Ready now? Let's go.
   (*use arms as wings to fly*)

I am a great big elephant.
I take big steps so slow.
I'd love to have you join me.
Ready now? Let's go
   (*take slow, big steps*)

I am a little puppy.
I love to run and run.
Come and do it with me.
We will have such fun.
   (*run like a puppy*)

RIGHT HAND, LEFT HAND

This is my right hand,
I'll raise it up high.
   (*raise the right hand up high*)
This is my left hand.
I'll touch the sky.
   (*raise the left hand up high*)
Right hand,
   (*show right palm*)
Left hand,
   (*show left palm*)
Roll them around
   (*roll hands over and over*)
Left hand,
   (*show palm*)
Right hand,
   (*show palm*)
Pound, pound, pound.
   (*hit fists together*)

SEE, SEE, SEE

See, see, see
   (*shade eyes with hands*)
Three birds are in a tree.
   (*hold up three fingers*)
One can chirp
   (*point to thumb*)
And one can sing
   (*point to index finger*)
One is just a tiny thing.
   (*point to middle finger, then rock baby bird in arms*)
See, see, see
Three birds are in a tree.
   (*hold up three fingers*)

STAND UP TALL

Stand up tall
Hands in the air.
Now sit down
In your chair.
Clap your hands
And make a frown.
Smile and smile.
Hop like a clown.

TEAPOT

I'm a little teapot,
   (*place right hand on hip, extend left, palm out*)
Short and stout.
Here's my handle.
And here's my spout.
When I get all steamed up, I just shout:
"Tip me over, and pour me out."
   (*bend to left*)
I can change my handle
   (*place left hand on hip and extend right hand out*)
And my spout.
"Tip me over, and pour me out."
   (*bend to the right*)

TEDDY BEAR

Teddy bear, teddy bear, turn around.
Teddy bear, teddy bear, touch the ground.
Teddy bear, teddy bear, climb the stairs.
Teddy bear, teddy bear, jump into bed.
Teddy bear, teddy bear, turn out the lights.
Teddy bear, teddy bear, blow a kiss.
Teddy bear, teddy bear, say goodnight.
Goodnight.

TEN LITTLE DUCKS

Ten little ducks swimming in the lake.
   (*move ten fingers as if swimming*)
Quack! Quack!
   (*snap fingers twice*)
They give their heads a shake.
   (*shake fingers*)
Glunk! Glunk! Go go little frogs.
   (*two claps of hands*)
And away to their mothers,
The ten ducks run.
   (*move hands in running motion from front to back*)

TEN LITTLE FINGERS

I have ten little fingers and ten little toes.
   (*children point to portions of body as they repeat words*)
Two little arms and one little nose.
One little mouth and two little ears.
Two little eyes for smiles and tears.
One little head and two little feet.
One little chin, that makes _____ complete.

THIS LITTLE PIGGY

This little piggy went to market.
   (*point to one finger at a time*)
This little piggy stayed home.
This little piggy had roast beef.
This little piggy had none.
This little piggy cried, "Wee, wee, wee."
And ran all the way home.

THREE FROGS

Three little frogs
   (*hold up three fingers of left hand*)
Asleep in the sun.
   (*fold them over*)
We'll creep up and wake them.
   (*make creeping motion with fingers of right hand*)
Then we will run.
   (*hold up three fingers while right hand runs away*)

THREE LITTLE DUCKIES

Three little duckies
   (*hold up three fingers*)
Swimming in the lake.
   (*make swimming motions*)
The first ducky said,
   (*hold up one finger*)
"Watch the waves I make."
   (*make wave motions*)
The second ducky said,
   (*hold up two fingers*)
"Swimming is such fun."
   (*smile*)
The third ducky said,
   (*hold up three fingers*)
"I'd rather sit in the sun."
   (*turn face to sun*)
Then along came a motorboat.
With a Pop! Pop! Pop!
   (*clap three times*)
And three little duckies
Swam away from the spot.
   (*put three fingers behind back*)

THREE LITTLE MONKEYS

Three little monkeys jumping on the bed.
   (*hold up three fingers*)
One fell off and bumped his head.
Mama called the doctor and the doctor said,
No more monkeys jumping on the bed.
   (*shake pointer finger as if scolding*)

Two little monkeys jumping on the bed,
   (*hold up two fingers*)
One fell off and bumped his head.
Mama called the doctor and the doctor said,
No more monkeys jumping on the bed.
   (*shake pointer finger as if scolding*)

One little monkey jumping on the bed.
   (*hold up one finger*)
He fell off and bumped his head.
Mama called the doctor and the doctor said,
No more jumping on the bed.
   (*shake pointer finger as if scolding*)

TWO LITTLE APPLES

(*hold hands above head, form circles with thumb
    and forefinger of each hand*)
Away up high in the apple tree,
Two red apples smiled at me.
    (*smile*)
I shook that tree as hard as I could.
    (*put hands out as if on tree—shake*)
And down they came.
    (*hands above head and lower to ground*)
And ummmmm were they good!
    (*rub tummy*)

TWO LITTLE BLACKBIRDS

Two little blackbirds sitting on a hill.
    (*show two fingers*)
One named Jack.
    (*hold up one finger on right hand*)
One named Jill.
    (*hold up one finger on the left hand*)
Fly away Jack.
    (*move right hand behind back*)
Fly away Jill.
    (*move the left hand behind back*)
Come back Jack.
    (*return right hand*)
Come back Jill.
    (*return left hand*)
(Children's names can be substituted for Jack and Jill in
    this finger play.)

TWO LITTLE KITTENS

(*hold up two fingers, cup hands together to form a ball*)
Two little kittens found a ball of yarn
As they were playing near a barn.
    (*bring hands together pointed upward for barn*)
One little kitten jumped in the hay,
    (*hold up one finger, make jumping then wiggling motion*)
The other little kitten ran away.
    (*make running motion with other hand*)

ZOO ANIMALS

This is the way the elephant goes.
    (*clasp hands together, extend arms, move back and forth*)
With a curly trunk instead of a nose.
The buffalo, all shaggy and fat.
Has two sharp horns in place of a hat.
    (*point to forehead*)
The hippo with his mouth so wide
Let's see what's inside.
    (*hands together and open wide and close them*)
The wiggly snake upon the ground
Crawls along without a sound.
    (*weave hands back and forth*)
But monkey see and monkey do is the
funniest animal in the zoo.
    (*place thumbs in ears and wiggle fingers*)

Songs

Music is a universal language and a natural form of expression for children of all ages. Toddlers need to have a wide variety of music experiences that are casual and spontaneous. They enjoy lullabies that are slow, soft, and soothing. In addition to lullabies, classical, folk and music from different ethnic and cultural groups should all be included. Children like songs about animals and familiar objects, which tell a story and contain frequent repetition. Choose simple songs with a strong melody that represent their age, abilities, and interests. Chances are children will more easily remember these songs. While singing, remember to convey enthusiasm.

Music is a valuable experience for young children. They enjoy listening to music while engaged in activities and napping. Music promotes the development of listening skills and builds vocabulary. It is a tool that provides an opportunity for learning new concepts such as up/down, fast/slow, heavy/light, and loud/soft. Music releases tension, stimulates the imagination, and promotes the development of auditory memory skills.

ALL ABOUT ME

Brushing Teeth
(Tune: "Mulberry Bush")
This is the way we brush our teeth,
Brush our teeth, brush our teeth.
This is the way we brush our teeth,
So early in the morning.

Good Morning
Good morning to you.
Good morning to you.
We're all in our places,
With bright shining faces,
Good morning to you.

ANIMALS

The Animals on the Farm
(Tune: "The Wheels on the Bus")
The cows on the farm go moo, moo, moo,
Moo, moo, moo, moo, moo, moo.
The cows on the farm go moo, moo, moo,
All day long.

The horses on the farm go nay, nay, nay,
Nay, nay, nay, nay, nay, nay.
The horses on the farm go nay, nay, nay,
All day long.

OTHER VERSES:
Pigs—oink
Sheep—baa
Chicken—cluck
Turkeys—gobble

The Ants Go Marching One by One
The ants go marching one by one.
Hurrah! Hurrah!
The ants go marching one by one.
Hurrah! Hurrah!
The ants go marching one by one.

The little one stops to suck her thumb
And they all go marching,
Down in the ground
To get out of the rain.
Boom Boom Boom

OTHER VERSES:
Two by two
The little one stops to tie his shoe
Three by three
The little one stops to scratch her knee
Four by four
The little one stops to shut the door
Five by five
The little one stops to wave goodbye.

Circus
(Tune: "Did You Ever See a Lassie")
Let's pretend that we are clowns, are clowns, are clowns.
Let's pretend that we are clowns.
We'll have so much fun.
We'll put on our makeup and make people laugh hard.
Let's pretend that we are clowns.
We'll have so much fun.

Let's pretend that we are elephants, are elephants, are elephants.
Let's pretend that we are elephants.
We'll have so much fun.
We'll sway back and forth and stand on just two legs.
Let's pretend that we are elephants.
We'll have so much fun.

Let's pretend that we are on a trapeze, a trapeze, a trapeze.
Let's pretend that we are on a trapeze.
We'll have so much fun.
We'll swing high and swoop low and make people
shout "oh"!
Let's pretend that we are on a trapeze.
We'll have so much fun!

Easter Bunny
(Tune: "Ten Little Indians")
Where, oh, where is the Easter Bunny,
Where, oh, where is the Easter Bunny,
Where, oh, where is the Easter Bunny,
Early Easter morning?

Find all the eggs and put them in a basket,
Find all the eggs and put them in a basket,
Find all the eggs and put them in a basket,
Early Easter morning.

Itsy Bitsy Spider
The itsy bitsy spider went up the water spout
Down came the rain and washed the spider out
Out came the sun and dried up all the rain
And the itsy bitsy spider went up the spout again.
(This is also a popular finger play.)

Kitty
(Tune: "Bingo")
I have a cat. She's very shy.
But she comes when I call Kitty
K-I-T-T-Y
K-I-T-T-Y
K-I-T-T-Y
and Kitty is her name-o.

(Variation: Let children think of other names.)

Old MacDonald Had a Farm
Old MacDonald had a farm,
E-I-E-I-O.
And on his farm he had some cows,
E-I-E-I-O.
With a moo, moo here and a moo, moo there,
Here a moo, there a moo, everywhere a moo, moo.
Old MacDonald had a farm,
E-I-E-I-O.

OTHER VERSES:
Sheep—baa, baa
Pigs—oink, oink
Ducks—quack, quack
Chickens—chick, chick

Two Little Black Bears
(Tune: "Two Little Blackbirds")
Two little black bears sitting on a hill
One named Jack, one named Jill.
Run away Jack
Run away Jill.
Come back Jack
Come back Jill.
Two little black bears sitting on a hill
One named Jack, one named Jill.

CLEANUP SONGS

Cleanup Time 1
(Tune: "London Bridge")
Cleanup time is already here,
Already here, already here.
Cleanup time is already here,
Already here.

Cleanup Time 2
(Tune: "Hot Cross Buns")
Cleanup time.
Cleanup time.
Put all of the toys away.
It's cleanup time.

Do You Know What Time It Is?
(Tune: "The Muffin Man")
Oh, do you know what time it is,
What time it is, what time it is?
Oh, do you know what time it is?
It's almost cleanup time.
     (Or, it's time to clean up.)

A Helper I Will Be
(Tune: "The Farmer in the Dell")
A helper I will be.
A helper I will be.
I'll pick up the toys and put them away.
A helper I will be.

It's Cleanup Time
(Tune: "Looby Loo")
It's cleanup time at the preschool.
It's time for boys and girls
To stop what they are doing.
And put away their toys.

Oh, It's Cleanup Time
(Tune: "Oh, My Darling Clementine")
Oh, it's cleanup time,
Oh, it's cleanup time,
Oh, it's cleanup time right now.
It's time to put the toys away,
It is cleanup time right now.

Passing Around
(Tune: "Skip to My Loo")
Brad, take a napkin and pass them to Sara.
Sara, take a napkin and pass them to Tina.
Tina, take a napkin and pass them to Eric.
Passing around the napkins.

(Fill in the appropriate child's name and substitute for "napkin" any object that needs to be passed at mealtime.)

Put Your Coat On
(Tune: "Oh, My Darling Clementine")
Put your coat on.
Put your coat on.
Put your winter coat on now.
We are going to play outside.
Put your coat on right now.
(Change "coat" to any article of clothing.)

This Is the Way
(Tune: "Mulberry Bush")
This is the way we pick up our toys,
Pick up our toys, pick up our toys.
This is the way we pick up our toys,
At cleanup time each day.
*(Substituting "before bedtime" opposed to "cleanup time"
   could modify this song.)*

Time to Clean up
(Tune: "Are You Sleeping?")
Time to clean up.
Time to clean up.
Everybody help.
Everybody help.
Put the toys away, put the toys away.
Then sit down. *(Or, then come here.)*
(Specific toys can be mentioned in place of "toys.")

We're Cleaning Up Our Room
(Tune: "The Farmer in the Dell")
We're cleaning up our room.
We're cleaning up our room.
We're putting all the toys away.
We're cleaning up our room.

FAVORITES

London Bridge
London Bridge is falling down,
Falling down, falling down.
London Bridge is falling down.
My fair lady.

Twinkle, Twinkle, Little Star
Twinkle, twinkle, little star,
How I wonder what you are!
Up above the world so high,
Like a diamond in the sky.
Twinkle, twinkle, little star,
How I wonder what you are!

Where Is Thumbkin?
Where is thumbkin?
Where is thumbkin?
Here I am,
Here I am.
How are you today, sir?
Very well, I thank you.
Fly away, fly away.

OTHER VERSES:
Pointer
Tall man
Ring man
Pinky

FEELINGS

Feelings
(Tune: "Twinkle, Twinkle, Little Star")
I have feelings.
You do, too.
Let's all sing about a few.
I am happy. *(smile)*
I am sad. *(frown)*
I get scared. *(wrap arms around self)*
I get mad. *(sneer and wrinkle nose)*
I am proud of being me. *(hands on hips)*
That's a feeling, too, you see.
I have feelings. *(point to self)*
You do, too. *(point to someone else)*
We just sang about a few.

If You're Happy and You Know It
If you're happy and you know it
Clap your hands.
   (clap twice)
If you're happy and you know it
Clap your hands.
   (clap twice)
If you're happy and you know it
Then your face will surely show it.
If you're happy and you know it
Clap your hands.
   (clap twice)

If you're sad and you know it
Say boo-hoo.
   (rub your eyes)
If you're sad and you know it
Say boo-hoo.
   (rub your eyes)
If you're sad and you know it
Then your face will surely show it.
If you're sad and you know it
Say boo-hoo.
   (rub your eyes)

If you're mad and you know it
Wrinkle your nose.
   (wrinkle nose)
If you're mad and you know it
Wrinkle your nose.
   (wrinkle nose)
If you're mad and you know it
Then your face will surely show it.
If you're mad and you know it
Wrinkle your nose.
   (wrinkle nose)

PEOPLE

Are You Sleeping?

Are you sleeping?
Are you sleeping?
Brother John, brother John,
Morning bells are ringing,
Morning bells are ringing.
Ding, ding, dong!
Ding, ding, dong!

Do You Know This Friend of Mine?
(Tune: "The Muffin Man")

Do you know this friend of mine,
This friend of mine,
This friend of mine?
Do you know this friend of mine?
Her name is _____.
Yes, we know this friend of yours,
This friend of yours,
This friend of yours.
Yes, we know this friend of yours.
Her name is _____.

The Muffin Man

Oh, do you know the muffin man,
The muffin man, the muffin man?
Oh, do you know the muffin man,
Who lives on Drury Lane?

Oh, yes we know the muffin man,
The muffin man, the muffin man.
Oh, yes we know the muffin man,
Who lives on Drury Lane.

Oh, how do you know the muffin man,
The muffin man, the muffin man?
Oh, how do you know the muffin man,
Who lives on Drury Lane.

Cause [Papaw] is the muffin man,
The muffin man, the muffin man.
[Pawpaw] is the muffin man,
Who lives on Drury Lane.

(Substitute names of other males who are important in the child's life, such as Daddy or Uncle Todd.)

This Old Man

This old man
He played one
He played knick knack on a drum
With a knick knack, paddy whack
Give the dog a bone
This old man came rolling home.

OTHER VERSES:
He played two
He played knick knack on my shoe.
He played three
He played knick knack on a tree
He played four
He played knick knack at my door
He played five
He played knick knack on a hive.

TRANSPORTATION

Row, Row, Row, Your Boat

Row, row, row your boat.
Gently down the stream.
Merrily, merrily, merrily, merrily,
Life is but a dream.

The Wheels on the Bus

The wheels on the bus go round and round.
Round and round, round and round.
The wheels on the bus go round and round.
All around the town.

OTHER VERSES:
The wipers on the bus go swish, swish, swish.
The doors on the bus go open and shut.
The horn on the bus goes beep, beep, beep.
The driver on the bus says, "Move on back."
The people on the bus go up and down.

Appendix H

Rhythm Instruments

Using rhythm instruments is a method of teaching young children to express themselves. Rhythm instruments can be common household objects or purchased through school supply stores or catalogs. Examples include:

Commercially Purchased	Household Items
Drums	Pots
Jingle sticks	Pans
Cymbals	Lids
Rattles	Wooden spoons
Wrist bells	Aluminum pie pans
Shakers	Metal whisks
Maracas	Plastic bowls
Sandpaper blocks	

You can also improvise and construct these instruments—save cans, cardboard tubes that have plastic lids from nuts, chips, and coffee. These items can be used as drums. If you place noise-making objects inside the cans or tubes, they can be used as shakers. However, make sure that you secure the lid using a high-quality adhesive tape that children cannot remove.

Appendix I

Recipes

Play dough and clay are satisfying materials for toddlers. Play dough is softer than clay and is usually preferred by the young toddler because it is pliable and easy to manipulate. When provided a handful of play dough, without encouragement, a child will begin to poke, push, roll, pinch, tear, squeeze, and pound it. Clay, on the other hand, is a firmer or stiffer medium, which requires more refined muscular development to successfully manipulate. As a result, clay typically is more appropriate for older toddlers and children.

Modeling materials such as play dough and clay are valuable tools for the young child. Play dough and play dough accessories provide young children with an opportunity to:

♡ explore materials using their senses
♡ represent their thoughts and ideas
♡ learn the physical nature of materials
♡ develop the ability to make choices
♡ learn to appreciate the value of tools in the human hands

♡ heighten perceptual powers
♡ develop small muscle coordination skills
♡ develop hand–eye coordination skills
♡ express their feelings, explore, and experiment

Colors can be added to play dough to increase interest. Food coloring is the preferred medium to add color to the dough because it will not rub off on a child's hands. Food coloring can be added directly to the liquids required in the recipe. Otherwise, colored tempera can be added to the flour. With this method, the dough requires kneading. A gallon-size, self-sealing plastic bag is a convenient way to mix and knead dough colored with tempera paint.

Give each child a piece of play dough the size of an orange or small grapefruit. Unless using Formica™, Corian™, or granite surface, cover the children's work area with a washable or disposable cover. Establish rules for playing with dough. Such rules might include the following: (1) dough should only be used at the table or other place you designate; (2) children should not be allowed to interfere with other children's use of dough; and (3) after using any modeling medium, children must wash their hands. While using play dough, toddlers need to be constantly supervised. Although nontoxic, play dough should not be consumed as it can upset a child's stomach.

Recipes for Doughs and Clays

Clay Dough

3 cups flour
3 cups salt
3 tablespoons alum

Combine ingredients and slowly add water, a little at a time. Mix well with spoon. As mixture thickens, continue mixing with your hands until it has the feel of clay. If it feels too dry, add more water. If it is too sticky, add equal parts of flour and salt.

Play Dough

2 cups flour
1 cup salt
1 cup hot water
2 tablespoons cooking oil
4 teaspoons cream of tartar
food coloring

Mix well. Knead until smooth. This dough may be kept in a plastic bag or covered container and used again. If it gets sticky, more flour may be added.

Favorite Play Dough

Combine and boil until dissolved:
2 cups water
½ cup salt
food coloring or tempera paint
Mix in while very hot:
2 tablespoons cooking oil
2 tablespoons alum
2 cups flour

Knead (approximately 5 minutes) until smooth. Store in covered airtight containers.

Cornstarch and Soda Play Dough

2 cups cornstarch
4 cups baking soda
2½ cups water
food coloring, if desired

In a pan, combine the baking soda, cornstarch, and water. Cook over a medium heat, while stirring constantly. When the mixture thickens and forms a ball, remove from the heat. Knead when cool and, if desired, add the food coloring. Note: If you are preparing the play dough for only one child, divide the recipe in half.

Cornstarch Play Dough

½ cup salt
¼ cup water
½ cup cornstarch
food coloring

Mix all ingredients thoroughly and cook over low heat, stirring constantly until the dough forms a ball. Add food coloring in desired color.

Laundry Modeling Dough

1½ cups laundry lint
1 cup warm water
⅓ cup flour
1 drop cinnamon or clove oil

Place lint and water in saucepan and stir. The lint will absorb most of the water. Add flour, stirring constantly. Add oil and cook over medium heat. When small peaks form, remove to a heatproof working surface and cool for ten minutes. (Note: This dough does not keep well, so use it immediately.)

Microwave Play Dough

2 cups flour
½ cup cornstarch
2 cups water
1 cup salt
1 tablespoon alum
1 tablespoon cooking oil
food coloring

Combine flour, salt, cornstarch, and alum in a 2-quart bowl. Mix the water, oil, and food coloring. Pour over dry ingredients and stir. Microwave 4½ to 5 minutes until thick, stirring every minute. Cool mixture. If desired, knead in color.

Sand Dough

4 cups sand
3 cups flour
¼ cup cornstarch
¼ cup oil
1 cup water

In bowl, mix sand and flour together. Add cornstarch, oil, and water. If needed, add more water for desired texture.

Baker's Clay #1

1 cup cornstarch
2 cups baking soda
1½ cups cold water

Combine ingredients. Stir until smooth. Cook over medium heat, stirring constantly until mixture reaches the consistency of slightly dry mashed potatoes.

Turn out onto plate or bowl, covering with damp cloth. When cool enough to handle, knead thoroughly until smooth and pliable on cornstarch-covered surface.

Store in tightly closed plastic bag or covered container.

Baker's Clay #2

4 cups flour
1½ cups water
1 cup salt

Combine ingredients. Mix well. Knead 5 to 10 minutes. Roll out to ¼-inch thickness. Cut with decorative cookie cutters or with a knife. Make a hole at the top.

Bake at 250 degrees for 2 hours or until hard. When cool, paint with tempera paint and spray with clear varnish or paint with acrylic paint.

Cloud Dough

3 cups flour
1 cup oil
scent (oil of peppermint, winter-green, lemon, etc.)
food coloring

Combine ingredients. Add water until easily manipulated (about ½ cup).

Sawdust Dough

2 cups sawdust
3 cups flour
1 cup salt

Combine ingredients. Add water as needed. This dough becomes very hard and is not easily broken. It is good to use for making objects and figures that one desires to keep.

Cooked Clay Dough

1 cup flour
½ cup cornstarch
4 cups water
1 cup salt
3 or 4 pounds flour
coloring if desired

Stir slowly and be patient with this recipe. Blend the flour and corn-starch with cold water. Add salt to the water and boil. Pour the boiling salt and water solution into the flour and cornstarch paste and cook over hot water until clear. Add the flour and coloring to the cooked solution and knead. After the clay has been in use, if too moist, add flour; if dry, add water. Keep in covered container. Wrap dough with damp cloth or towel. This dough has a very nice texture and is very popular with all age groups. May be kept 2 or 3 weeks.

Salt Dough

4 cups salt
1 cup cornstarch

Combine with sufficient water to form a paste. Cook over medium heat, stirring constantly.

Play Dough

5 cups flour
2 cups salt
4 tablespoons cooking oil
add water to right consistency

Powdered tempera may be added in with flour or food coloring may be added to finished dough. This dough may be kept in plastic bag or covered container for approximately 2 to 4 weeks. It is better used as play dough rather than leaving objects to harden.

Soap and Sawdust

1 cup whipped soap
1 cup sawdust

Mix well together. This gives a very different feel and appearance. It is quite easily molded into different shapes by all age groups. May be used for 2 to 3 days if stored in tight plastic bag.

Used Coffee Grounds

2 cups used coffee grounds
½ cup salt
1½ cups oatmeal

Combine ingredients and add enough water to moisten. Children like to roll, pack, and pat this mixture. It has a very different feel and look, but it's not good for finished products. It has a very nice texture.

Soap Modeling

2 cups soap flakes

Add enough water to moisten, and whip until consistency to mold. Use soap such as Ivory Flakes, Dreft, Lux, etc. Mixture will have very slight flaky appearance when it can be molded. It is very enjoyable for all age groups and is easy to work with. Also, the texture is very different from other materials ordinarily used for molding. It may be put up to dry, but articles are very slow to dry.

Fingerpaint Recipes

Liquid Starch Method

liquid starch (put in squeeze bottles)
dry tempera paint in shakers

Put about 1 tablespoon of liquid starch on the surface to be painted. Let the child shake the paint onto the starch. Mix and blend the paint. Note: If this paint becomes too thick, simply sprinkle a few drops of water onto the painting.

Soap Flake Method

Mix in a small bowl:
soap flakes
a small amount of water

Beat until stiff with an eggbeater. Use white soap on dark paper, or add food coloring to the soap and use it on light-colored paper. This gives a slight three-dimensional effect.

Uncooked Laundry Starch

A mixture of 1 cup laundry/liquid starch, 1 cup cold water, and 3 cups soap flakes will provide a quick fingerpaint.

Flour and Salt I

1 cup flour
1½ cups salt
¾ cup water
coloring

Combine flour and salt. Add water. This has a grainy quality, unlike the other fingerpaints, providing a different sensory experience. Some children enjoy the different touch sensation when 1½ cup salt is added to the other recipes.

Flour and Salt II

2 cups flour
2 teaspoons salt
3 cups cold water
2 cups hot water
food coloring

Add salt to flour, then pour in cold water gradually and beat mixture with eggbeater until it is smooth. Add hot water and boil until it becomes clear. Beat until smooth, then mix in coloring. Use ¼ cup food coloring to 8 to 9 ounces of paint for strong colors.

Instantized Flour, Uncooked Method

1 pint water (2 cups)
1½ cups instantized flour
    (the kind used to thicken gravy)

Put the water in the bowl and stir the flour into the water. Add color. Regular flour may be lumpy.

Cooked Starch Method

1 cup laundry starch dissolved in a
    small amount of cold water
5 cups boiling water added slowly
    to dissolve starch
1 tablespoon glycerine (optional)

Cook the mixture until it is thick and glossy. Add 1 cup mild soap flakes. Add color in separate containers. Cool before using.

Cornstarch Method

Gradually add 2 quarts water to 1 cup cornstarch. Cook until clear and add ½ cup soap flakes. A few drops of glycerine or oil of wintergreen may be added.

Flour Method

Mix 1 cup flour and 1 cup cold water. Add 3 cups boiling water and bring all to a boil, stirring constantly. Add 1 tablespoon alum and coloring. Paintings from this recipe dry flat and do not need to be ironed.

Rainbow Stew

1 cup cornstarch
4 cups water
½ cup sugar
food coloring (if desired)

Cook water, cornstarch, and sugar until thick. Mixture will be clear and glossy. Add food color to desired boldness.

Tips:

Be sure you have running water and towels nearby or provide a large basin of water where children can rinse off.

Fingerpaint on a smooth table, oil cloth, or cafeteria tray. Some children prefer to start fingerpainting with shaving cream on a sheet of oil cloth.

Food coloring or powdered paint may be added to the mixture before using, or allow children to choose the colors they want sprinkled on top of paint.

Sometimes reluctant children are more easily attracted to the paint table if the fingerpaints are already colored.

Bubble Solutions

Bubble Solution #1

1 cup of water
2 tablespoons of liquid detergent
1 tablespoon glycerine
½ teaspoon sugar

Bubble Solution #2

⅔ cup liquid dish detergent
1 gallon of water
1 tablespoon glycerine (optional)

Allow solution to sit in an open container for at least a day before use.

Bubble Solution #3

3 cups water
2 cups Joy liquid detergent
½ cup Karo syrup

Source: Herr, J. (2000). *Creative resources for the early childhood classroom* (3rd ed.). Albany, NY: Delmar.

Appendix J

Resources Related to Toddlers

The authors and Delmar Learning make every effort to ensure that all Internet resources are accurate at the time of printing. However, due to the fluid, time-sensitive nature of the Internet, we cannot guarantee that all URLs and Web site addresses will remain current for the duration of this edition.

The American Montessori Society Bulletin
American Montessori Society (AMS)
281 Park Avenue South, 6th Floor
New York, NY 10010-6102
(212) 358-1250; (212) 358-1256 FAX
www.amshq.org

Babybug
Cricket Magazine Group
PO Box 7437
Red Oak, IA 51591-2437
(800) 827-0227
www.babybugmag.com

The Black Child Advocate
National Black Child Development Institute (NBCDI)
1101 15th Street NW, Suite 900
Washington, DC 20005
(202) 833-2220; (202) 833-8222 FAX
www.nbcdi.org

Child and Youth Quarterly
Human Sciences Press
233 Spring Street, Floor 5
New York, NY 10013-1522
(212) 620-8000

Child Development and Child Development Abstracts and Bibliography
Society for Research in Child Development
University of Michigan
505 East Huron, Suite 301
Ann Arbor, MI 48104-1567
(734) 998-6578; (734) 998-6569 FAX
www.srcd.org

Child Health Alert
PO Box 610228
Newton Highlands, MA 02161
(781) 239-1762
ericps.ed.uiuc.edu/npin/nls/chalert.html

Childhood Education; Journal of Research in Early Childhood Education
Association for Childhood Education International (ACEI)
17904 Georgia Avenue; Suite 215
Olney, MD 20832
(301) 570-2111; (301) 570-2212 FAX
www.udel.edu/bateman/acei

Child Welfare
Child Welfare League of America (CWLA)
440 First Street NW, 3rd Floor
Washington, DC 20001-2085
(202) 638-2952; (202) 638-4004 FAX
www.cwla.org

Children Today
Superintendent of Documents
U.S. Government Printing Office
Washington, DC 20402
www.access.gpo.gov

Early Childhood Education Journal
Human Sciences Press
233 Spring Street, Floor 5
New York, NY 10013-1522
(212) 620-8000
www.wkap.nl/journalhome.htm/1082-3301

Developmental Psychology
American Psychological Association
750 First Street NE
Washington, DC 20002-4242
(202) 336-5500
www.apa.org

Dimensions of Early Childhood
Southern Association for Children Under Six
Box 56130 Brady Station
Little Rock, AR 72215
(800) 305-7322; (501) 227-5297 FAX

Early Child Development and Care
Gordon and Breach Publishing
Box 32160
Newark, NJ 07102
(800) 545-8398
www.gbhap.com

Earlychildhood NEWS
Earlychildhood.com
2 Lower Ragsdale, Suite 125
Monterey, CA 93940
(831) 333-5501; (800) 627-2829;
(831) 333-5510 FAX
www.earlychildhood.com

Early Childhood Research Quarterly
National Association for the Education of Young
Children (NAEYC)
1509 16th Street NW
Washington, DC 20036-1426
(202) 232-8777; (202) 328-1846 FAX
www.naeyc.org

Educational Leadership
Association for Supervision and Curriculum
Development (ASCD)
1703 North Beauregard Street
Alexandria, VA 22311-1714
(703) 578-9600; (800) 933-ASCD;
(703) 575-5400 FAX
www.ascd.org

Educational Researcher
American Educational Research Association
(AERA)
1230 17th Street NW
Washington, DC 20036
(202) 223-9485; (202) 775-1824 FAX
www.aera.net

ERIC/EECE
University of Illinois
Children's Research Center
51 Gerty Drive
Champaign, IL 61820-7469
http://ericps.ed.uiuc.edu/eece

Exceptional Children
Council for Exceptional Children
1110 North Glebe Road, Suite 300
Arlington, VA 22201-5704
(703) 620-3660; (888) CEC-SPED;
(703) 264-9494 FAX
www.cec.sped.org

Gifted Child Quarterly
National Association for Gifted Children
1707 L Street NW, Suite 550
Washington, DC 20036
(202) 785-4268
www.nagc.org

Instructor
Scholastic, Inc.
555 Broadway
New York, NY 10012
www.scholastic.com/instructor

Journal of Family and Consumer Sciences
American Association of Family and Consumer
Services (AAFCS)
1555 King Street
Alexandria, VA 22314
(703) 706-4600; (703) 706-4663 FAX
www.aafcs.org

Young Children
National Association for the Education of Young
Children (NAEYC)
1509 16th Street NW
Washington, DC 20036-1426
(202) 232-8777; (202) 328-1846 FAX
www.naeyc.org

Other information may be obtained through various
professional organizations.

The following groups may be able to provide you with
other resources:

American Association for Gifted Children
Box 90270
Durham, NC 27708-0270
www.aagc.org

American Association of Family and Consumer Services
(AAFCS)
1555 King Street
Alexandria, VA 22314
(703) 706-4600; (703) 706-4663 FAX
www.aafcs.org

American Montessori Association (AMS)
281 Park Avenue South, 6th Floor
New York, NY 10010
(212) 358-1250; (212) 358-1256 FAX
www.amshq.org

Association for Childhood Education International
(ACEI)
17904 Georgia Avenue, Suite 215
Olney, MD 20832
(301) 570-2111; (800) 423-3563;
(301) 570-2212 FAX
www.udel.edu/bateman/acei

Association for Supervision and Curriculum Development (ASCD)
    1703 North Beauregard Street
    Alexandria, VA 22311-1714
    (703) 578-9600; (800) 933-ASCD;
    (703) 575-5400 FAX
    www.ascd.org

Canadian Association for the Education of Young Children (CAYC)
    612 West 23rd Street
    Vancouver, BC V7M 2C3
    www.cayc.ca

Children's Defense Fund
    25 E Street NW
    Washington, DC 20001
    (202) 628-8787
    www.childrensdefense.org

Child Welfare League of America
    440 First Street NW, 3rd Floor
    Washington, DC 20001-2085
    (202) 638-2952; (202) 638-4004 FAX
    www.cwla.org

Council for Exceptional Children
    1110 North Glebe Road, Suite 300
    Arlington, VA 22201-5704
    (703) 620-3660; (888) CEC-SPED;
    (703) 264-9494 FAX
    www.cec.sped.org

International Reading Association
    800 Barksdale Road
    PO Box 8139
    Newark, DE 19714-8139
    (302) 731-1600; (302) 731-1057 FAX
    www.reading.org

National Association for the Education of Young Children (NAEYC)
    1509 16th Street NW
    Washington, DC 20036-1426
    (202) 232-8777; (202) 328-1846 FAX
    www.naeyc.org

National Association for Gifted Children
    1707 L Street NW, Suite 550
    Washington, DC 20036
    (202) 785-4268
    www.nagc.org

National Black Child Development Institute (NBCDI)
    1101 15th Street NW, Suite 900
    Washington, DC 20005
    (202) 833-2220; (202) 833-8222 FAX
    www.nbcdi.org

National Committee to Prevent Child Abuse
    2950 Tennyson Street
    Denver, CO 80212
    (303) 433-2451; (303) 433-9701 FAX
    www.childabuse.org

National Education Association (NEA)
    1201 16th Street NW
    Washington, DC 20036
    (202) 833-4000
    www.nea.org

Society for Research in Child Development
    University of Michigan
    505 East Huron, Suite 301
    Ann Arbor, MI 48104-1567
    (734) 998-6578; (734) 998-6569 FAX
    www.srcd.org

Appendix K

Developmental Checklist

Child's Name: _____

Observer's Name: _____

Observation Date: _____

PHYSICAL DEVELOPMENT		OBSERVED
Birth to Three Months	Date	Comments
Acts reflexively—sucking, stepping, rooting		
Swipes at objects in front of body, uncoordinated		
Holds head erect and steady when lying on stomach		
Lifts head and shoulders		
Rolls from side to back		
Follows moving objects with eyes		
Four to Six Months		
Holds cube in hand		
Reaches for objects with one hand		
Rolls from back to side		
Reaches for objects in front of body, coordinated		
Sits with support		
Transfers objects from hand to hand		
Grabs objects with either hand		
Sits in tripod position using arms for support		
Seven to Nine Months		
Sits independently		
Stepping reflex returns, so that child bounces when held on a surface in a standing position		
Leans over and reaches when in a sitting position		
Gets on hands and knees but may fall forward		
Crawls		
Pulls to standing position		
Claps hands together		
Stands with adult's assistance		
Learns pincer grasp, using thumb with forefinger to pick up objects		
Uses finger and thumb to pick up objects		
Brings objects together with banging noises		

The developmental milestones listed are based on universal patterns of when various traits emerge. Because each child is unique certain traits may develop at an earlier or later age.

PHYSICAL DEVELOPMENT		OBSERVED
Ten to Twelve Months	Date	Comments
Supports entire body weight on legs		
Walks when hands are held		
Cruises along furniture or steady objects		
Stands independently		
Walks independently		
Crawls up stairs or steps		
Voluntarily releases objects held in hands		
Has good balance when sitting; can shift positions without falling		
Takes off shoes and socks		
Thirteen to Eighteen Months		
Builds tower of two cubes		
Turns the pages of a cardboard book two or three at a time		
Scribbles vigorously		
Walks proficiently		
Walks while carrying or pulling a toy		
Walks up stairs with assistance		
Nineteen to Twenty-Four Months		
Walks up stairs independently, one step at a time		
Jumps in place		
Kicks a ball		
Runs in a modified fashion		
Shows a decided preference for one hand		
Completes a three-piece puzzle with knobs		
Builds a tower of six cubes		
Twenty-Five to Thirty-Six Months		
Maneuvers around obstacles in a pathway		
Runs in a more adult-like fashion; knees are slightly bent, arms move in the opposite direction		
Walks down stairs independently		
Marches to music		
Uses feet to propel wheeled riding toys		
Rides a tricycle		
Usually uses whole arm movements to paint or color		
Throws a ball forward, where intended		
Builds tower using eight or more blocks		
Imitates drawing circles and vertical and horizontal lines		
Turns pages in book one by one		
Fingers work together to scoop up small objects		
Strings large beads on a shoelace		

Additional Observations for Physical Development

The developmental milestones listed are based on universal patterns of when various traits emerge. Because each child is unique certain traits may develop at an earlier or later age.

LANGUAGE AND COMMUNICATION DEVELOPMENT		OBSERVED
	Date	Comments
Birth to Three Months		
Communicates with cries, grunts, and facial expressions		
Prefers human voices		
Coos		
Laughs		
Smiles and coos to initiate and sustain interactions with caregiver		
Four to Six Months		
Babbles spontaneously		
Acquires sounds of native language in babble		
Canonical, systematic consonant–vowel pairings; babbling occurs		
Participates in interactive games initiated by adults		
Takes turns while interacting		
Seven to Nine Months		
Varies babble in loudness, pitch, and rhythm		
Adds *d, t, n,* and *w* to repertoire of babbling sounds		
Produces gestures to communicate often by pointing		
May say *mama* or *dada* but does not connect words with parents		
Ten to Twelve Months		
Uses preverbal gestures to influence the behavior of others		
Demonstrates word comprehension skills		
Waves good-bye		
Speaks recognizable first word		
Initiates familiar games with adults		
Thirteen to Eighteen Months		
Has expressive vocabulary of 10 to 20 words		
Engages in "jargon talk"		
Engages in telegraphic speech by combining two words together		
Experiences a burst of language development		
Comprehends approximately 50 words		
Nineteen to Twenty-Four Months		
Continues using telegraphic speech		
Able to combine three words		
Talks, 25 percent of words being understandable		
Refers to self by name		

The developmental milestones listed are based on universal patterns of when various traits emerge. Because each child is unique certain traits may develop at an earlier or later age.

LANGUAGE AND COMMUNICATION DEVELOPMENT		OBSERVED
Nineteen to Twenty-Four Months (continued)	Date	Comments
Joins three or four words into a sentence		
Comprehends approximately 300 words		
Expressive language includes a vocabulary of approximately 250 words		
Twenty-Five to Thirty-Six Months		
Continues using telegraphic speech combining three or four words		
Speaks in complete sentences following word order of native language		
Displays effective conversational skills		
Refers to self as *me* or *I* rather than by name		
Talks about objects and events not immediately present		
Uses grammatical markers and some plurals		
Vocabulary increases rapidly, up to 300 words		
Enjoys being read to if allowed to participate by pointing, talking, and turning pages		

Additional Observations for Language and Communication Development

COGNITIVE DEVELOPMENT		OBSERVED
Birth to Three Months	Date	Comments
Cries for assistance		
Acts reflexively		
Prefers to look at patterned objects, bull's-eye, horizontal stripes, and the human face		
Imitates adults' facial expressions		
Searches with eyes for sources of sounds		
Begins to recognize familiar people at a distance		
Discovers and repeats bodily actions such as sucking, swiping, and grasping		
Discovers hands and feet as extension of self		

The developmental milestones listed are based on universal patterns of when various traits emerge. Because each child is unique certain traits may develop at an earlier or later age.

LANGUAGE AND COMMUNICATION DEVELOPMENT (continued)		OBSERVED
Four to Six Months	Date	Comments
Recognizes people by their voice		
Enjoys repeating acts, such as shaking a rattle, that produce results in the external world		
Searches with eyes for source of sounds		
Enjoys watching hands and feet		
Searches for a partially hidden object		
Uses toys in a purposeful manner		
Imitates simple actions		
Explores toys using existing schemas such as sucking, banging, grasping, shaking, etc.		
Seven to Nine Months		
Enjoys looking at books with familiar objects		
Distinguishes familiar from unfamiliar faces		
Engages in goal-directed behavior		
Anticipates events		
Finds objects that are totally hidden		
Imitates behaviors that are slightly different than those usually performed		
Begins to show interest in filling and dumping containers		
Ten to Twelve Months		
Solves sensorimotor problems by deliberately using schemas, such as shaking a container to empty its contents		
Points to body parts upon request		
Drops toys intentionally and repeatedly looks in the direction of the fallen object		
Waves good-bye		
Shows evidence of stronger memory capabilities		
Follows simple, one-step directions		
Categorizes objects by appearance		
Looks for objects hidden in a second location		
Thirteen to Eighteen Months		
Explores properties of objects by acting on them in novel ways		
Solves problems through trial and error		
Experiments with cause-and-effect relationships such as turning on televisions, banging on drums, etc.		
Plays body identification games		
Imitates novel behaviors of others		
Identifies family members in photographs		

The developmental milestones listed are based on universal patterns of when various traits emerge. Because each child is unique certain traits may develop at an earlier or later age.

COGNITIVE DEVELOPMENT		OBSERVED
Nineteen to Twenty-Four Months	Date	Comments
Points to and identifies objects on request, such as when reading a book, touring, etc.		
Sorts by shapes and colors		
Recognizes self in photographs and mirror		
Demonstrates deferred imitation		
Engages in functional play		
Finds objects that have been moved while out of sight		
Solves problems with internal representation		
Categorizes self and others by gender, race, hair color, etc.		
Twenty-Five to Thirty-Six Months		
Uses objects for purposes other than intended		
Uses private speech while working		
Classifies objects based on one dimension, such as toy cars versus blocks		
Follows two-step directions		
Concentrates or attends to self-selected activities for longer periods of time		
Points to and labels objects spontaneously, such as when reading a book		
Coordinates pretend play with other children		
Gains a nominal sense of numbers through counting and labeling objects in a set		
Begins developing concepts about opposites such as big and small, tall and short, in and out		
Begins eveloping concepts about time such as today, tomorrow, and yesterday		

Additional Observations for Cognitive Development

The developmental milestones listed are based on universal patterns of when various traits emerge. Because each child is unique certain traits may develop at an earlier or later age.

SOCIAL DEVELOPMENT	OBSERVED	
Birth to Three Months	Date	Comments
Turns head toward a speaking voice		
Recognizes primary caregiver		
Bonds to primary caregiver		
Finds comfort in the human face		
Displays a social smile		
Is quieted by a voice		
Begins to differentiate self from caregiver		
Four to Six Months		
Seeks out adults for play by crying, cooing, or smiling		
Responds with entire body to familiar face by looking at a person, smiling, kicking legs, and waving arms		
Participates actively in interactions with others by vocalizing in response to adult speech		
Smiles at familiar faces and stares solemnly at strangers		
Distinguishes between familiar and nonfamiliar adults and surroundings		
Seven to Nine Months		
Becomes upset when separated from a favorite adult		
Acts deliberately to maintain the presence of a favorite adult by clinging or crying		
Uses adults as a base for exploration, typically		
Looks to others who are exhibiting signs of distress		
Enjoys observing and interacting briefly with other children		
Likes to play and responds to games such as patty-cake and peekaboo		
Engages in solitary play		
Develops preferences for particular people and objects		
Shows distress when in the presence of a stranger		
Ten to Twelve Months		
Shows a decided preference for one or two caregivers		
Plays parallel to other children		
Enjoys playing with siblings		
Begins asserting self		
Begins developing a sense of humor		
Develops a sense of self-identity through the identification of body parts		
Begins distinguishing boys from girls		

The developmental milestones listed are based on universal patterns of when various traits emerge. Because each child is unique certain traits may develop at an earlier or later age.

SOCIAL DEVELOPMENT		OBSERVED
Thirteen to Eighteen Months	Date	Comments
Demands personal attention		
Imitates behaviors of others		
Becoming increasingly aware of the self as a separate being		
Shares affection with people other than primary caregiver		
Shows ownership of possessions		
Begins developing a view of self as autonomous when completing tasks independently		
Nineteen to Twenty-Four Months		
Shows enthusiasm for company of others		
Views the world only from own, egocentric perspective		
Plays contentedly alone or near adults		
Engages in functional play		
Defends possessions		
Recognizes self in photographs or mirrors		
Refers to self with pronouns such as *I* or *me*		
Categorizes people by using salient characteristics such as race or hair color		
Shows less fear of strangers		
Twenty-five to Thirty-Six Months		
Observes others to see how they do things		
Engages primarily in solitary or parallel play		
Sometimes offers toys to other children		
Begins to play cooperatively with other children		
Engages in sociodramatic play		
Wants to do things independently		
Asserts independence by using "no" a lot		
Develops a rudimentary awareness that others have wants or feelings that may be different than their own		
Makes demands of or "bosses" parents, guardians, and caregivers		
Uses physical aggression less and uses words to solve problems		
Engages in gender stereotypical behavior		

Additional Observations for Social Development

The developmental milestones listed are based on universal patterns of when various traits emerge. Because each child is unique certain traits may develop at an earlier or later age.

EMOTIONAL DEVELOPMENT		OBSERVED
Birth to Three Months	Date	Comments
Feels and expresses three basic emotions: interest, distress, and disgust		
Cries to signal a need		
Quiets in response to being held, typically		
Feels and expresses enjoyment		
Shares a social smile		
Reads and distinguishes adults' facial expressions		
Begins to self-regulate emotional expressions		
Laughs aloud		
Quiets self by using techniques such as sucking a thumb or pacifier		
Four to Six Months		
Expresses delight		
Responds to the emotions of caregivers		
Begins to distinguish familiar from unfamiliar people		
Shows a preference for being held by a familiar person		
Begins to assist with holding a bottle		
Expresses happiness selectively by laughing and smiling more with familiar people		
Seven to Nine Months		
Responds to social events by using the face, gaze, voice, and posture to form coherent emotional patterns		
Expresses fear and anger more often		
Begins to regulate emotions through moving into or out of experiences		
Begins to detect the meaning of others' emotional expressions		
Looks to others for clues on how to react		
Shows fear of strangers		
Ten to Twelve Months		
Continues to exhibit delight, happiness, discomfort, anger, and sadness		
Expresses anger when goals are blocked		
Expresses anger at the source of frustration		
Begins to show compliance to caregivers' requests		
Often objects to having playtime stopped		
Begins eating with a spoon		
Assists in dressing and undressing		
Acts in loving, caring ways toward dolls or stuffed animals, typically		
Feeds self a complete meal when served finger foods		
Claps when successfully completing a task		

The developmental milestones listed are based on universal patterns of when various traits emerge. Because each child is unique certain traits may develop at an earlier or later age.

EMOTIONAL DEVELOPMENT		OBSERVED
Thirteen to Eighteen Months	Date	Comments
Exhibits autonomy by frequently saying "no"		
Labels several emotions		
Connects feelings with social behaviors		
Begins to understand complicated patterns of behavior		
Demonstrates the ability to communicate needs		
May say "no" to something they want		
May lose emotional control and have temper tantrums		
Shows self-conscious emotions such as shame, guilt, and shyness		
Becomes frustrated easily		
Nineteen to Twenty-Four Months		
Expresses affection to others spontaneously		
Acts to comfort others in distress		
Shows the emotions of pride and embarrassment		
Uses emotion words spontaneously in conversations or play		
Begins to show sympathy to another child or adult		
Becomes easily hurt by criticism		
Experiences a temper tantrum when goals are blocked, on occasion		
Associates facial expressions with simple emotional labels		
Twenty-Five to Thirty-Six Months		
Experiences increase in number of fears		
Begins to understand the consequences of basic emotions		
Learns skills for coping with strong emotions		
Seeks to communicate more feelings with specific words		
Shows signs of empathy and caring		
Loses control of emotions and throws temper tantrums		
Able to recover from temper tantrums		
Enjoys helping with chores such as cleaning up toys or carrying grocery bags		
Begins to show signs of readiness for toileting		
Desires that routines be carried out exactly as has been done in the past		

Additional Observations for Emotional Development

Appendix L

Sample Running Record

Child's name:_____

Date of birth:_____

Location:_____

Date and time:_____

Observer's name:_____

Behavioral Description of Observations:	Interpretations of/Reflections on Observations:

Sample Running Record

Child's name: ___Christina R.___

Date of birth: ___2-10-96___

Location: ___Inside, before and during snack___

Date and time: ___March 2, 2xxx___ ___2:00–2:25 p.m.___

Observer's name: ___Jane U.___

Behavioral Description of Observations:	Interpretations of/Reflections on Observations:
Christina is playing with a toy truck. She says, "Katy, can I keep it?" She repeats this two times until a teacher responds, "No, the toys are for all the children to use at school." She drops the truck on the floor and walks over to the shelf. She picks up a guitar and plays it while walking around the room looking at the other children. The teacher says, "It's snack time. Wash your hands, Christina." Christina says to the boy beside her, "It's snack time." She walks to the snack table and sits down.	Working on ownership issues. Social development: Helping classmate to follow routine of classroom.
Christina sits in a hunched position between a boy and a girl. She says, "Look, bananas" in an excited voice while reaching for the plate. She grabs the plate and takes two bananas. The teacher says, "Start with one banana. If you eat the first one, you can have one more." Christina peels the banana using her thumb and fore-finger on her right hand. She puts the entire banana in her mouth and grabs for a second banana. The teacher says, "Chew up your banana. I don't want you to choke. Thank you for sitting while you are chewing." Christina smiles and takes a second banana and peels it in the same manner as before. She takes a large bite of the banana, eating half of it at once. She grabs her glass of milk with both hands and takes a large gulp. She burps loudly. The teacher says, "Excuse you." Christina leaves the table and dumps the uneaten part of the banana in the waste can. She uses a rag (the teacher gave her) to wash each finger individually and then wipes her face.	She didn't wash her hands, and the teacher didn't catch it! Okay with this limit. Continues eating snack. Good fine motor skills to peel own banana. She seems very hungry—when did she last eat? Receptive to positive reinforcement by teacher, seemed pleased with own behavior. In the process of learning manners. She didn't repeat the statement, though. Good self-help skills.
She walks in a stiff legged motion to another area of the classroom.	Always on the move!!

Appendix M

Panel Documentation

A panel is a two-dimensional display to communicate with others the learning that occurred during an activity. Panels present the learning of a group of children; thus, different children and their work must be featured. For ease of reading, you should neatly handwrite or type your message. Then, adhere all sections mentioned in the following list on a foam board, poster board, or trifold board.

A panel should contain the following information:

♡ Title of the activity
♡ A record of the children's *actual* words while engaging with the materials or interacting with peers
♡ Artifacts to document representations of the children's thinking—drawings paintings, writings, and/or graphs—or photographs of the children's work on sculptures, creative drama/movements, or roles during dramatic play
♡ A narrative that highlights and explains what learning and interactions occurred

To fulfill the goal of communicating with others, the panel will need to be displayed in a prominent location. Invite others to look at and converse about the children's work. Include the children as part of the audience by reviewing their work as a way to promote language, cognitive, and social development. Also, build on the experience during future activities.

For additional resources on making panels, see:

Gandini, L., & Pope Edwards, C. (Eds.). (2001). *Bambini: The Italian approach to infant/toddler care.* New York: Teachers College Press.

Helm, J. H., Beneke, S., & Steinheimer, K. (1998). *Windows on learning: Documenting young children's work.* New York: Teachers College Press.

Pope Edwards, C., Gandini, L., & Forman, G. (Eds.). (1993). *The hundred languages of children.* Norwood, NJ: Ablex.

Lesson Plan

Name: _____ Date: _____

Developmental area: _____

Child's developmental goals:

Materials:

Preparation:

Nurturing strategies:

Variations:

Appendix O

Toddler Daily Communication: Home to Center

Toddler's name: _____ Parent's name: _____

Day/date: _____ Time of arrival: _____ Time of departure: _____

Child picked up by: _____

FILLED IN BY PARENT:

Toddler seems: [ ] Normal, typical

                         [ ] Bit fussy

                         [ ] Not acting like usual

Toddler slept: [ ] Soundly

                         [ ] Woke up several times

                         [ ] Did not sleep well

Toddler ate: [ ] Meal before coming _____

                         [ ] Snack before coming _____

                         [ ] Nothing

Toddler changed/used toilet: [ ] Bowel movement   Time _____

                                       [ ] Wet   Time _____

SPECIAL INSTRUCTIONS FOR TODAY:

_____

_____

_____

_____

Parent's signature: _____

Caregiver's signature: _____

Toddler Daily Communication: Center to Home

Date: _____ Check-in time: _____

Read toddler's daily communication: Home to center _____

_____

INTERACTIONS/ACTIVITIES: *(Description of adult interaction, developmental tasks, and activities that sustained child's interest)*

_____

_____

_____

Breakfast:

[ ]   Ate well   [ ]   Ate a little bit   [ ]   Not hungry today   _____

Lunch:

[ ]   Ate well   [ ]   Ate a little bit   [ ]   Not hungry today   _____

Nap time:

[ ]   Slept   [ ]   Quietly rested   _____

Toileting:

[ ]   Diapers only   [ ]   Sat on toilet   [ ]   Used toilet

[ ] Bowel movement Time _____   [ ] Wet Time _____

NOTES TO PARENTS:

_____

_____

_____

Caregiver's signature: _____

Parent's signature: _____

We need: [ ] Diapers/underpants [ ] Change of clothing

      [ ] Blankets   [ ] Other: _____

Adapted with permission from New Horizon Child Care, Inc.